QUASI-RELIGIOUS SOCIETIES

A Historical Synopsis and a Commentary

THE CATHOLIC UNIVERSITY OF AMERICA
CANON LAW STUDIES
No. 261

Quasi-Religious Societies

A Historical Synopsis and a Commentary

BY

THE REV. BERNARD JOSEPH RISTUCCIA, C.M., J.C.L.
PRIEST OF THE CONGREGATION OF THE MISSION

A DISSERTATION

SUBMITTED TO THE FACULTY OF THE SCHOOL OF CANON LAW OF THE CATHOLIC UNIVERSITY OF AMERICA IN PARTIAL FULFILLMENT OF THE REQUIREMENTS FOR THE DEGREE OF DOCTOR OF CANON LAW

THE CATHOLIC UNIVERSITY OF AMERICA PRESS
WASHINGTON, D. C.
1949

IMPRIMI POTEST:

DANIEL M. LEARY, C.M.V.,

Provincial Superior.

Philadelphia, Pa., March 27, 1948

NIHIL OBSTAT:

JEROME D. HANNAN, A.M., LL.B., S.T.D., J.C.D.,

Censor Deputatus.

Washington, D. C., June 10, 1947

IMPRIMATUR:

✠ MICHAEL J. CURLEY, D.D.

Archbishop of Baltimore-Washington.

Washington, D. C., June 10, 1947

MURRAY AND HEISTER
WASHINGTON, D. C.

PRINTED BY
TIMES AND NEWS PUBLISHING CO.
GETTYSBURG, PA., U.S.A.

TO

THE IMMACULATE MOTHER OF GOD

TABLE OF CONTENTS

TABLE OF CONTENTS (Continued)

PART II

Canonical Commentary

TABLE OF CONTENTS (Continued)

TABLE OF CONTENTS (Continued)

TABLE OF CONTENTS (Continued)

TABLE OF CONTENTS (Continued)

TABLE OF CONTENTS (Continued)

FOREWORD

There exist in the Church today groups of men and women who, although living a life in common and striving after perfection through the practice of the evangelical counsels, nevertheless are not numbered among the religious communities which go to make up the institution known as the religious life. The reason why these groups are not considered as religious communities in the proper meaning of the term is that a legal distinction is made in the Code of Canon Law between the members of these groups and the members of religious institutes.

The Code in canon 488, defines a religious institute as one which is approved by ecclesiastical authority, and in which the members, according to the laws of each society, pronounce public vows, either temporary or perpetual.[1]

On the other hand, a quasi-religious society is established in imitation of the religious communities and is defined by canon 673 as a society of men or women in which the members, living a life in common in imitation of the religious life, do not pronounce the three public vows of religion.[2]

It can readily be seen that the basis for the distinction between the two groups under consideration rests on the question of the public vows of religion. The profession of the public vows of religion makes one a member of a religious institute, while admission into a society in which public vows are not pronounced makes one a member of a quasi-religious society.

Because of the resemblance of the societies which are dealt with in Book II, Title XVII of the Code to religious institutes they will be called throughout this work *quasi-religious* societies, and the members of these societies will be called *quasi-religious.* On the other hand, religious communities in the proper sense of the term will be consistently called *religious institutes.*

This dissertation will attempt to apply to the quasi-religious so-

[1] Can. 488.

[2] Can. 673.

cieties the canons of the Code equally applicable to the religious institutes and quasi-religious societies. Because of the comprehensive nature of this dissertation it will not be possible to go into a detailed explanation of the canons which are thus applied. Rather, the general principles of the various canons will be delineated in their relation to quasi-religious societies. Consequently, only those general interpretations or explanations which these canons may warrant in their application to quasi-religious societies will be the subject of this work.

The individual constitutions of the several societies are beyond its scope. Therefore, in spite of what might be said in the subsequent pages, those constitutions which have been approved by the Holy See since the publication of the Code retain their force even though they might contain prescriptions contrary to it. Likewise, the prescriptions of individual constitutions which contain laws more demanding or more rigorous than those presented herein as the law of the Code, but still not contrary to the Code, retain their force.

In several instances, when the opinions of authors are referred to as substantiating certain statements referring to quasi-religious societies, the opinions of the authors concerned were expressed not specifically in regard to quasi-religious societies, but rather in regard to religious institutes. These references, however, seem valid in virtue of the fact that the particular conclusions under consideration are equally applicable to both quasi-religious societies and religious institutes.

The writer takes this occasion to thank the Congregation of the Mission of the Eastern Province for the opportunity to pursue a course of graduate study in canon law. He likewise expresses his gratitude to the Faculty of the School of Canon Law of The Catholic University of America for their kindly, considerate and helpful criticism and for their many kindnesses over the past three years, especially relative to the writing of this dissertation.

PART I

Historical Synopsis

CHAPTER I

The Historic Growth of the Quasi-Religious Societies to the Council of Trent

ARTICLE I. INTRODUCTION

The historic background of the institution known as the quasi-religious societies cannot be traced back beyond the life of Saint Benedict. It was only after the establishment of the Benedictine rule that the religious life properly so called adopted any uniform and specific regulations which had to be fulfilled in order that a community might be legally recognized as a religious group.[1] Consequently, those societies which existed in imitation of these legally recognized religious groups, without demanding all the requirements specified in the Benedictine rule, were the forerunners of the quasi-religious societies now recognized in Book II, Title XVII of the Code of Canon Law.[2]

Previous to the Benedictine influence the religious life had gone through various stages of development. Monachism was the first form of the religious life. It embraced a twofold element, the anchoretic life and the cenobitic life. The anchoretic life was followed by the hermits and the solitaries who were not bound by a common rule and who were not obliged to the fulfillment of religious exercises in common. The cenobitic life was followed by those monks who favored a community form of life, and these monks lived a common life in a monastery under the authority of a superior.[3]

Monachism remained the principal form of the religious life through the early centuries of the Christian era, though it under-

---

[1] Schäfer, *Compendium de Religiosis ad norman Codicis Iuris Canonici* (3. ed., Romae: S.A.L.E.R., 1940), p. 21 (hereafter cited as *De Religiosis*).

[2] Cans. 673-681.

[3] Cayré, *Manual of Patrology* (translated from the French by H. Howitt, 2 Vols., Paris: Desclee and Co., 1936-1940), I, 502.

went several changes under the influence of some of the early desert fathers. The Fathers chiefly influential in the development of the religious life were Saint Anthony (251-356),[4] Saint Pachomius (292-346),[5] Schenute (350-466),[6] Saint Basil (330-379)[7] and Saint Augustine (354-430).[8]

The monastic form of the religious life at the beginning of the sixth century consisted of several entirely distinct groups of religious, each following a different rule. There was lacking entirely any kind of uniformity or coherence among the various rules. This diversity along with the confusion which it necessarily occasioned was to a great extent the cause of the laxity and abuse which crept into the religious life at that time. Undoubtedly there was a definite need for a reform in the monastic way of life.[9]

ARTICLE II. THE BENEDICTINE INFLUENCE ON THE RELIGIOUS LIFE

The impetus for this needed reform and reorganization of the religious life was supplied by Saint Benedict (480-543). In the rule of Saint Benedict there is found for the first time a systematized set of regulations for the governing of the religious life. The series of moral, social, liturgical and penal ordinances which Saint Benedict expressed in his rule more than supplied the necessary correctives which the disorganized and languid religious life of his age required.

The rule of Saint Benedict was adopted by several communities within a very short time, and eventually it became almost the exclusive code of laws for all the western monasteries.[10] This rule was also extended to women religious through the influence of

---

[4] Montalembert, *The Monks of the West* (2 vols., Boston, 1872), I, 179; Migne, *Patrologiae Cursus Completus Series Graeca* (161 vols., Paris, 1856-1866), XXVI, 838-976 (hereafter cited as *MPG*).

[5] Montalembert, *op. cit.*, I, 180; Migne, *Patrologiae Cursus Completus Series Latina* (221 vols., Paris, 1844-1864), XXIII, 62-83 (hereafter cited as *MPL*).

[6] Michael Ott, "Schenute," *The Catholic Encyclopedia* (15 vols., 2 Supplements and Index, New York: Appleton Co., 1907-1922), XII, 527.

[7] Cayré, *op. cit.*, I, 406-407; *MPG,* XXXI, 890-1078.

[8] Montalembert, *op. cit.*, I, 298; *MPL,* XXXII, 1377-1384.

[9] Montalembert, *op. cit.,* II, 696.

[10] Schäfer, *De Religiosis,* p. 21.

Saint Scholastica, the twin sister of Saint Benedict, so that from the sixth until the thirteenth century this rule was followed by practically all the communities of women religious.[11]

In this rule of Saint Benedict was seen for the first time the real soul of the religious life, namely, a public profession of the vows of poverty, chastity and obedience in an approved religion.[12]

ARTICLE III. THE CANONESSES

Assistance on the part of women in the work of the Church dates back to very early times. Various rules were enacted for each group which engaged in furnishing this assistance. However, the first general rule for their guidance is attributed to Saint Augustine.[13] The rule was addressed to Felicitas, superioress of the monastery of Hippo, and to Rusticus, a priest to whose charge Saint Augustine had entrusted the religious of the monastery.[14] The title of Canonesses was first applied to these women in the ninth century. It was used with reference to those communities of women who, while they professed a common life, yet did not carry out to its full extent the original Rule of Saint Augustine.[15]

These women were called Canonesses inasmuch as the regulation of their life practically paralleled that of the chapters of canons regular, which had been recently revived through the introduction of the *Regula Vitae Communis* of Saint Chrodegang, Bishop of Metz (✠ 766). These Canonesses occupied themselves with the recitation of the divine office, the care of the holy vestments, and the education of the young.[16]

Mention of them was made for the first time as early as 813 in

---

[11] Augustine, *A Commentary on the Code of Canon Law* (8 vols., St. Louis: B. Herder, 1920-1938, Vol. III, 5. ed., 1938), III, 19.

[12] Butler, *Benedictine Monachism* (2. ed., London, New York: Longmans Green & Co., 1924), pp. 122, 125, 147.

[13] Currier, *History of Religious Orders* (New York, 1894), p. 169.

[14] *MPL,* XXXIII, 958-965.

[15] Mansi, *Sacrorum Conciliorum Nova et Amplissima Collectio* (53 vols. in 60, Parisiis, 1901-1927), XIV, 104 (hereafter cited as Mansi); Hefele-Leclercq, *Histoire des Conciles* (10 vols. in 19, Paris: Letouzey et Ané, 1907-1938), IV, 17 (hereafter cited as Hefele).

[16] Dunford, "Canonesses," *Catholic Encyclopedia,* III, 256.

the Council of Chalon-sur-Saône. The fifty-third canon of this Council distinguished between women religious strictly so called, *moniales*, and other groups of holy women called *sanctimoniales* or *canonesses*.[17]

Contrary to the general rule whereby all religious communities after the time of Saint Benedict made some form of profession and pronounced the vows of religion, these women took no vows at all, nor did they make any form of public profession.[18]

In a certain sense these communities of Canonesses could be termed the legal forerunners of those communities whose members now are called quasi-religious. These Canonesses constituted the first community which according to the legal requirements of the period was not a religious community strictly so called; yet they constituted a community whose members lived after the fashion of a religious community.

The legal requirements for the constitution of a religious community at that time consisted in a form of public profession and in a certain pronouncement of vows, as was prescribed in Saint Benedict's Rule. These requirements had been implicitly demanded by the First National Council of Germany (743), when in the seventh canon the Fathers of that Council stated that "monks and nuns should strive to live, govern and order their lives according to the Holy Rule of Benedict."[19] At an even earlier time the Synod of Autun (677) in its fifth canon had enjoined that the Rule of Saint Benedict was to be followed by all the religious communities in that diocese.[20] As has been already stated, the Canonesses took no vows at all, nor did they make any form of public profession.

ARTICLE IV. THE MILITARY ORDERS

One of the most important periods of the middle ages had arrived. Europe was suddenly awakened as if by an electric shock,

---

[17] *Monumenta Germaniae Historica, Legum Sectio III, Concilia* (3 tomes, ed. A. Boretius et V. Krause, Hannoverae: 1833-1924), II, 284 (hereafter cited as *MGH*).

[18] C. 43, *De electione et electi potestate,* I, 6, in VI°.

[19] Mansi, XII, 367.

[20] Mansi, XI, 124.

and found its attention turned suddenly towards the East. The followers of Mahomet had been constantly gaining ground and were rapidly moving westward, until finally Egypt, a portion of Spain, and at length Jerusalem were taken, the Holy City falling in 1086. The conquerors of the Holy Land began to exercise the most cruel atrocities upon the numerous pilgrims who went there from all corners of the world to visit the places made sacred by the life and death of Christ.[21]

The Christian answer to this menace was the institution which came to be known as the Military Orders. The first of the Military Orders was that of the Knights of Malta, also known as the Hospitallers of Saint John, founded originally for the practice of works of mercy towards the sick, but which a few years later assumed a military character, and took up the work of defending the Faith by force of arms. In 1118 Raymond du Puy, their second superior, gave his subjects a rule which obliged them to take the three solemn vows of poverty, obedience and chastity.[22]

A second Order of Knighthood, called the Knights Templar, was instituted in 1118. At the same time other Orders such as the Teutonic Order, the Order of Calatrava and Alcantara, and the Military Order of Mt. Carmel, came into existence with the same object, namely, that of fighting against the infidels in defense of the Christian Faith.[23]

The question has been raised whether or not these various Orders were religious bodies. It is difficult to answer that question absolutely one way or the other. However, with proper distinctions it could be said that profession in those Military Orders, if it was accompanied with the vows, not only of poverty and of obedience, but also of perfect and total chastity, implied for the professed members the full status of religious.[24] The Hospitallers of Saint John and the Teutonic Order were Orders of this type. Other

---

[21] Currier, *History of Religious Orders,* p. 10.

[22] Currier, *op. cit.,* p. 11; Suarez, *Opera Omnia* (ed. nova, a Carolo Berton, 28 vols., Parisiis: Apud Ludovicum Vivès, 1856-1861), Tom. IV, lib. I, cap. 3, no. 4.

[23] Currier, *op. cit.,* p. 12.

[24] Reiffenstuel, *Ius Canonicum Universum* (5 vols. in 7, Parisiis, 1864-1870), lib. III, tit. 31, n. 30.

Military Orders, in which the vows of poverty, of obedience and of conjugal chastity were taken, could not be considered religious Orders strictly so called, for the reason that there was lacking one of the essential requirements for a religious profession, namely, the vow of perfect and total chastity, which according to Saint Thomas is a *de iure divino* requirement for a true religious profession.[25] The Military Orders of Alcantara, of Calatrava, of Saint Lazarus, and of Mt. Carmel were examples of this latter group.[26]

ARTICLE V. THE THIRD ORDERS

The definite beginning of the quasi-religious group as introduced through the communities of the Canonesses was further developed through the formation of the Third Orders.

In addition to the already existing requirements of public profession and of vows, there was enacted in the thirteenth century the further requisite of the permission of the Holy See as a condition essential for the erection of a religious community. Pope Innocent III, in the IV General Council of the Lateran (1215), was the one who first legislated on the necessity of this papal permission.[27]

The profession of solemn vows became a necessary requirement for religious profession in the time of the pontificate of Boniface VIII (1294-1303). This pontiff, in settling the dispute as to what determined the solemnity of vows, decreed that the vows taken in a community approved by the Church were solemn vows.[28] In view, then, of the just mentioned decree of Pope Innocent III, it could safely be said that solemn vows were at that time taken by all religious alike.

The Third Orders, established principally by Saints Francis (1181-1226) and Dominic (1170-1221), were founded in favor

---

[25] St. Thomas, *Summa Theologica* (6 vols., Romae, 1886-1887), Ia IIae, q. 186, a. 4; Reiffenstuel, lib. III, tit. 31, n. 32.

[26] Currier, *op. cit.*, p. 217; Reiffenstuel, lib. III, tit. 31, n. 30; Suarez, *Opera Omnia*, Tom. IV, lib. I, cap. 5, n. 1.

[27] Mansi, XXII, 1002; c. 9, X, *de religiosis domibus, ut episcopo sint subiectae*, III, 36.

[28] Cap. un., *de religiosis domibus*, III, 17, in VI°.

of the men and women who, although they were under the necessity of living a secular life in the world, still desired to attain a high degree of Christian perfection.[29] The rules and regulations drawn up for these Third Orders were so arranged and selected that the Tertiaries were given a way of life adapted to their secular lives in the world and in society; they did not strictly constitute a religious rule. The principal distinction between the then existing religious rules, on the one hand, and the rules of the Tertiaries, on the other, was that in the Tertiary rule there was no mention of solemn vows, nor was the requirement of the cloister stressed or even set as essential on the part of women members.[30] This was the first instance in which women who had made a religious profession were at the same time allowed to remain outside the monastic conventual cloister.[31]

A further distinction between the religious life strictly so called and the life of the Tertiaries turned about the question of the necessary papal approval. The decree of Innocent III demanded an explicit papal approval for religious foundations. However, the Tertiary Order of Saint Francis, which was founded in 1221, was not explicitly approved until the publication, in 1289, of the Bull "*Supra montem*" of Nicholas IV (1288-1292).[32] Nevertheless, the various privileges accorded to the Tertiary Orders many years before 1289 showed quite clearly that the Holy See had approved of their existence despite the fact that they lacked an explicit papal approbation.

In 1221 Pope Honorius III (1216-1227) freed the Tertiaries from the obligations of bearing arms in military service and from the need of taking oaths. In 1228 Pope Gregory IX (1227-1241) permitted the Tertiaries to take oaths when it was deemed necessary for them to do so in order to maintain peace, in order to confess their faith, and in order to clear themselves of calumny.

---

[29] Currier, *op. cit.*, p. 253.

[30] *C. 2 de statu monachorum vel canonicorum regularium*, III, 10, in Clem.

[31] Cf. cap. un., *de statu regularium*, III, 16, in VI°.

[32] *Bullarum Diplomatum et Privilegiorum Sanctorum Romanorum Pontificum Taurinensis Editio* (24 vols. et Appendix, Augustae Taurinorum-Neapoli, 1857-1872), IV, 90 (hereafter cited as *Bull. Rom. Taur.*).

Pope Gregory IX likewise granted them the privilege of not being obliged to accept public office.[33]

In view of the fact that the rules of the Tertiaries did not prescribe the taking of vows, the obedience which these rules called for did not bind the Tertiaries under the threat of grave sin in the event of any violation. This was expressly stated in the twentieth chapter of the Bull "*Supra montem*" of Pope Nicholas IV. The twentieth chapter stated in part:

> . . . Coeterum, in praemissis omnibus ad quae fratres vestri ordinis, non ex divinis praeceptis, vel statutis tenentur Ecclesiae, nullum ipsorum ad culpam mortalem volumus obligare. . . .[34]

In the thirteenth century, not many years after the foundations of the Tertiary Orders, there was a tendency among them to unite into communities. Although for a time these newly formed communities did not take any vows of religion, nevertheless they more and more withdrew themselves from the world, and they more and more closely approximated the true religious Orders, so that it was not very long before they added to their rules the obligations of solemn vows and of the observance of the cloister.[35]

ARTICLE VI. THE BEGUINS

From the time of Saint Benedict until the thirteenth century the three public vows taken at a public religious profession formed, as it were, the essence of all communities in which the religious life was practiced.[36] Nevertheless the rather revolutionary practice of the Tertiary Orders and of the Canonesses in forming communities in which the three public vows were not professed was a manifestation found also among other communities. One of the earliest known of the religious communities which allowed their members to live as religious without being bound as religious was

---

[33] Potthast, *Regesta Pontificum Romanorum inde ab anno post Christum natum 1198 ad annum 1304* (2 vols., Berolini, 1874-1875), n. 8159.

[34] *Bull. Rom. Taur.*, IV, 94.

[35] Currier, *op. cit.*, p. 256.

[36] Currier, *History of Religious Orders*, p. 607.

the community of women founded by Blessed Mary of Oignies (✠ 1213) shortly before the year 1200. This community was called the Beguins.[37]

The rules of the Beguins introduced several new elements into the development of the quasi-religious communities. The members of this community took private vows in place of the customary public profession, and instead of being perpetual their profession was only temporary. Their vows lasted only as long as the person remained in the community. The profession of the Beguins called for the professing of the private vows of chastity and obedience in the presence of the parish priest, under whose jurisdiction the local community was placed.[38] It was only natural that a community with such weak bonds in the matter of supervision and with such elasticity within its rules would soon present the occasion for many abuses and laxities among its members. Such proved to be the case within the community of the Beguins.

The Council of Trier (1227) condemned the Beguins for the dogmatic errors in their teaching.[39] The Synod of Fritzlar in 1259 spoke of the "pestilence of the Beguins," and the community was again reproved for its erroneous teaching.[40] Finally, at the general Council of Vienne in France (1311-1312), the community was suppressed.[41] Some of the local Beguin communities had not fallen into the errors and abuses which led to the suppression of the institute itself. These members who had remained true to their rule and orthodox in their teachings were protected by Pope John XXII (1316-1334), and allowed to live together in a community form of life.[42]

---

[37] Cf. K. Behlmeyer, "Beginen," *Lexikon für Theologie und Kirche* (2. ed., 10 vols., Freiburg: Herder & Co., 1930-1938), II, 89-90.

[38] Stanton, *De Societatibus sive Virorum sive Mulierum in Communi Viventium sine Votis* (2. ed., Halifaxiae: apud Custodiam Librariam Maioris Seminarii a. Sanctissimo Corde B.V.M., 1936), p. 20 (hereafter cited as *De Societatibus*).

[39] Mansi, XXIII, 32.

[40] Hefele, VI, 62.

[41] Hefele, VI, 543; c. 1, *de religiosis domibus,* III, 11, in Clem.

[42] Currier, *op. cit.,* p. 606; cap. un., *de religiosis domibus,* tit. VII, in Extrav. Ioan. XXII.

ARTICLE VII. THE OBLATES OF SAINT FRANCES OF ROME

In the year 1425 Francesca de'Ponziani (1384-1440) founded a community of young women and widows, which she called the Oblates, and eventually placed them under the direction of the Olivetan Fathers, a branch of the white monks of the Benedictine Order.[43] The rule which Saint Frances gave to her associates was indeed based on the Benedictine Rule, but it had several special provisions. The members took no vows; rather, they made an oblation of themselves to God, and hence took the name of Oblates.[44]

The rule prescribed a year of novitiate, but if after profession the members wished to leave the community in order to enter the state of marriage they were free to do so. They were not bound by the observance of the cloister. The superioress could give the members of the community permission to remain at their own homes for an indefinite period.[45]

This community of the Oblates was approved by Pope Eugene IV (1431-1447) on July 4, 1433, and some years later this same pontiff conferred on the members of the community the right to share in the favors, privileges and pious acts of the religious Orders.[46]

---

[43] Heimbucher, *Die Orden und Kongregationen der katholischen Kirche* (2. ed., 3 vols., Paderboan: Ferdinand Schöningh, 1907-1908), I, 310-311.

[44] Migne, *Encyclopédie Théologique* (3 series, 168 vols., Serie I, Vols. XX-XXIII, *Dictionnaire des Orders Religieux,* Paris, 1847-1859), XXII, 9-10 (hereafter cited as *Dictionnaire des Orders Religieux*).

[45] Currier, *op. cit.,* p. 535.

[46] Baronius, *Annales Ecclesiastici* (ed. A. Theiner, 37 vols., Vols. I-XXVIII, Silvae Ducis, 1864-1875; Vols. XXIX-XXXVII, Parisiis, 1876-1883), XXVIII, 157.

CHAPTER II

Quasi-Religious Societies from the Council of Trent until the Seventeenth Century

ARTICLE I. INTRODUCTION

Following the Council of Trent (1545-1563) there was an expansive development in all the phases of the religious life. It was perhaps the Church's insistence on reform measures, as expressed in the decrees of that famous Council, relative to the training of clerics for the priesthood, that gave rise, more than any other factor, to this development in the religious life.[1] New religious communities, putting into effect the decrees of the Council which called for the establishment of seminaries and the reform of the clergy, sprang up everywhere. This development was particularly notable among the communities of quasi-religious which were founded. This ecclesiastical institution thenceforth developed very rapidly and became solidly entrenched as a permanent part of the religious life in the Church's legislation. The final and ultimate official recognition of this institute came when the Code of Canon Law devoted to it an entire title in its general legislation for the religious life.[2]

ARTICLE II. THE VISITANDINES

The development of the quasi-religious societies was given an added impetus by the saintly Francis de Sales (1567-1622), Bishop of Geneva and Annecy (1602-1622). This gentle saint had been favored by God with a vision which revealed to him that he was to found a community for women in their maturity who because of their infirm health or widowhood might desire to leave the world and to consecrate themselves to God under obedience to a religious rule. Saint Francis de Sales wished that this community should not

[1] Cf. Conc. Trident., sess. XXIII, *de ref.* c. 18.

[2] Cf. cans. 673-681.

be bound by vows, for he believed that there were enough such communities already existing in the Church. For the founding of this community he secured the co-operation of the Baroness Jane Frances Frémyot de Chantal (1572-1641).[3]

The first profession in the community of the Visitation, which was pronounced by only three candidates, consisted of a simple offering of themselves to God. They pronounced no vows, nor did they bind themselves to the strict observance of the cloister.[4] When this community spread beyond the diocese of Annecy and founded a new house in the archdiocese of Lyons, Cardinal de Marquemont did not approve of the non-taking of vows or of the non-observance of the cloister. Saint Francis de Sales after much hesitation finally agreed to change the constitutions of the community, and thus the Visitandines became a community professed with solemn vows and thenceforward also observed the strict rule of the cloister.[5]

ARTICLE III. THE OBLATES OF SAINT PHILIP NERI

In the post-Tridentine development of the institute of quasi-religious, the Company of the Oratory was the first of the communities to appear in lending its effort and zeal to the promotion of sanctity and piety in the clerical state.

The company of the Oratory was founded by Saint Philip Neri in 1575 in the city of Rome. Saint Philip, born in Florence in 1515, from his earliest days had shown signs of a singularly pious and holy life. He was ordained a priest in the year 1551 in the city of Rome, and immediately launched forth on a life of self-sacrificing sacerdotal zeal and energy. Saint Philip was first stationed in the parish of San Girolamo della Carità. In an upper room connected with the same parish church he laid the foundations of his community. It was there that he began to give conferences to the clergy and to inaugurate exercises of devotion for the priests.

Soon a regular group of priests formed a sort of company and

[3] Currier, *op. cit.*, pp. 417-418.

[4] Currier, *op. cit.*, p. 419; Migne, *Dictionnaire des Orders Religieux*, XXII, 921-924.

[5] Stanton, *op. cit.*, p. 29, in which he quotes Bougaud, *Histoire de S. Chantal* (Paris, 1899), I, 524 ff.

placed themselves under his direction. In 1564 Saint Philip and his disciples were given the Church of the Florentines, and so the Saint transferred his activities to this new foundation. The community took the name of Priests of the Company of the Oratory in view of the first foundation of their group in the Oratory of the Church of San Girolamo. In 1575 this group obtained the Church of Santa Maria in Vallicella. Here they built a large edifice, called the *Chiesa Nuova,* where they permanently established the Company of the Oratory. On the 15th of July of the year 1575 Pope Gregory XIII (1572-1585), in the Bull *"Copiosus,"* formally approved this new congregation.[6]

The community spread rapidly. New houses were founded in Naples, Milan, San Severino, Palermo and other Italian cities. This rapid spread of the community and the problems that naturally arose made it imperative that the company develop a complete set of rules and constitutions. This was finally accomplished seventeen years after the death of Saint Philip, and the new constitutions were approved by Pope Paul V (1605-1621) in the Bull *"Christifidelium"* on the 24th of February, 1612.[7]

It had been the fervent will of Saint Philip that no vows should be taken in the Congregation of the Oratory. This same wish was legalized and definite provisions were accordingly made in these new constitutions. The fourth chapter of the constitutions reads in part:

> Cum nostra Congregatio solo charitatis mutuae nexu, neque ullis adstricta votorum, iuramenti, aut promissionis huiusmodi vinculis, olim per beatum patrem Philippum Nerium fuerit divina inspiratione instituta, atque haec fuerit eius et omnium Congregationis patrum mens semper unanimis; decretum est, si quando aliqui qui ex nostris putaverunt ab hoc statu recedendum, et alligare patres, fratresque ullis votorum, iurisiurandi, aut promissionis vinculis, etiam si isti maiorem partem conficiant, ut sit ipsis quidem liberum, quam velint, ingredi Re-

[6] Currier, *History of Religious Orders,* pp. 607-608; Passardière, *L'oratoire de St. Philippe de Neri* (2 parts, Draguignan, 1879), Part 1, pp. 17-25; *Bull. Rom. Taur.*, VIII, 541.

[7] *Bull. Rom. Taur.*, XII, 36; Passardière, *op. cit.,* Part I, pp. 64-76.

> ligionem, sed altera pars, quamvis numero longe impar, habeat omnia bona Congregationis quocumque loca posita, quandiu perseveraverit in hoc statu, nec aliter quicquam dare, vel acquisitum vel acquirendum, teneatur. . . .[8]

Saint Philip did not wish his members to pronounce vows since he believed that there was a sufficient number of religious Orders already existing for all persons who wished to lead the monastic life of a Regular. He saw no reason for founding another such Order.

Saint Philip was greatly encouraged by the approval of Pope Gregory XIII, who stated that he willed always that in the Church of God there should exist and flourish such congregations of reformed secular priests who would not be bound by any vows.[9]

Since no vows or oaths or promises were pronounced in the community, no one was held by profession to practice poverty. It was decreed, however, that each member had to be able to support himself in a manner befitting the life of a cleric. Furthermore, a member was to use his means to help defray the expenses of the congregation and promote the works of charity.[10]

The members of the community were free to leave whenever their consciences dictated that it was the proper thing to do, either because they considered themselves no longer worthy of the congregation, or because other reasons of charity or religion made their departure essential.[11]

The principal ends of the Oratory were threefold: prayer, preaching and the dispensing of the sacraments. Prayer included the carrying out of the liturgical office and the assistance at choir on feast days. The constitutions insisted on a frequent personal use of the sacraments as well as the administration of them to others, and for promoting the latter a priest was to sit daily in the confessional. Preaching comprised the presentation to the faithful of four sermons every day.

---

[8] *Bull. Rom. Taur.*, XII, 40.

[9] Perraud, *L'Oratoire de France* (Paris, 1866), p. 20.

[10] Passardière, *op. cit.*, Part I, pp. 44-47.

[11] Antrobus, *The Excellencies of the Oratory of St. Philip Neri* (London, 1881), pp. 338-342.

The Oratory continued to spread very rapidly. Houses were founded in Italy, Spain, Portugal, Poland, South America and even in distant India. To this day it continues its work in various parts of the world.[12]

ARTICLE IV. THE OBLATES OF SAINT AMBROSE

This congregation owes its origin to Saint Charles Borromeo (1538-1584), Archbishop of Milan (1560-1584) and Cardinal of the Church. Saint Charles had been created cardinal and assigned to the See of Milan by his uncle, Pope Paul IV, in 1560. The Oratory of Saint Philip had not yet been established in the archiepiscopal city. Feeling the need of having a clergy of zealous workers, Saint Charles decided to organize a congregation of secular priests upon whom he could depend to fulfill the needs of his archdiocese.[13]

He accordingly chose certain ecclesiastics who he thought would be suitable for such work, and he added to their number certain others who freely offered their services to his cause. He gave to this group the name Oblates, because they had offered themselves voluntarily, and he placed the congregation under the protection of the Blessed Virgin and of Saint Ambrose.[14]

Saint Charles himself drew up the rules for the community. Before submitting them to Rome for approval, he showed them to Saint Philip Neri, the founder of the Oratorians, and to Saint Felix of Cantalice (1512-1587). It was Saint Felix who persuaded him not to impose a vow of poverty on his subjects. Finally, the rules and constitutions having been approved by these saintly men, they were presented to the Holy Father for his acceptance. On the 16th of August in the year 1578 Pope Gregory XIII blessed the congregation with the official ecclesiastical approbation of the Holy See.[15]

The rules specified that the prospective member of this congregation was to take only a simple vow of obedience in the presence

[12] Antrobus, *The Excellencies of the Oratory of St. Philip Neri*, pp. 47-52.

[13] Migne, *Dictionnaire des Orders Religieux*, XXII, 18-21.

[14] Currier, *op. cit.*, p. 620.

[15] Stackpoole-Kenny, *St. Charles Borromeo* (New York: Benziger Bros., 1911), pp. 170-172.

of the Archbishop of Milan. The Archbishop was to be recognized as the superior of the congregation to such an extent that no command other than his should be obeyed, and this only, in things lawful and pertaining to the institute. No other occupations were to be entered upon other than those involved in the duty of assisting the Archbishop in the care of his diocese. These duties consisted in the visiting of various cities and there giving missions and retreats, in fulfilling the office of vicars and curates in vacant churches, in the conducting of schools and of seminaries, and, in general, in the various priestly duties which were to be fulfilled in the efficient and proper administration of a diocese.[16]

It is quite evident from the formula of profession that the vow of obedience which was to be rendered to the Archbishop and his successors was the only official and legal bond which held all the members to the community. The formula read in part:

> . . . Ego N., omnipotenti Deo, et Sanctissimo Patri nostro Ambrosio, coram Beatissima Virgine, Dei Matre Maria . . . ac tibi quoque locum sanctissimi Patris nostri Ambrosii hic obtinenti, Reverendissime Domine Pater Archiepiscope, ceterisque deinceps Archiepiscopis Sanctae Mediolanensis Ecclesiae successoribus tuis promitto, spondeo ac voveo perpetuam obedientiam in his omnibus, quae mihi praecipientur. . . .[17]

Regarding the question of poverty, it was left to the will of the individual candidate whether or not he wished to take a voluntary vow of poverty in addition to the above mentioned obligatory vow of obedience to the Archbishop of Milan.[18]

This voluntary vow of poverty could assume one or the other of two forms. One form of the vow called upon the candidate to relinquish the complete dominion of his property; the other form of the vow permitted the candidate to maintain the dominion of his possessions, but he willingly submitted the use of his goods

---

[16] Migne, *Dictionnaire des Orders Religieux,* XXII, 22.

[17] *Institutionum ad Oblatos S. Ambrosii Pertinentium Epitome,* Caroli S.R.E. Cardinalis Tit. Sanctae Praxedis Archiep. Mediol. iussi Edita (Mediolani, 1716), pp. 507-18.

[18] Currier, *op. cit.,* p. 620.

to the will of his superiors. To forestall any worries of conscience or other difficulties, it was expressly stated that, in whichever form the vow was pronounced, it was always to be considered as a simple vow, regardless of the publicity attached to the ceremony, or of the number of witnesses, or of any solemnity that might be employed on the occasion of the profession.[19]

The members of the society were able to leave the institute for any just or righteous cause. The permission, however, for their departure could be granted only by the Archbishop of Milan.[20]

The entire congregation was divided into six assemblies or quasi-provinces. There were two such assemblies or communities in Milan, and four outside the city. Each assembly, although completely subject to the Archbishop of Milan, was immediately under the guidance of a superior and a spiritual director.[21]

ARTICLE V. SECULAR CLERICS LIVING IN COMMON

As a result of the Thirty Years' War the Catholic Faith suffered a serious setback. The fire of the Faith had been cooled, and the morals and religious discipline not only of the laity but also of the clergy had been considerably relaxed. Because of this frightful state in which the Church found herself, Bartholomew Holzhauser (1613-1658), a saintly priest of the diocese of Salzburg, decided to dedicate his life and talents to the increase of zeal and piety among the faithful both lay and clerical.[22]

He planned to found a community of secular priests who would lead an apostolic life in common, and become models of priestly perfection and zealous leaders of the faithful. He would send the more learned of his disciples to be teachers in the seminaries, and thus call into being a new generation of priests. These same priests, inspired by the learning and zeal of their instructors, would supply the impetus to a restoration of faith and morals among the laity and the clergy in a war-wearied nation.

[19] *Institutionum ad Oblatos S. Ambrosii Pertinentium Epitome*, p. 3.

[20] *Ibid.*, p. 18.

[21] "Traite des Congregations Seculières," *Analecta Juris Pontificii*, V (1861), 65.

[22] Heimbucher, *Die Orden und Kongregationen der katholischen Kirche*, III, 553-554.

He started his community at Salzburg, and with the aid of saintly priests the first seminary came into existence. The results of this first establishment were so successful that the Bishop of Chiemsee in Bavaria offered him the vicarage of Saint John in the Leoggental (Leukental). Father Holzhauser accepted the benefice, and started his community in Bavaria.[23]

Although the institution of secular clerics of the common life had been established in 1643, the first real efforts to secure papal approbation did not take place until some years after the death of the saintly founder. Finally in 1680, at the request of several princes and prelates, Pope Innocent XI (1676-1689) confirmed and approved the constitutions of the society. Four years later, in 1684, the constitutions were further enlarged upon and necessary corrections were made.[24]

The constitutions did not call for any profession of the vows of religion. Instead of the customary bonds of poverty, chastity and obedience, the candidates were to take an oath of obedience to the ordinary of the diocese where the community house was located. The oath was called an *agreement.* The candidates were likewise bound by this oath to be obedient to their superiors in matters of a private nature pertaining to their own spiritual advancement and the welfare of the community.[25]

The candidates likewise pronounced an oath of perseverance whereby they obliged themselves never to be separated from the institute of their own accord. Only the Holy Father was empowered to dispense the members from this oath of stability.[26]

No oath was pronounced concerning the matter of poverty, but the members were held to a community of goods, which imposed upon them the obligation of disposing of their legally acquired goods in the promotion of the common pious purposes, and also the obligation of so arranging their last wills and testaments that after their death the property left might likewise be used for pious causes.[27]

---

[23] Migne, *Dictionnaire des Orders Religieux,* XXII, 373.

[24] *Bull. Rom. Taur.,* XIX, 244, 530; Heimbucher, *op. cit.,* III, 556.

[25] *Bull. Rom. Taur.,* XIX, 242, 245; Migne, *Dictionnaire des Orders Religieux,* XXII, 533.

[26] *Bull. Rom. Taur.,* XIX, 530.

[27] *Bull. Rom. Taur.,* XIX, 244-245.

ARTICLE VI. THE CONGREGATION OF THE MISSION

Saint Vincent de Paul (1581-1660), the founder of the Congregation of the Mission, was born at Pouy near Dax in France. He began his ecclesiastical studies at an early age, and in 1600 was ordained a priest. In 1608 he joined the family of Emanuel de Gondy, Count of Joigny, in the capacity of tutor for the de Gondy children. During the years of his service in the de Gondy household, Saint Vincent was frequently called upon by Madame de Gondy, a very devout Catholic, to preach mission sermons to the poor serfs attached to the de Gondy estates. This humble ministry to the poor was the sowing of the seeds which not many years later would flower into the establishment of the Congregation of the Mission and provide the poor of generations to come with sacerdotal ministrations.[28]

In 1625 Madame de Gondy established a foundation to provide for the giving of a mission every five years to the rural population of her extensive estates. After many unsuccessful attempts to secure the aid of already established religious communities for the accomplishment of this foundation, she persuaded Saint Vincent de Paul to gather some zealous priests into a sort of company for the purpose of delivering these missions to the long neglected poor. Saint Vincent accepted the foundation, and prepared immediately to secure the necessary sacerdotal aid and the proper ecclesiastical approbation.

It was not a very difficult problem to find in Paris enough priests whom Saint Vincent considered as suitable associates in this work for the poor, and in the year 1626 the Archbishop of Paris approved this new community which had adopted the title of Priests of the Congregation of the Mission. In 1627 King Louis XIII (1610-1643) of France, added his seal of royal authority to the act of foundation approved just the year previous by the ecclesiastical authorities.[29]

---

[28] Coste, *Life and Labors of St. Vincent de Paul* (translated from the French by Joseph Leonard, C.M., 3 vols., London: Burns, Oates and Washbourne, 1934-1935), I, 60-63; Currier, *op. cit.*, p. 441.

[29] Pisani, *The Congregations of Priests from the XVI-XVIII Century* (translated by Mother Mary Reginald, O.P., St. Louis: Herder and Co., 1930), pp. 72-75; Coste, *Life and Labors of St. Vincent de Paul*, I, 145-159.

Some years elapsed before the approbation of Rome was given to the *Congregation of the Mission.* This was due chiefly to the opposition of the clergy, who feared that in these new congregations there would rise up inconvenient censors of their own lives. Another cause was the opposition of the bishops, who did not look with favor on institutions which enjoyed a certain ecclesiastical autonomy, and were to a certain extent removed from the jurisdiction of the local ordinaries. It required six years of laborious negotiations before Pope Urban VIII (1625-1644) on the 12th of January, 1633, by means of the Bull *"Salvatoris Nostri"* approved the society of the Priests of the Congregation of the Mission. This Bull did not approve the fully developed rules and constitutions of the congregation; it merely concerned itself with the scope of its works, its subjection to the ordinaries with regard to the actual works of the missions, and the election of Saint Vincent as the first superior of the congregation.[30]

In 1665 Pope Alexander VII, in the Brief *"Ex commissa Nobis,"* approved the full constitutions of the community. By this document the nature of its vows and the exemption of the community from the jurisdiction of the ordinaries, with regard to all matters except those which touched the actual missions, were given ecclesiastical approbation.[31]

The nature of the vows taken by the priests of the congregation is of particular interest to the scope of this dissertation. It had always been the mind of Saint Vincent that the members of his community should never be considered as religious. He believed that if they were bound by the obligations and the duties of the religious life they would not be able to carry out efficiently the varied works of the institute which demanded their services at all hours of the day and in so many different works of the priestly life.

Although Saint Vincent was determined that his subjects should not be classed as religious, still he did desire to bind them to the life and works of the community in a manner similar to the bond which resulted from the profession of the vows of religion.

[30] Pisani, *Congregation of Priests from the XVI-XVIII Century,* pp. 75-77; *Acta Apostolica, Bullae, Brevia et Rescripta in Gratiam Congregationis Missionis* (Parisiis, 1873), pp. 3-7 (hereafter this work will be cited as *Acta*).

[31] *Bull. Rom. Taur.,* XVI, 67.

To bring about this desired result Saint Vincent called upon his subjects to pronounce private vows of chastity, poverty, obedience and stability. These vows were not to be received in the name of the Church or by the superiors of the congregation, but were to be pronounced before the Blessed Sacrament in the presence of the superior as witness, and for a guarantee of the obligations assumed by the missioner to the community, and of the reciprocal obligations assumed by the community towards the missioner. As a result of a profession of this nature, consisting of the pronouncing of private vows, a person could not be considered a religious in the strict sense of the word, since there was no acceptance of the vows either by the Church or by the community, which condition was required before one could strictly be considered a religious. Nevertheless, by a profession of this kind the subject for all practical purposes was bound to the community by all the obligations and responsibilities which would have resulted from religious profession accepted in the strict sense.[32]

The word *private* with reference to vows had not as yet been recognized in the canonical terminology. Accordingly in the Brief, *"Ex commissa Nobis,"* of Alexander VII, the expression *simple vow* was used. However, it can indirectly be proved that a private vow was meant. In the first place the very description of the nature and of the ceremony of the profession, which directly manifested that the vows were not received by any authority, implied that the vows were to be distinguished from both the solemn and the simple vows of religion, both of which had to be received either by the Church or by the institute. Further proof is offered by the fact that, although at the time of the foundation of the community profession with simple vows was sufficient to constitute one a religious, nevertheless the Congregation of the Mission was always considered and recognized as a secular community and not as a religious body. This was expressly stated by Alexander VII in the Brief *"Alias Nos"* (1659) : ". . . Dicta Congregatio non censeatur propterea in numero ordinum religiosorum, sed sit de corpore cleri saecularis."[33]

---

[32] Coste, *Le grand saint du grand siècle Monsieur Vincent* (3 vols., Desclée de Brouwer & Co., Paris: 1931), II, 20-22.

[33] *Bull. Rom. Taur.,* XVI, 488.

The approval of the congregation in the Brief *"Ex commissa Nobis"* of Alexander VII read in part:

> . . . Praefatam Congregationem Missionis . . . tenore praesentium confirmamus et approbamus cum emissione votorum simplicium castitatis, paupertatis, et obedientiae, nec non stabilitatis in dicta Congregatione ad effectum se, toto vitae tempore, saluti pauperum rusticanorum applicandi, post biennium probationis facienda; in quorum tamen votorum emissione nemo intersit, qui ea acceptet, sive nomine Congregationis, sive Nostro. . . .[34]

A most unusual privilege was granted to the community in this same Brief, when the pontiff accorded them exemption from the local ordinaries in all things except with regard to the official functions of the members while engaged in the works of the mission. The words of exemption read as follows:

> Statuentes ut dicta Congregatio Missionis exempta sit a subiectione locorum Ordinariorum in omnibus, excepto quod personae quae a Superioribus eiusdem Congregationis deputabuntur ad missiones aliquas subsint ipsis Ordinariis tantum quoad missiones et ea quae illas concernunt.[35]

As a result of this privilege of exemption all that concerns the spiritual and community affairs of the members of the congregation are the concern of the superiors, and not of the bishop.

The extent and meaning of the vow of poverty in the congregation was definitely established by Pope Alexander in the Brief *"Alias Nos,"* in which it was stated that the members would retain the dominion of their immovable goods and their simple benefices. However, the constitutions imposed on them the duty of applying the accruing revenues, with the permission of their superiors, to either works of piety or to the relief of their parents and relatives whenever these might be in want.[36]

---

[34] *Bull. Rom. Taur.*, XVI, 67; Coste, *Life and Labors of St. Vincent de Paul*, I, 494-495.

[35] *Bull. Rom. Taur.*, XVI, 68.

[36] *Bull. Rom. Taur.*, XVI, 488-489; Coste, *Life and Labors of St. Vincent de Paul*, I, 497.

The governing of the community was distributed through various offices. The Superior General, elected for life and with residence in Paris, was made the first and principal superior. To aid him in the work of governing the community, he was given four Assistants elected by the General Assembly. Provision was also made for a Secretary General and a Procurator General, both chosen by the Superior General. Supreme authority was placed in the General Assembly, which was required to meet every twelve years. The office of Visitor was established, the incumbents to be appointed by the Superior General as his representatives in each province. Local government was placed in the hands of a local superior in immediate charge of each house.[37]

ARTICLE VII. THE SULPICIANS

The Council of Trent in 1563 had decreed that seminaries were to be erected in the metropolitan and cathedral cities, and that in these seminaries young clerics were to be trained for their priestly mission.[38]

It was this pronouncement of the Fathers of the Council of Trent that had been an inspiration to Saint Vincent de Paul in his zealous efforts to establish seminaries for the future clergy of France. This flame of zeal, enkindled by Saint Vincent, soon caught within its circle of warmth the heart and mind of one of his associates, Monsieur Olier (1608-1657). Monsieur Olier had studied very closely the efforts and successes of Saint Vincent. The achievements of this saint had made a lasting impression upon his mind, and filled him with a desire to continue this work of training clerics for the holy and responsible duties of the sacred priesthood.[39]

Shortly after his ordination to the priesthood Monsieur Olier began to put his dreams into reality. He established a seminary for clerics at Vaugirard, a suburb of Paris, in January, 1642, and his work was an immediate success. Several zealous priests soon

---

[37] Coste, *Life and Labors of St. Vincent de Paul,* I, 476.

[38] Conc. Trident., sess. XXIII, *de ref.,* c. 18.

[39] Currier, *History of Religious Orders,* p. 623; Heimbucher, *Die Orden und Kongregationem der katholischen Kirche,* III, 442-443.

joined him, and the news of the success of this establishment spread very quickly. In August of the same year Monsieur Olier was placed in charge of the parish of Saint Sulpice, and the seminary of Vaugirard was transferred thither. Monsieur Olier then organized his disciples into a regular company, and he was chosen the first superior. No rules were immediately drawn up, since it was the wish of the founder that the rules be evolved through the test of time.[40]

It was not until 1651 that Monsieur Olier submitted the first copy of his constitutions to the General Assembly of his company, and it was some twelve years later in 1664 that the constitutions received ecclesiastical approbation from the Papal Legate of France, Cardinal Flavius Chigi.[41] During the several years which elapsed between the founding of the community and its final approbation, the Society of Saint Sulpice had founded several seminaries at the requests of the local ordinaries.[42]

Monsieur Olier had died in 1657. It was the second Superior General of the society, Alexander le Ragois de Bretonvilliers (1657-1676), who completed the work of organizing the rules and constitutions of the community, and thereupon submitted them to Cardinal Chigi for the necessary ecclesiastical approval. However, it must be noted that this approval did not establish the community as a religious congregation; it merely approved the single foundation of Saint Sulpice, and left the members of the society in the status of the secular clergy in which they had been when the society was first founded. The approval made this point quite clear, since it was addressed to "Superiores et presbyteri saeculares seminarii, Sancti Sulpitii nuncupati, in suburbio Sancti Germani prope Parisios siti et fundati."[43]

It had always been the will of Monsieur Olier that the members of his community should never become a religious body. He insisted that they always remain secular priests, and that they should live the life of diocesan priests. The professors and students in

---

[40] Faillon, *Vie de M. Olier* (4. ed., 3 vols., Paris, 1853), III, 13-20; Heimbucher, *op. cit.*, III, 443-444.

[41] Faillon, *Vie de M. Olier,* III, 274-276.

[42] Heimbucher, *op. cit.*, III, 444.

[43] Faillon, *Vie de M. Olier,* III, 275.

their seminaries were expected to live according to rule, obeying the superiors appointed under it and bound by the obligations imposed by it.[44] No mention was made in the constitutions of any profession by vow, oath or promise. However, by reason of their admission into the Society, the members assumed an implied obligation to obey the prescriptions of their institute and the commands of their superiors.[45]

In order to enter the society a candidate had to spend at least five years in a house of the community. This length of time could be lessened, but only by the superior with the advice of his councillors and for a good and sufficient reason. The society was not to be over-eager in seeking out new members; only those candidates were to be accepted who were willing to live a life of service in the training of the clergy. The houses of the company were not to be so large that order and discipline could be preserved only with difficulty.[46]

The constitutions urged the practice of priestly poverty, and all the members of the society had to renounce any dignity or benefice which was incompatible with his residence or his employment in the community. The acceptance of any dignity or benefice without the permission of the Vicar General was forbidden to the members.

The constitutions likewise left each member free to leave the institute whenever his conscience dictated to him that there was a sufficiently grave reason to do so.[47]

Each house of the institute was considered a separate establishment, each directly subject to the local ordinary, while the internal rule and discipline of each house was controlled by a local superior, who was appointed by the Superior General. The unity of the entire society existed not in any legal dependence or relationship, but rather in the spirit which animated the members in their life and practice.[48]

---

[44] Faillon, *Vie de M. Olier,* III, 242-246.

[45] Herbermann, *The Sulpicians in the United States* (New York: Encyclopedia Press, 1916), p. 31.

[46] Faillon, *Vie de M. Olier,* III, 185-186; Stanton, *De Societatibus,* p. 73.

[47] Herbermann, *The Sulpicians in the United States,* p. 31; Faillon, *Vie de* M. Olier, III, 246.

[48] Faillon, *Vie de M. Olier,* III, 242-244.

ARTICLE VIII. THE EUDISTS

Father Eudes de Mezerai (1601-1680), founder of the company known as the Society of Jesus and Mary, had been for many years a member of the Congregation of the Oratory. Just prior to his founding of the society he had been appointed superior of the Oratory at Caën. While engaged in the works of the ministry as a member of the Oratorians, he had become conscious of the necessity for good and zealous priests who might be able to carry on fittingly the works of the priesthood. He became convinced that the best means for providing such worthy priests was to establish really worthy seminaries. He fully realized that the priests could give to others only what they themselves received during their years of priestly formation. It was this realization that filled his soul and heart with the burning desire to dedicate his life to the formation of godly priests.

Father Eudes, after spending some time in seeking wise and prudent guidance and in becoming fully convinced of the righteousness of his action, left the Oratory and immediately started to put into action his long desired hopes. Eight priests joined Father Eudes in his new enterprise, and in 1643 this band of priests founded a seminary at Caën. They took as their title The Society of the Sacred Hearts of Jesus and Mary. The seminary at Caën remained for some time the only house of the Society. The priests devoted themselves entirely to the work of training the young clerics for their future life in the ministry.[49]

The first statutes of the society were approved by the Holy See in 1654. Practically all these documents were lost after the Revolution, and only a part of one chapter remains.[50]

In 1664 the Bishop of Bayeux, Jacques d'Angennes, gave to the society letters of approval, permitting them to institute a seminary and to erect a congregation of ecclesiastics under the name of the Priests of the Society of Jesus and Mary. In the years which preceded their official Roman approbation, the society undertook

---

[49] Heimbucher, *op. cit.*, II, 448-449; Georges, *St. Jean Eudes* (3. ed., Paris: P. Lethielleux, 1936), pp. 55-65.

[50] Boulay, *Vie de Venerable Jean Eudes* (4 vols., Paris, 1906), II, append., 28, IV, 301.

the direction and the erection of several seminaries, always however after having first secured the approval of its constitutions from the local ordinary.[51]

It had always been the firm conviction of Eudes that the members of his company should never pronounce the vows of religion. He reasoned that if priests could find the inspiration and the means of rising to perfection, not in a religious profession, but rather in the dignity of their vocation, they would be in a much more suitable position to inspire young clerics with a lofty idea of the sacred priesthood and the sanctity which it demanded. Another reason for his insistence on the non-pronouncement of vows was that he believed that the bishops would be more inclined to give the direction of their seminaries to priests over whom they would have the fullest jurisdiction, than to entrust these seminaries to communities of priests which by reason of their religious nature would be in varying degrees removed from episcopal jurisdiction.[52]

It was because of this reasoning that Father Eudes, in the first copy of his constitutions, insisted that the members of the society should not take the customary vows of religion, but rather should be bound by a link of charity. This union of charity was to oblige the members to obedience to the rule as though they had taken a vow of obedience.[53] The formula of profession as found in the constitutions calls for a promise of fidelity to the observance of the rules and constitutions.

> . . . Moi n—, proteste en la face du ciel et de la terre que je vous reconnais et adore, ô mon Seigneur Jesus, comme le Souverain et le Père de cette sainte Congrègation, . . . et que je m'engage moyennant votre sainte grâce, à y vivre et mourir pour vous y servir et honorer en toute la perfection qui me sera possible, par une entière abnégation de ma propre volonté pour suivre la vôtre, qui me sera manifestée par celle de mes Supérieurs et par les Constitutions de cette même Congregation. Pour cet effet, je me donne a vous de tout mon coeur, ô mon Jésus, promettant d'être fidèle, pour l'amour de

[51] Stanton, *De Societatibus*, p. 74.

[52] Georges, *St. Jean Eudes*, pp. 59-63; Montez, *Father Eudes and His Foundations* (Boston, 1874), pp. 96-97; Stanton, *De Societatibus*, p. 56.

[53] Costaggini, *Vita del Beato Giovani Eudes* (Roma: Typografia Pontificia del Instituto Pio IX, 1909), p. 108; Currier, *op. cit.*, p. 618.

vous, à cet engagement et vous suppliant de m'en donner la grâce. . . .[54]

Although the profession made no mention of obedience to the bishops, still it was the absolute will of Saint John Eudes that the members of the society should be under the complete jurisdiction of the local ordinaries, just as any other of his diocesan subjects, with the single reservation that only in the private and personal matters concerned with the rules or constitutions should a subject depend upon a superior of the society for his conduct. The local ordinary had the full right of visitation and correction, and all other episcopal powers.[55]

In place of any vow or promise of poverty there existed among the members a custom whereby they distributed their personal revenues in good works. With the permission of their superiors the members could provide for their parents whenever these happened to be in need.[56]

The internal government of the society lay in the hands of the General Assembly. The Assembly consisted of the Superior General, of subordinate superiors, and of individual deputies from the various houses. The Superior General was to be the president and the first officer of the Assembly. He held his office for life, while the local superiors were to be elected for terms of three years. This General Assembly had the right to modify the constitutions relative to things exterior and temporal, provided that it was for the harmony of the common life.[57]

Underlying the whole spirit and activities of the Society, there was present a most firm attachment to the direction and the doctrine of the Holy See. This was brought about by the devotion of Saint Eudes to the person of Christ as represented in the Holy Father. The Saint demanded that as long as the society existed it was to take all orders from Rome as coming from the center of unity and Faith.[58]

---

[54] Stanton, *De Societatibus*, p. 132.

[55] Costaggini, *Vita del Beato Giovani Eudes*, p. 108; Migne, *Dictionnaire des Orders Religieux*, XXI, 249; *Analecta Juris Pontificii*, V (1861), 96-97.

[56] Currier, *op. cit.*, p. 618; *Analecta Juris Pontificii*, V (1861), 97.

[57] Migne, *Dictionnaire des Orders Religieux*, XXI, 249; Stanton, *De Societatibus*, p. 76.

[58] Costaggini, *Vita del Beato Giovani Eudes*, p. 108.

CHAPTER III

Quasi-Religious Societies from the Eighteenth Century until the Code

ARTICLE I. THE PALLOTTINE FATHERS

Vincent Pallotti (1795-1850), the founder of the Pious Society of the Missions, had from the first days of his priesthood been filled with a longing to spread the faith of Christ over the entire world. His dream was to found a society composed of both men and women who would be of one heart and mind and who, inspired solely by the love of God, would work together for the spread of the Catholic Faith. He hoped to see this association so increase its membership that it would soon spread over the entire world and include within its scope every land, every home and every soul. His aim, in brief, was to make every one a Catholic, every Catholic a good Catholic, and every good Catholic an apostle.

Pallotti soon interested a number of friends, both lay and cleric, with his plan. This group formed the foundation of his apostolate. Funds were soon gathered to further the cause. To insure the proper use of the money and to protect the group against any false reports, Pallotti decided to create a formal society which would have the approbation of the Church. Pope Gregory XVI (1831-1846), on July 11, 1835, bestowed upon the society his approval and blessing. The newly formed company took the name of the Society of the Catholic Apostolate. With a view to greater efficiency through a more organized control, the society was divided into three classes, the active members, the praying members and the supporting members. The first group consisted of those who could give their time to the works of the company, the second group consisted of those who could not contribute any material help but whose prayers and sacrifices were to enrich the works of the society, and thc third group consisted of those who contributed financially to the society.[1]

Pallotti soon realized that such a vast organization could not be directed by him alone. He planned, therefore, to form a group of leaders who, united under one superior, would direct the organization in accordance with the purposes of the Apostolate. Pallotti himself became the leader of this group. It was made up of secular priests who were willing to devote their entire time to the works of the Apostolate. This group of secular clergy took the name of the Congregation of the Catholic Apostolate. However, that title soon became the cause of much controversy due to the fact that several of the clergy thought that the title included within its scope many of the works of the Society of the Propagation of the Faith, and some even held that the society by assuming this title was arrogating to itself the works of the Holy See. It was not until the death of Pallotti that the disputes concerning the works and the title of the society were finally settled. The final form of their title reads "The Pious Society of the Missions." The word *Pious* is to be understood in the sense of the Latin *pia,* which connotes the idea of being devoted or dedicated to God.[2]

When Pallotti drew up the first rules for this organized body of the Apostolate, he did not contemplate the taking of any vows or the making of any formal promises on the part of the members. The love of Christ was to be the only bond holding them to the society. In fact, the founder did not intend to draw up a detailed set of constitutions; he maintained that the Gospel should be the complete guide for his subjects.[3]

Within a few years it became evident that for the good order and the prosperous outcome of the works of the society a determined set of rules and constitutions had to be composed. Accordingly, Pallotti drew up the necessary documents, and in place of the bond of charity the members were now called upon to pro-

---

[1] Herbert, *Venerable Vincent Pallotti, Apostle and Mystic* (revised and enlarged by Nicholas M. Wilwers, P.S.M., Milwaukee: The Pallottine Fathers, 1942), pp. 27-33.

[2] Migne, *Dictionnaire des Orders Religieux,* XXIII, 1041-1042.

[3] Herbert, *Venerable Vincent Pallotti,* pp. 35-36.

nounce promises of fidelity to the society, which promises would have the force of a contract binding the members to the institute.

The constitutions called for a two year novitiate after which there was to be a temporary profession of one year. This year of temporary profession was to be followed by a perpetual profession, in which the members were to promise the observance of a life in common, the practice of poverty, of chastity and of obedience, and perseverance for life in the membership of the society.[4]

The formula of profession read in part:

> . . . Ego, n.n., me totum eidem omnipotenti Deo trado, dono, et offero, ac Dominum nostrum Jesum Christum sequi statuo; et ideo promitto Piae Societati Missionum eiusque Superioribus perseverantiam, obedientiam, castitatem, paupertatem ac vitam communem perfectam, secundum euisdem Societatis Constitutiones.[5]

The promise of poverty as pronounced in the society permitted the members to retain their possessions and to dispose of them by will. However, as long as they were members of the society their property was to be administered for pious causes.[6]

To relieve all doubts of conscience the constitutions stated that of the four virtues promised at profession only the promise of perseverance, which constituted the contract between the society and the members, was binding under the pain of mortal sin, whereas the remaining promises bound solely in fidelity and under pain of venial sin.[7]

ARTICLE II. THE FATHERS OF THE PRECIOUS BLOOD

Blessed Father Gaspar del Bufalo, the founder of the Priests of the Congregation of the Precious Blood, was born at Rome in 1786. He was ordained a priest in 1808. Immediately upon his ordination he devoted himself wholeheartedly to the work of

---

[4] Heimbucher, *Die Orden und Kongregationen der katholischen Kirche,* III, 485.

[5] Stanton, *De Societatibus,* p. 133.

[6] Heimbucher, *op. cit.,* III, 585.

[7] Herbert, *Venerable Vincent Pallotti,* p. 159.

preaching mission sermons. In October of the year 1814 he preached a retreat to the Augustinian Canons Regular at Giano in the diocese of Spoleto. While engaged in this work he came to know of an old abandoned church and monastery, which had been dedicated to Saint Felix. The sight of this edifice inspired Bufalo with the plan of founding there a company of clerics who might devote themselves to the work of preaching missions.

Shortly afterwards Bufalo returned to Rome and there discussed his plan with Cardinal Cristaldi. The prudent Cardinal encouraged him in his hopes, but he advised Bufalo first to seek the approval of the Pontiff. The then reigning Pontiff, Pius VII (1800-1823), not only approved his plans, but even donated a sum of money to Bufalo to assist him in the establishing of his institute.

In 1814 the Pontiff gave Bufalo the abandoned church of Saint Felix, and the work was formally begun. A number of priests interested in the work of the missions attached themselves to Bufalo, and soon other foundations were established. In 1820 the community had prospered so well that the Pope ordered them to open six houses in Albano, with the hope that the preaching of missions in that territory would remedy the evils caused by the local banditti.[8]

Bufalo completed the first copy of the rules and constitutions shortly before his death, which occurred in 1837. He insisted that the members of the congregation should pronounce no vows. His reason for this was that he believed the members of the company, being chiefly drawn from the ranks of the secular clergy, would more voluntarily and faithfully perform their duties if they were not bound by the customary vows of religion. In place of these vows the congregation was to be united by a bond of charity. In their constitutions the members were to be obedient to the commands of their superiors and to be always at their disposal.[9]

As a safeguard lest the bond of a religious profession by vows

---

[8] Heimbucher, *op. cit.*, III, 474-475; Migne, *Dictionnaire des Orders Religieux*, III, 215-225.

[9] *Blessed Gaspar del Bufalo* (by a member of the same Congregation, Carthagena, Ohio, 1933), p. 79; Sardi, *Vita del B. Gaspare de Bufalo* (Roma, 1904), pp. 164-165.

might ever develop in the congregation, the fourth article of the constitutions was thus drawn up: "Alumni non solum nullo peculiari voto ligantur, sed nec iuramento, nec sponsione permanendi, ut semper omni vinculo soluti censeantur. . . ."

The administration of the society was placed in the hands of a General Directory composed of the Moderator General, elected for life, and of four missionaries, elected by the General Chapter for a term of twelve years. The General Chapter was to convene every twelfth year. It was to consist of the members of the General Directory, of the various provincials, of one delegate for the first fifty missionaries, and of an additional delegate for each twenty-five missionaries over and above the first fifty in each established province.[10]

ARTICLE III. THE PAULISTS

Isaac Hecker (1819-1888), the founder of the Congregation of Missionary Priests of Saint Paul, had been a convert to the Catholic Faith. Following his conversion he entered the Congregation of the Most Holy Redeemer at St. Trond in Belgium in 1845. He was ordained a priest in 1849. After his ordination Father Hecker was sent to America as a member of the first group of Redemptorists who came to the American Continent to labor for the conversion of infidels and non-Catholics to the true fold. He was very fond of his mission, and proved himself a most competent missionary and leader in the works of the mission.

In 1857 a disagreement arose between the Redemptorists in America and the members of the community in Rome. The dispute concerned the establishment of a new house in America, where English would be the language used by the members of the congregation. Father Hecker, representing the American group, went to Rome to lay his case before the Rector General. In all probability Hecker acted in good faith, not adverting to the fact that one of the statutes of the constitutions of the congregation, under the pain of expulsion, forbade any member of the company to go to the General without his permission. In virtue of

[10] *The Messenger of the Precious Blood,* XXI (1915), 281-282.

this regulation Hecker was expelled from the congregation in 1857. The matter was brought to the attention of the Holy Father. After mature consideration, Pius IX (1846-1878) dispensed Father Hecker from his vows. At the same time the Pontiff dispensed four companion priests of Father Hecker from their vows professed in the same Congregation of the Most Holy Redeemer. These four American missionaries had petitioned the Holy See for their dispensation after the expulsion of Hecker.[11]

Upon the granting of these dispensations Father Hecker returned to America. The five former Redemptorists continued their missionary work in America, and formed themselves into a missionary society under the direction of Father Hecker. This new society drew up a set of rules and constitutions very similar to the rules and constitutions of the Redemptorist community. This set of rules, termed by the members a Programme of Rule, was signed by the five members and submitted to the Archbishop of New York for his approval. Archbishop Hughes (1850-1864) on July 7, 1858, approved the Programme, and thus the new society under the title of The Missionary Priests of Saint Paul the Apostle was formally recognized as a corporate body in the Church.[12]

When Father Hecker drew up the first plans for the community, he did not wish his subjects to be bound by any profession of the vows of religion. He preferred, rather, that a principle of voluntary loyalty and service should be the only bond of union existing in the society. He did not entirely abandon the idea of vows, but he wished to put off the question until a later date, when experience, counsel, and divine guidance might aid him in his final decision. He summed up the entire question in the following sentence: "The true Paulist should be ready to take vows at any moment."[13]

In the thirty-ninth article of the constitutions is found the following formula of profession, which calls on the candidate to pronounce, in the place of the customary vows of religion, a perpetual

---

[11] Elliott, *The Life of Father Hecker* (2. ed., New York, 1894), pp. 230-280.

[12] Currier, *History of Religious Orders,* pp. 620-630; Elliott, *The Life of Father Hecker,* pp. 281-284.

[13] Elliott, *The Life of Father Hecker,* pp. 293-295.

voluntary agreement to obey the rules and constitutions of the congregation.

> Ego, N.N., cum firmiter prudenterque persuasum habeam ante conspectum Dei me divinitus ad vitam religiosam vocari in Societatem a S. Paulo Apostolo, *promitto* me regulis Societatis obediturum, christianam religiosamque perfectionem servaturum, laboribus apostolici ministerii assidue incubiturum et in hac voluntate usque ad vitae finem perseveraturum.[14]

In order to specify most clearly the voluntary nature of this promise, the final draft of the constitution stated: "This declaration by no means produces any obligation, either direct or indirect, of a vow, an oath, or a perpetual contract or justice. Moreover, it will never be lawful to substitute or even propose to substitute any other bond of union between the associates of the Institute in place of the spontaneous consent and compact above determined and defined."[15]

Although Father Hecker did not forbid the prescribing of a profession of vows at some later date, nevertheless, as has been already stated, when the constitutions were rewritten in their final form, the method of profession not only remained unaltered, but furthermore any future profession by vows was permanently forbidden. Probably the reason for this lay in the fact that, as Father Hecker himself thought, the spirit of the Paulist community was one of a too extreme individualism for a religious community. It must have been quite obvious to the drafters of the final constitutions, as it had been very evident to Father Hecker, that a generous insistence on the principle of individuality could hardly be compatible with any simultaneous insistence on a community spirit, as is demanded in a religious community. As Father Hecker himself stated, "A Paulist is to emphasize individuality; that is to make individual liberty an essential element in every judgement that touches the life and welfare of the community and that of its mem-

[14] Stanton, *De Societatibus*, pp. 133-134.

[15] *Constitutions of the Priests of the Mission of St. Paul the Apostle* (New York, 1920), p. 5.

bers. Those who emphasize the community element are inclined to look upon this as a dangerous and impracticable experiment."[16]

Under the constitutions a candidate was to spend a year of novitiate before pronouncing the formula of profession. The first profession was to be a temporary one of one year. A yearly profession was to be renewed for two more years. After the last renewal a final profession was to be pronounced.[17]

Although the question of poverty was not mentioned in the formula of profession, nevertheless the constitution did impose the practice of the virtue of poverty, whereby it was forbidden to the members to use any personal income for their individual support or convenience, and thus made all the members dependent on the community for all the things which they might need. The members were to retain dominion of their personal property and were free to dispose of it by will or through any other lawful method. The use of their property, however, was subject to the will of the superior.[18]

The ultimate government of the congregation was placed in the hands of the General Chapter. The highest superior of the company was the Superior General, elected by the Chapter. The Superior General, his consultors, and the delegates from each house of the Institute were to constitute the General Chapter. Each individual house was governed by a local superior, who was appointed by the Superior General for a term of three years.[19]

ARTICLE IV. THE JOSEPHITES

Section 1. The Society in Europe

In the earlier half of the nineteenth century, when the clergy of Europe were doing so much to encourage the work of the missions

---

[16] Elliott, *The Life of Father Hecker*, p. 294; Gillis, *The Paulists* (New York: The Macmillan Co., 1923), pp. 50-51.

[17] *Constitutions of the Priests of the Mission of St. Paul the Apostle*, p. 15; *The Paulists and Their Works* (New York: Paulist Press, 1923), p. 19.

[18] *Constitutions of the Priests of the Mission of St. Paul the Apostle*, pp. 18-19.

[19] *Constitution of the Priests of the Mission of St. Paul the Apostle*, pp. 30-36, 46-47.

in America, the lack of effort on the part of England was particularly noticeable. Finally, in 1836 Dr. Wiseman (1802-1865), then rector of the English College in Rome, took the first steps in fostering the American Missions in England. It appears that at this time Dr. Wiseman was tormented by scruples. He consulted the saintly Father Pallotti, who assured him that this cross would not be lifted from his shoulders until England should possess a foreign missionary college. These words were prophetic, for when Wiseman had returned to England he became acquainted with Herbert Vaughan (1832-1903), then a member of the Oblates of Saint Charles. There existed in the mind of Father Vaughan this very desire of establishing a missionary college to aid the foreign fields. Wiseman encouraged Vaughan to tour this country in an effort to raise funds in order that this college might be established. In 1868 property was purchased at Mill Hill in London. The following year Archbishop Manning (1808-1892), successor to Cardinal Wiseman, laid the corner-stone of the college. Dr. Vaughan became the first Superior General of the society, and under his guidance the society soon established houses in Holland and in the Tyrol.[20]

The society adopted the title of Saint Joseph's Society of the Sacred Heart for Foreign Missions. The principal aim of the company was the propagation of the Gospel among the unevangelized people beyond Europe. The society was placed under the direction and control of the Sacred Congregation for the Propagation of the Faith. The subjects of the society were ordained under the title of *the Mission,* and were required by the Sacred Congregation for the Propagation of the Faith to take an oath to devote themselves always to the works of the missions.[21]

According to the articles of the constitutions the candidates were to serve a postulancy period of one scholastic year. If after that period a candidate received a two-thirds majority vote in his favor, he was allowed to pronounce a temporary oath of perseverance and obedience for a two year period. The temporary profession was

---

[20] Currier, *History of Religious Orders,* pp. 631-632; Heimbucher, *Die Orden und Kongregationen der katholischen Kirche,* III, 502-503.

[21] Currier, *op. cit.,* p. 632.

then followed by a final profession. The oath of profession read as follows:

> Ego. N.N., filius N.N., diocesis N.N., alumnus Societatis Sancti Josephi pro Missionibus Exteris, ante conspectum Omnipotentis Dei, . . . spondeo et iuro me totam vitam operi Missionum huic Societati commissarum, vel in posterum committendarum, consecraturum esse, atque obedientiam Superiori Generali secundum Societatis Constitutiones praestaturum esse. . . .

Article 206 of the constitutions stated that the constitutions do not bind under sin, and that the oath of obedience binds in conscience only when the proper superior specifically makes it known to the subject that he so intends to bind him.[22]

Section 2. The Society in America

Until 1887 aspirants for the negro missions were all obliged to go to Mill Hill in London where the Society of Saint Joseph had its house of studies. However, in view of the increasing number of vocations and because of the difficulty of crossing the ocean, it was decided in 1887 by a joint action of Cardinal Gibbons (1834-1921) and Bishop Vaughan (1832-1903) to open a seminary in Baltimore for the American candidates of the society.

In March of the year 1891, Father John R. Slattery, the superior of the American seminary, with the knowledge and permission of Cardinal Gibbons, sent to Bishop Vaughan a request asking that he permit the establishment of an independent organization in America. In January, 1892, Vaughan wrote to every priest, giving him the free choice either of joining the new society or of remaining allied to the English community.

The new society was placed under the protection of Cardinal Gibbons, and he appointed Father Slattery the head of the organization. There was drawn up a set of rules corresponding exactly to those which governed the community previous to the separation of the two groups. The priests were still subject to the Sacred Con-

---

[22] Constitutions of the Society as quoted by Stanton, *De Societatibus*, pp. 130, 134, 148.

gregation for the Propagation of the Faith, and were ordained under the same title of *the Mission.*[23]

ARTICLE V. THE MARYKNOLL MISSIONARIES

In the nineteenth century the seminaries in America were in large number conducted by the Sulpician Fathers. It had always been a standard principle among the members of this society to inspire in their seminaries a love for the work of the missions. The establishment of the Society for the Propagation of the Faith was due in great extent to this zeal for the missions always urged and encouraged by the Sulpicians. The first founders of the Society of Maryknoll received their inspiration from these missionary-minded priests. A Sulpician priest, Father André, a professor in the seminary at Baltimore, was the first to plant in the mind and heart of Father Thomas Frederick Price (1861-1919) this desire to advance the cause of the missions among the American people. This same Father André, some years later while he was a professor at the seminary in Boston, came into contact with Father James Anthony Walsh (1867-1936), the other founder of the Maryknoll movement. Once again there was sowed the seed of missionary zeal and faith, and Father Walsh, like his future associate Father Price, resolved to spend his life for that cause.

Father Price had spent the first years following his ordination doing mission work in his native North Carolina. Meanwhile Father Walsh realized his mission dreams in the capacity of an active member in the Society for the Propagation of the Faith, becoming in a few years its director in the city of Boston. Neither of these zealous priests ever gave up the idea and hope of seeing a society established in America for the purpose of supplying missionaries for the pagan peoples of the world. Finally, at the International Eucharistic Congress of Montreal in 1910, these two similarly-minded ecclesiastics met. They were already acquainted with one another's ideas by reason of the articles each had often written on the subject of an American Mission Society, so it was a natural

---

[23] Currier, *op. cit.*, pp. 634-637; Ott, "St. Joseph's Society for the Colored Missions," *Catholic Encyclopedia*, VIII, 521; Heimbucher, *op. cit.*, III, 503.

consequence that they should then and there decide to undertake themselves the founding of this society.

In April, 1911, they presented their plans to the Bishops assembled at Washington. The Bishops of America heartily approved their plans, and thereupon the work was officially begun. In June of that same year their plans were submitted to Rome and approved by His Holiness Pope Pius X (1903-1914).[24]

The co-founders had agreed that the seminary where the future missionaries would be trained and educated would necessarily have to be free from any diocese. They desired that the whole organization should be entirely under the direction and guidance of the Sacred Congregation for the Propagation of the Faith in the same manner as the other missionary seminaries in Europe. The seminary was to be "national in character, organized and sustained by priests of the United States, guided of course by the best traditions of similar institutions abroad."[25]

After much consideration and prudent counsel, the two priests decided to found their first institute within the Archdiocese of New York. After a conference with Archbishop Farley (1842-1918) the society was welcomed into the Archdiocese on October 13, 1911.[26]

From the very start Father Price insisted that his co-founder be the first superior of the society, and with Cardinal Farley's approval Father Walsh became Superior General of the Foreign Mission Society of America. It was Father Price's desire to see the society permanently established, so that he might then withdraw and join some religious group, a longing he had hoped to satisfy for many years. As events worked out he was constantly needed so that he could never realize this dream.[27]

When Rome granted the two priests permission to found their society, they had been instructed to keep the Sacred Congregation for the Propagation of the Faith informed on their progress. This instruction was carried out in detail. On July 15, 1915, Maryknoll

---

[24] Considine, *March into Tomorrow* (Maryknoll, New York: Field Afar Press, 1942), pp. 8-10; Powers, *The Maryknoll Movement* (Maryknoll, New York: Field Afar Press, 1920), pp. 48-65.

[25] Powers, *The Maryknoll Movement*, pp. 57-58.

[26] Powers, *The Maryknoll Movement*, p. 62.

[27] Powers, *The Maryknoll Movement*, p. 70.

received the *Decretum Laudis,* approving the rule of the society for ten years. The society was placed under the immediate jurisdiction of the Sacred Congregation for the Propagation of the Faith. The decree had been transmitted to the society through Cardinal Farley.[28]

In the summer of 1918 the Holy See gave striking evidence of its confidence in the young society by granting it the privilege of ordaining subjects under the title of *the Mission,* the number however being limited to ten candidates at each yearly ordination. A few years later this number was increased, and in 1923 the society was given the general privilege of ordaining its subjects either under the title of *the Mission* or under the title of *the mensa Communis.* Previous to these privileges it had been necessary to secure an adopting bishop for each candidate for Holy Orders, excepting the few that the society was permitted to ordain on the title of *the Mission.*[29]

Under the constitutions a candidate for the society was required to undergo a novitiate period of one year. Following this time the candidate was required to make a temporary profession for one year. This temporary profession was to be repeated annually two more times. Following the third temporary profession, a final profession was to be pronounced.[30]

The formula of profession called for an oath and promise of perseverance and obedience. The 14th Article of the constitutions reads as follows:

> I ...., son of ...., of the Diocese of ...., member (or probationer) of the Catholic Foreign Mission Society of America, in the presence of God and of the Immaculate Virgin Mary, Mother of God and Queen of the Apostles, and of the Holy Apostles Peter and Paul, on bended knee *promise and swear* that I will consecrate my whole life (or that I will consecrate myself for one year) to the work of the Mis-

---

[28] *Field Afar,* IX (1915), 146, as quoted by Powers, *The Maryknoll Movement,* p. 109.

[29] *Maryknoll Letter Files,* as quoted by Powers, *The Maryknoll Movement* p. 110.

[30] Stanton, *De Societatibus,* p. 130.

> sions committed, or to be committed in the future, to this Society, and that I will observe the Constitutions of the Society, and obey my legitimate Superior.

Concerning the oath thus taken, the 15th Article of the constitutions reads:

> The clause of the oath which reads, "promise and swear that I will consecrate my whole life (or that I will consecrate myself for one year) to the work of the Missions committed, or to be committed in the future, to this Society" shall be considered as binding *sub gravi,* because of the gravity of the matter of which it treats.

The 288th Article reads: "The constitutions of themselves do not bind under pain of sin."[31]

In the first ceremony of departure for the mission fields in 1918, in Saint Peter's Cathedral, Scranton, the avowed purpose to remain for life in the society was read by the departing missionaries then leaving for China.[32]

---

[31] Constitutions of the Society as quoted by Stanton, *De Societatibus,* pp. 134, 148.

[32] Powers, *The Maryknoll Movement,* p. 106.

PART II

Canonical Commentary

CHAPTER IV

Preliminary Notions Concerning Quasi-Religious Societies

ARTICLE I. CANONICAL RECOGNITION OF THESE SOCIETIES AS FOUND IN CANON 673

The canonical recognition of the quasi-religious societies by the Code of Canon Law is found in the prescription of canon 673, § 1. The first paragraph of canon 673 reads as follows:

> *Societas sive virorum sive mulierum, in qua sodales vivendi rationem religiosorum imitantur in communi degentes sub regimine Superiorum secundum probatas constitutiones, sed tribus consuetis votis publicis non obstringuntur, non est proprie religio, nec eius sodales nomine religiosorum proprie designantur.*

A society of men or women who lead a community life after the manner of religious under the government of superiors and according to approved constitutions, but without the three customary vows of religion, is not a religious organization properly so called, nor are its members religious in the strict sense of the term.

The first paragraph of canon 673 might be called a descriptive definition of the type of society treated in Book II, Title XVII of the Code. The first section of the first paragraph stresses the resemblances between the quasi-religious societies and the religious institutes strictly so called. In the second part of this paragraph there is brought out the essential difference between these two groups. Their close resemblance may more readily be seen by a consideration of canon 488.

In the first section of canon 488, there is given the canonical definition of the religious life properly so called. The first number of canon 488 reads as follows:

> RELIGIONIS, [*notio est*] *societas, a legitima ecclesiastica auctoritate approbata, in qua sodales, secundum proprias*

> *ipsius societatis leges, vota publica, perpetua vel temporaria, elapso tamen tempore renovanda, nuncupant, atque ita ad evangelicam perfectionem tendunt.*

A religious group is a society approved by legitimate ecclesiastical authority, the members of which society strive after evangelical perfection by living according to the special laws of the society itself and by taking public vows, either perpetual or temporary, to be renewed, if temporary, when the time of the vows expires.

A brief comparison between these two canons should produce a better understanding of the canonical position of the quasi-religious societies and their relations with the religious institutes strictly so called. The resemblances between these two groups consist essentially in their mutual enjoyment of the material elements of the religious life. These material elements are three in number, namely, the living of a common life, subjection to the rule of legitimate superiors, and the possession of approved constitutions. These three elements, as they exist especially in the quasi-religious societies, will now be considered.

Section 1. The Common Life

The common life as it exists in both these groups partakes of a twofold notion: a). The social life which signifies an incorporation in the society. This incorporation is realized by the voluntary subjection of the individual to the society and the voluntary acceptance of the individual by the society; and b). The actual common dwelling under the same roof and a common participation in the ordinary needs of life, viz., food and clothing. The second note contained in the element of the common life is prescribed by several canons of the Code.[1]

This element of the common life is of particular importance in a consideration of the societies treated in Title XVII, because it is essentially this element which distinguishes the quasi-religious societies from the associations of the faithful in general, comprising the various groups of the faithful living in the world in some imitation of the religious life.[2]

---

[1] Cans. 587, § 2; 594, § 1; 2389.

[2] Schäfer, *De Religiosis*, p. 1030.

Maroto (1875-1937),[3] in discussing this point, makes mention of an inquiry which concerned itself with a group of women who, while pursuing the duties of school-teaching in the public schools of a certain diocese, formed themselves into a society modeled after a religious group. They bound themselves by rules to live a life in strict imitation of the religious life. In order to achieve this purpose they drew up a set of constitutions and had them approved by the local ordinary. The constitutions provided for a postulancy of six months, a novitiate of one year under the direction of a novice mistress, and the pronouncing of three year temporary private vows of poverty, chastity and obedience in the presence of a superior. This temporary profession was to be followed by a perpetual profession.

An inquiry was made asking whether this group of women was to be considered as a quasi-religious society or merely as an association of the faithful. In his reply to this inquiry, Maroto stresses the point that these women did not live a completely common life owing to the fact that each one remained in her own home in the world. In this sense they differ greatly from both the quasi-religious societies and the religious institutes which live a completely social form of common life. It is because of this lack of a completely social form of common life on the part of this society of women, that Maroto considers them to be a society of the faithful and not a quasi-religious society.

Maroto states in his treatment of the question that some authors hold the opinion claiming that a completely social form of a common life is not of its nature an essential requisite of the religious life. He refers especially to Wernz (1842-1914)[4] and Vermeersch (1858-1936)-Creusen.[5]

Despite this opinion of some authors, Maroto claims that the general principle still holds, namely, that according to the norms of law in force today the completely social form of a common life is actually an essential element of the religious life. He likewise

[3] "Commentarium Codicis,"—*Commentarium pro Religiosis,* V (1924), 342-352 (hereafter this periodical will be cited *CpR*).

[4] *Ius Decretalium* (2. ed., 6 vols., Romae et Prati, 1906-1913), III, n. 590.

[5] *Epitome Iuris Canonici* (3 vols., Romae, 1921-1923), I, n. 438 (hereafter cited as *Epitome*).

claims that for an institute in which there does not flourish the full practice of the common life there is need of a special privilege of the Holy See in order to be recognized as a religious institute.

Maroto further claims that if some institute should exist in which a completely social form of common life does not flourish, and if this institute has the approbation of only the ordinary or even of the Holy See, but not specifically as a religious body, then such an institute would not be a religious institute or a quasi-religious society, but rather a pious association of the faithful.

As proof of his claims Maroto stressed the common practice of the Roman Curia. He states that the Sacred Congregation of Religious generally refuses to allow an ordinary to establish a society which does not practice a completely social form of common life. Even in the few cases in which such societies were allowed to be established the Sacred Congregation later refused to approve them as societies of papal approbation, or even to accord them a decree of praise.

It may also be stated in further proof of this opinion that even Vermeersch, who claims that a completely social form of common life is not of the very essence of a religious institute, nevertheless, in speaking of the erection of religious institutes states: "De societate autem quae vita communi caret, . . . ipse status religiosus hodie existere nequit."[6]

Section 2. Subjection to the Guidance of Superiors

It would be absolutely impossible for any society to exist unless there was present some legitimate authority in which there would reside the power of commanding and guidance. This necessity of authority in a religious institute or a quasi-religious society is self-evident. The subjection of the members to this authority in every religious institute is implicitly contained in the voluntary entrance of the subject into the society and in the voluntary acceptance of the subject by the society. The very word *subject,* which is used in the language of religious constitutions, and the word *superior* connote a subjection and a subordination on the one hand and a recognized right of legislation and of direction on the other.

---

[6] *Epitome,* I, n. 460.

Section 3. The Possession of Approved Constitutions

A. Definition of Constitutions

Constitutions may be defined as the fundamental laws of a society approved by the local ordinary or by the Holy See. Rules, on the other hand, might be considered as the statutes inspected and approved by the chapter of a society in accordance with the intent of the constitutions.[7]

Formerly constitutions differed from rules in three ways: 1) The rules were more ancient and they were common to many religious groups; 2) The rules were more general and undetermined; and 3) The rules were specially approved by the Pope and considered entirely reserved to the Pontiff as to their modification.

The constitutions, however, were proper to each society and contained all that was necessary for ruling the society and the attainment of its ends. The constitutions likewise contained the means which had to be used to attain these ends and at the same time foster the spirit of the society. Generally, but not necessarily, these constitutions were approved by the Holy See. Furthermore, if the constitutions did not have papal approbation, they could be changed without the permission of the Pontiff. Today, however, the constitutions of any society are in general the primary and fundamental laws of a society, and they are approved by the ordinary or by the Holy See. The rules today are considered as the particular and minor norms of government, e.g., the rules of the novitiate, the rules for the lay brothers, clerics, etc.[8]

B. Interpretation of the Constitutions

The constitutions of societies of quasi-religious follow the same general principles of interpretation as do the constitutions of religious institutes. The relation between the constitutions of quasi-religious societies and the Code are the same as the relations exist-

[7] Wernz-Vidal, *Ius Canonicum ad Codicis Norman Exactum* (7 tomes in 8 vols., Tom. III, *De Religiosis,* Romae: apud Aedes Universitatis Gregorianae, 1933), III, n. 47 (hereafter cited as *De Religiosis*).

[8] Larraona, "Commentarium Codicis," *CpR,* IV (1923), 137-138.

ing between the constitutions of religious institutes properly so called and the legislation of the Code.

When a society without vows has received the decree of praise and consequently is recognized as a society of papal law, only the Holy See can issue authentic interpretations of their constitutions. Therefore neither the superior general nor a general chapter has this power of interpretation unless it has been delegated to them by the Holy See. If such delegated power is claimed by any of these persons, they have the obligation of proving the possession of this power.[9]

In religious institutes or quasi-religious societies of diocesan law the power of interpretation of the constitutions must be determined by the prescriptions of the particular constitutions.[10]

C. Constitutions and the Code

The general principles governing the relations between the constitutions of religious institutes and the prescriptions of the Code are contained in canon 489 of the common law. This canon reads as follows:

> *Regulae et particulares constitutiones singularum religionum, canonibus huius Codicis non contrariae, vim suam servant; quae vero eisdem opponuntur, abrogatae sunt.*

If the rules or particular constitutions of a religious body are not contrary to the canons of the Code they retain their force, while on the other hand whatever is opposed to the prescriptions of the Code is abrogated.

These principles are to be observed even in the case of those societies or religious institutes whose constitutions were approved by the Holy See before the promulgation of the Code. Accordingly, if in such constitutions there are laws contrary to the prescriptions of the Code, even though these laws had papal approval at the time of their enactment, nevertheless they are now to be considered as abrogated and the constitutions must be revised to eliminate them.[11]

---

[9] Schäfer, *De Religiosis,* p. 111.

[10] Schäfer, *De Religiosis,* p. 111.

[11] Schäfer, *De Religiosis,* p. 106.

However, it must be remembered that rules and constitutions which are contrary to the prescriptions of the Code but which contain privileges, or apostolic indults, or a provision deriving from immemorable custom, retain their vigor unless they are expressly revoked. Likewise constitutions contrary to the Code but which have been approved by the Holy See after the promulgation of the Code retain their force.

In the application of canon 489 it must likewise be kept in mind that constitutions are not contrary to the Code if they contain prescriptions which are stricter than the prescriptions of the common law, or if they contain obligations which are more demanding than the Code.[12]

Finally, because the constitutions of religious institutes and of quasi-religious societies are considered as true particular laws, canon 6 must be applied whenever there is a case of these constitutions reproducing prescriptions of the old law not contained in the Code.[13]

If constitutions reproduce prescriptions of the old law not contained in the Code, then these old laws are not abrogated, for canon 6, n. 6, in abrogating old laws not now contained in the Code is referring only to general laws formerly in force, so that the constitutions of religious institutes as particular laws are not touched by the prescriptions of canon 6, n. 6.[14]

D. Constitutions and Decrees

An interesting question in connection with the subject of the constitutions of religious institutes and of quasi-religious societies concerns itself with the relations between these constitutions and the general decrees of the Holy See. While the Code itself does not establish the juridical force of these decrees, nevertheless the law does demand that the various moderators of the Sacred Congregations make known to the Holy Father any grave or extra-

---

[12] Larraona, "Commentarium Codicis,"—*CpR,* IV (1923), 168.

[13] Cf. cans. 163; 168; 488, n. 1; 495, § 2; 507, § 1; Cocchi, *Commentarium in Codicem Iuris Canonici ad Usum Scholarum* (8 vols. in 5, Lib. II, pars II, *De Religiosis,* 3. ed., Taurinorum Augustae: Marietti, 1932), II, n. 7 (hereafter cited as *De Religiosis*).

[14] Larraona, "Commentarium Codicis,"—*CpR,* IV (1923), 168.

ordinary declarations, and that they receive his approbation before they undertake the publication of any of these grave pronouncements.[15]

Although strictly considered the decrees thus published by the various Roman Congregations do not proceed from the legislative power of the Church, nevertheless it seems that such general pronouncements which have been approved by the Pope, and then promulgated according to law in the *Acta Apostolica Sedis,* and declared to be binding on all whom they concern, should be regarded as having the force of a general law.

Some authors in discussing this question make a distinction between the specific and the general approval of the Pope, and they claim that a decree which has the specific approval of the Pope has the strict force of a general law, while a decree generally approved by the Pope, has a qualified force of general law.[16]

Merkelbach (1871-1942) claims that if a general decree which has been approved by the Pope contains resolutions, declarations or general decisions which explain the sense of the law, it then has the force of a general law.[17]

Accordingly it seems to be the opinion of the authors that a general decree of a Congregation which has been approved by the Pope, at least in a general way and which has been published in the *Acta Apostolica Sedis,* for all practical purposes has the force of a general law, and obliges all those for whom it was intended.

Inasmuch as the constitutions of religious institutions are particular laws, the relations existing between these constitutions and the general decrees of the Holy See, which are general laws, must be regulated according to the prescriptions of canon 22. This canon states that a later law abrogates a previous one when the later law expressly states this, or when it is directly contrary to the previous law, or if the new law completely changes the matter of the

---

[15] Cf. can. 244.

[16] Genicot-Salsmans, *Institutiones Theologiae Moralis* (14. ed., 2 vols., Buenos Aires: Typis Desclée de Brouwer, 1939), I, 77; Noldin-Schmitt, *Summa Theologiae Moralis* (26. ed., 3 vols., Oeniponte: Typis et Sumptibus Fel. Rauch, 1940), I, n. 134.

[17] *Summa Theologiae Moralis ad Mentem D. Thomae et ad Normam Iuris Novi* (3. ed., 3 vols., Parisiis: Desclée de Brouwer, 1939), I, 320.

previous law. However, a universal later law does not abrogate a previous particular law unless that fact be expressly mentioned.

According to these principles, if a decree of the Holy See stated something contrary to what is already expressed in the constitutions of a particular institute or society, and the decree was a general one obliging all religious institutes and societies, the constitutions nevertheless need not be changed unless the general decree expressly demanded it.

A practical application of this conclusion occurred on the occasion of the recent decree of the Sacred Congregation for Religious which prescribed certain obligations as resting upon ordinaries in connection with religious institutes and quasi-religious societies of diocesan law within their territories. The decree itself will be discussed in the following chapter, but it should be noted here that there is found in the concluding paragraph of this decree a fine example of an application of the principle just discussed. This paragraph stated that the matter of the decree was made known to Pope Pius XI in an audience granted to the secretary of the Congregation on November 25, 1922. It then stated that formal approval was granted by the Pope, and that all whom the decree concerned were obliged by its prescriptions. The concluding sentence of this last paragraph read: "*Contrariis quibuscumque minime obstantibus. . . .*"

The concluding phrase of the paragraph contained an express abrogation of any contrary prescription. Consequently the particular contrary law of any constitution was abrogated by the prescriptions of this general later law, by virtue of the expressed abrogation of all contrary prescriptions.[18]

E. Approval of Constitutions

It will be noted that canon 673, § 1, speaks of *probatae constitutiones* (approved constitutions). The Sacred Congregation of Religious issued three decrees relating to the proper correction of constitutions and customs of religious institutes of pontifical law and of quasi-religious societies of pontifical law. These corrections are required in constitutions which are not in harmony with the Code.

---

[18] *Acta Apostolicae Sedis, Commentarium Officiale* (Romae, 1909-), XIV (1922), 644-646 (hereafter cited as *AAS*).

The first decree was published on June 26, 1918, and it prescribed that all religious institutes and quasi-religious societies of pontifical law were required if necessary, to correct their constitutions in accordance with the prescriptions of canon 489. Furthermore, the corrected texts of the constitutions were to be sent to the Holy See for its approval. It was likewise provided that this revised text together with the report on the state of the community should be submitted together when, in accordance with the prescriptions of canon 510, the papal report was next due.[19]

The second decree was published by the same Sacred Congregation on March 31, 1919. This decree ordered all the books containing customs, uses, and prayers proper to each institute and society of pontifical law to be submitted to the Sacred Congregation for its approval. There was added a reminder to the ordinaries of the various dioceses to notify the respective institutes and societies of their obligations in this matter. The decree further stated that, whenever any ordinary in the future petitioned the Holy See for a decree of praise for any religious institute or quasi-religious society of diocesan law, he had to submit to the Sacred Congregation of Religious all books of customs, uses, and prayers along with the other necessary information.[20]

On October 26, 1921, the Sacred Congregation of Religious issued a third decree which explained the manner in which the necessary revision of the constitutions was to be made. It appeared that the earlier decrees were not clearly understood by several communities, and in consequence faulty texts had been submitted to the Sacred Congregation. Accordingly the Sacred Congregation issued a set of rules which were to be observed in the making of the necessary corrections and in the submitting of the revised texts.[21]

This third decree contained the following conclusions: 1) Only those constitutions by which an institute or society was actually governed were to be corrected and submitted for approval. Furthermore, only those constitutions which had clearly been approved by the Holy See were included within the prescriptions of these decrees: 2) the responsibility of making the necessary corrections

[19] *AAS,* X (1918), 290.

[20] *AAS,* XI (1919), 239.

[21] Schäfer, *De Religiosis,* pp. 109-110.

rested entirely with the superiors of the institutes and societies concerned; 3) two copies of the corrected constitutions were to be submitted to the Sacred Congregation; 4) only those parts of the constitutions were to be corrected and submitted for approval which were previously opposed to the prescriptions of the Code. Furthermore, whenever anything was added to the constitutions in order to supply for what was previously lacking, this addition also had to be submitted. If matter was added to the constitutions, the very words of the common law were required to be used in so far as this regulation could be followed; and, 5) lest any discrepancy should arise in the texts of those constitutions which might be used by several different houses of the same community or by *sui iuris* monasteries, the Sacred Congregation of Religious demanded that a copy of the corrected text be accepted by every house which used the same constitutions.[22]

Although the three decrees just considered were intended only for religious institutes and quasi-religious societies of pontifical law, nevertheless in religious institutes and quasi-religious societies of diocesan law the local ordinary has the right to demand that their rules and constitutions be corrected in accordance with the prescriptions of canon 489. He could also demand that the corrected texts be shown to him for his approval.[23]

ARTICLE II. THE LACK OF PUBLIC VOWS

This chapter thus far has had for its subject matter the similarities between the quasi-religious societies and the religious institutes. However, the first paragraph of canon 673 further clarifies the canonical position of the quasi-religious societies by showing negatively the relation between the quasi-religious societies and the religious institutes, i.e., by stressing the essential differences between them. This paragraph states that quasi-religious societies are not bound by the three public vows customarily pronounced in religious institutes, namely, the vows of poverty, of chastity, and of obedience. It then affirms that in the strict sense these societies are

[22] *AAS,* XIII (1921), 538.

[23] Schäfer, *De Religiosis,* p. 111.

not religious institutes, and that their members are not to be called religious.[24]

From the very grammatical structure of the canon it can logically be deduced that the only reason why quasi-religious societies are not considered as true religious institutes is the fact that their members do not pronounce the three customary *public vows* of religion. From an examination of the constitutions of some of these societies it will be discovered that they do pronounce the three customary vows of religion, but the vows thus pronounced are not *public vows* in the legal sense of the word. Rather, from a juridical viewpoint, they pronounce *private vows*. The meaning of these terms will be discussed below.

Consequently, it can be concluded that the only absolute distinction between quasi-religious societies and religious institutes is the legal nature of their vows. The word *absolute* is used to denote this distinction, since it is the only one universally applicable, although actually in some cases there are other distinctions. For example, the members of several quasi-religious societies pronounce no vows at all, but take oaths or promises or perhaps pronounce only one of the customary vows.

A vow is a deliberate promise made to God of accomplishing a greater good which lies within the realm of achievement. The promise freely made must be fulfilled under an obligation deriving from the virtue of religion.[25]

In accordance with the prescription of canon 1308, § 1, if the vow is received in the name of the Church by a legitimate ecclesiastical superior, the vow is considered by the common law to be *public;* otherwise it is a *private* vow.

It is important to note that the juridical publicity of the vow is independent of public knowledge, and thus it exists not as something that is necessarily contraposed to the idea of an occult fact. The fact of the vow's acceptance by a legitimate ecclesiastical authority comprises the note of publicity attaching to the vows of religion in the juridical sense.[26]

---

[24] Societas . . . in qua . . . in communi degentes . . . tribus consuetis votis publicis non obstringuntur, non est proprie religio, nec eius sodales nomine religiosorum proprie designantur, can. 673, § 1.

[25] Can. 1307, § 1.

[26] Schäfer, *De Religiosis,* p. 58.

ARTICLE III. PRIVATE VOWS

It must likewise be remembered that the public and external formalities attached to the pronouncement of a vow do not affect its public or private nature. For instance, among the priests of the Congregation of the Mission the vows pronounced by the subjects are approved by the Church, which determines the conditions concerning their validity or their lawfulness. Furthermore, the vows are pronounced aloud before the superiors of the community or their delegates. Necessary permission must be secured before a subject may pronounce his vows. Once the vows have been pronounced only the Pope, or the Superior General may dispense from them.

Even though a vow might have inherent in it the effect of a public vow, it is not for that reason necessarily a public vow. For instance, the vows of the Congregation of the Mission have the effect of a public vow to this extent at least that, if a person had taken a vow to enter a religious institute and later pronounced the vows of the Congregation of the Mission, he is freed from his promise, although in a strict sense he has not entered a religious institute. In this instance the private vows have the effect of relieving the candidate from the promise of becoming a religious, an effect which from a legal viewpoint can be attributed only to a public vow.[27]

Despite all the conditions and the effect attached to the vows of the Congregation of the Mission, they still remain private vows in the eyes of the Church, since in no official manner are they received in the name of the Church. This reception of the vows in the name of the Church is usually effected by means of a formula of acceptance pronounced by the superior legitimately appointed to receive them. However, no specific formula is required for the producing of this effect. The constitutions of each institute must be consulted if one is to see which superiors have this power.

The private vow was discussed here at length, since its characteristics approach very closely those of the public vow. Furthermore, of all the bonds existing among quasi-religious societies, the private vow best illustrates the precise point of distinction between quasi-religious societies and religious institutes. However, it must be remembered that the private vow is not the only bond of union

---

[27] Coste, *Le grand saint du grand siècle Monsieur Vincent,* III, 34-35.

among members of quasi-religious societies. Canon 673 does not specify any particular formal element of union that must exist among the members of these societies. It merely speaks of an analogy with the religious life existing in them.

ARTICLE IV. OTHER BONDS OF UNION

The formal element of the public vow inherent in religious institutes is imitated in various ways by the quasi-religious societies. This is done by means of private vows among the priests of the Congregation of the Mission, the Daughters of Charity of St. Vincent de Paul, the Mercy Fathers, and the members of the Beguin community. The Mill Hill Fathers, the Society of Saint Columban, the Society of the African Missions and the Maryknoll societies take oaths instead of vows. The members of the Eudist, Pallottine, Precious Blood and Paulist societies all make promises. There are still other quasi-religious societies, v.g., the Oratorians and the Sulpicians, which pronounce neither oaths nor vows nor any form of solemn promises.[28]

ARTICLE V. INCORPORATION INTO THESE SOCIETIES

Because of the varied forms of bond present in these societies, and more especially because of the complete lack of any bond in some societies, it is extremely difficult to establish exactly wherein lies the element that unites their members to them. In the case of the religious institutes, the very law gives the effect of public incorporation to the pronouncement of public vows. Since quasi-religious societies are recognized by the common law, they too must possess some means of producing this effect of public incorporation.

Goyeneche, in discussing the question of the dominative power of the superiors of quasi-religious societies, a question which will be treated in a later chapter, states that, although these societies are not properly to be regarded as religious institutes, nevertheless they do have a public character. He also states that except for the lack of public vows they show, with regard to their juridical structure, no difference from religious institutes. The author then claims

[28] Wernz-Vidal, *De Religiosis*, nn. 456-457.

that in order to effect the possession of dominative power by superiors of quasi-religious societies there is required not a formal vow, but only some juridically valid bond through which equivalently there is effected a public incorporation into the society.[29]

It seems to follow that the particular bond existing in these quasi-religious societies, which Goyeneche claims is sufficient to produce not only dominative power but also all the juridical effects proper to dominative power, should also produce the necessary binding force without which dominative power or any form of power would be not only impractical and useless but actually a usurpation. However, it seems that since these societies and their members are recognized by the common law, therefore the Church looks upon the very act of admission into these societies, according to the approved constitutions, as a legal and juridically recognized incorporation into the society. The bond producing this legal incorporation accordingly seems to arise from the implied obligation of obedience and fidelity assumed by the subject when he voluntarily seeks admission into the society and meets acceptance by the voluntary act of the society according to the approved constitutions.

The common law, to a certain extent, seems to favor this conclusion. Canon 675 applies to quasi-religious societies the prescriptions of canons 499-530, including therefore the prescription of canon 501, § 1. Canon 501, § 1 states:

> *Superiores et Capitula, ad normam constitutionum et iuris communis, potestatem habent dominativam in subditos.*

Superiors and chapters of religious institutes according to the norms of their constitutions and of the common law have dominative power over their subjects. If this canon be applied to quasi-religious societies, as is prescribed by canon 675, it follows that according to the norms of the common law the superiors of these societies have dominative power over their subjects. Furthermore, the superiors of clerical exempt quasi-religious societies possess true jurisdiction over their subjects. As has already been stated, it

---

[29] "Consultationes,"—*CpR,* I (1920), 144; Maroto, *Institutiones Iuris Canonici* (2 vols., Vol. I, 3. ed., Romae, 1919-1921), I, n. 459 (hereafter cited as *Institutiones*).

would be useless to speak of a superior's having dominative power or true jurisdiction over a subject unless there was implied a juridically valid bond uniting the subject to both the superior and the society, from which bond are derived the obligations of obedience and subjection on the part of the subject.[30]

Another reason offers itself in defense of the opinion that there exists by reason of a valid admission a juridically valid bond that unites the subjects of quasi-religious societies to their societies, even in the cases in which the latter do not provide for any pronouncement of vows, of oaths or of promises. The Code itself considers constitutions as private laws. However, the very nature of a law implies that there exist subjects who are legally related to the legislative source from which the law emanates, and who are legally obliged to obey the prescriptions of the law. In the application of these principles to quasi-religious societies it follows that their subjects are legally bound to them as the source of the private laws of the constitutions, and that their subjects are juridically obliged to obey these laws.

In conclusion it can be stated that the juridical bond that unites subjects to their institutes consists primarily and essentially in the valid acceptance of the subject into the institute. This acceptance produces a public incorporation of the subject into the institute. Incorporation, in turn, implies that the member is constituted a real part of the institute, subject to the laws and the obligations of the institute, and likewise entitled to all its favors and benefits. From this it follows that whether the members pronounce public vows, as is the case of religious institutes, or whether they pronounce private vows, oaths or promises, or finally whether they do not pronounce any of these, nevertheless in all these cases, as long as the members are validly accepted by the religious institute or the quasi-religious society according to approved constitutions, and as long as the institute or the society is canonically erected, every member is, according to the legal aspect, equally incorporated into the society or institute, and equally obliged to obey the prescriptions of his proper constitutions.

---

[30] Cf. Wernz-Vidal, *De Religiosis,* n. 458 note (4); Vermeersch-Creusen, *Epitome,* I, n. 675; Schäfer, *De Religiosis,* p. 1034.

It follows, too, that the public vows, the private vows, the oaths and the promises are at the most only means of producing the public legal incorporation from which all the obligations of obedience and all the benefits of unity with the organization arise. These various bonds are not of themselves the source of the obligations or of the benefits. Of course it must be held that the different types of vow, and the different vows, as also the oaths and promises, do contribute to the moral force of the union that holds the members in subjection to their respective superiors and organizations. In the light of a purely moral consideration a solemn vow produces a greater obligation of obedience than does a simple vow; so, too, a public vow begets effects different from those of a private vow, especially concerning the questions of dispensation, dismissal, transfer, etc. Nevertheless, it is the opinion of the writer that from a purely legal viewpoint the members of an Order, of a congregation, or of a quasi-religious society, are all equally united to their respective organizations. Furthermore as long as these members remain united to their organizations, all are according to law equally obliged to obey the constitutions of their institutes or societies in accordance with the prescriptions which are enacted in the constitutions themselves.

The opinion that this bond of union arises from the act of valid admission into the society or institute seems to be supported by Herbermann (1840-1916) in his work on the Sulpicians. The Sulpicians, it will be recalled, pronounce no form of vow, oath or promise. Herbermann states that although in the constitutions of the Sulpicians there is no mention of profession by vow, oath or promise, nevertheless by reason of the very admission of the subject into the society there is to be assumed for him the existence of an implied obligation to obey the prescriptions of the society and the commands of the superiors.[31]

Wernz (1842-1914)-Vidal (1867-1938), in discussing quasi-religious societies, state that the very entrance of the subject into them produces an implicit pact of subjection and subordination to their superiors. Otherwise there would not be satisfied what the very law demands when, in speaking of these societies, it states that

[31] *The Sulpicians in the United States,* p. 31.

their members are under the rule of superiors according to their constitutions.[32]

In clarification of the present writer's opinion it is stated that, once subjection and obedience to law on the part of particular subjects are legally established, it then becomes impossible from a legal viewpoint, to consider the subjects of any one law as being brought under a different kind of obligation in the matter of due obedience than are the subjects of any other law. There can of course arise circumstances in consequence of which one may become excused from obeying a law, or in view of which the perpetrated violation would constitute a greater moral offense, or as a result of which one may be made to suffer greater punishment, in the physical or in the moral order, than someone else who has violated the same law. However, the principle still remains that from a legal aspect all persons concerned are equally obliged in their obedience to the law, and that apart from divergent external circumstances no divergent effects would arise, for one is either obliged to obey a law or one is not obliged; in its essential nature and existence as a moral duty an obligation of obedience to law is an entity that is unaffected with variable degrees.

In the application of this principle to the case in question, it is evident that subjects of quasi-religious societies are obliged to obey their constitutions. This can be gathered from the application of the common law which gives the superiors of these societies dominative power, and in some cases even real jurisdiction over their subjects. As was stated in a previous paragraph, this granting of power would be useless and impractical if there were no obligation of obedience on the part of the subjects. Consequently, there is a legal obligation of obedience to the constitutions on the part of the subjects of these societies, just as there is an obligation of obedience to the constitutions on the part of members of religious Orders and congregations. In the light of the law both classes of subjects are equally a part of the association in which they have become incorporated. In other words, a Sulpician is just as much a member of the Sulpician society, as long as he is enrolled in the society, as a Franciscan or a Jesuit is a member of his respective institute, as long as he is legally incorporated in it.

[32] *De Religiosis,* n. 456; can. 673.

ARTICLE VI. CANONICAL DIVISION OF QUASI-RELIGIOUS SOCIETIES

In addition to the similarities which canon 673, § 1, reflects relative to quasi-religious societies and religious institutes there are other manifest qualities which both of these share in common. The division of the quasi-religious societies follows that of the religious institutes.

The second paragraph of canon 673 states that quasi-religious societies are divided into clerical and lay societies and into societies of diocesan or of pontifical approval. This division corresponds to the division of religious institutes as mentioned in canon 488, nn. 3, 4.

When one applies the definition of canon 488, n. 3, to quasi-religious societies one must conclude that a quasi-religious society is considered as a society of pontifical legal status when it has received a final approval, or at least an initial decree of praise, from the Holy See. Papal approbation is the last act of the Sacred Congregation of Religious by which the society together with its constitutions stands definitely approved. Generally, the approbation is at first granted for a certain length of time, followed later by a definitive approbation. The decree of praise usually precedes the granting of the definitive papal approbation. It consists in an express act whereby the Holy See through a special decree lends an initial commendation and praise to the existing society.[33]

If the erection of a society is made with pontifical authority, then the society is one of pontifical legal status from its inception. When a society has received at least the decree of praise from the Holy See and consequently becomes a society of pontifical law, it is removed from the jurisdiction of the ordinary only to the extent that the ordinary can no longer change the constitutions of the society, investigate its economical situation, or intervene in its internal government or discipline. In all other affairs the society, even though it be one of pontifical law, is not exempt from the jurisdiction of the ordinary, unless a special privilege of exemption has been granted it by the Holy See.[34]

---

[33] Blat, *Commentarium Textus Codicis Iuris Canonici* (5 vols. in 7, lib. II, pars II-III, *Ius de Religiosis et Laicis iuxta Codicis Ordinem,* 3. ed., Romae, apud "Angelicum," 1938), p. 31 (3)° (hereafter cited as *De Religiosis*).

[34] Schäfer, *Re Religiosis,* pp. 97-98, 128.

On the other hand, if a society upon its foundation by the local ordinary has not yet obtained from the Holy See at least the decree of praise, it remains entirely under the jurisdiction of the ordinary and is called a society of diocesan law. Even if in the course of time a society founded by a local ordinary should spread into the limits of several dioceses, as long as it has not received the decree of praise from the Holy See it remains a society of diocesan law.[35]

The division noted in canon 488, n. 4, when applied to quasi-religious societies, indicates that a society is either a clerical or a lay society.[36]

The word *plerique* as used in canon 488, n. 4, does not necessarily imply that a greater part of the members of a society must be priests if it is to be considered as a clerical society. It can be understood in the sense of simply many or several. The word *many* actually is opposed to *one* or a *few*. Therefore the fact that a few priests belong to a society will not be sufficient to establish that society as a clerical one. This would be true even though these few priests have been accorded so much power that the actual ruling of the society has been reserved to the priest members. Likewise an accidental change in the relative number of priests belonging to a society, for example, at a time of a pestilence or persecution, would not change the status of its lay or clerical character as attaching to the society and as demonstrable through its past tradition, its continued practice, or its accepted constitutions. Finally, it must be concluded that whether a society is to be considered as a clerical or as a lay society depends on a consideration of its primary end, i.e., whether or not the society by its canonical institution was destined for the performance of the functions of the apostolic ministry. If it was so destined, it is to be considered a clerical society. If, on the other hand, it was not so destined, it is to be listed as a lay society.[37]

Canon 673, § 2, in mentioning various canonical divisions which the quasi-religious societies have in common with religious institutes, does not enumerate all the canonical divisions which these two groups can have in common. For example, canon 488, n. 2, divides the religious institutes into those which are exempt and

---

[35] Schäfer, *De Religiosis*, p. 98.

[36] Cf. Can. 488, n. 4, in comparison with can. 673, § 2.

[37] Schäfer, *De Religiosis*, p. 95.

those which are non-exempt. This same division can be made with reference to the quasi-religious societies. It is possible for these societies to enjoy the privilege of exemption to the same extent as it is enjoyed by religious institutes.

The Congregation of the Mission, a quasi-religious society, in consequence of the Brief *"Ex commissa Nobis,"* issued by Pope Alexander VII on September 22, 1655, was granted the privilege of exemption. This privilege removed its members from the jurisdiction of the local ordinaries in all affairs except in the matters which pertained to the external missions to which they might be sent.[38]

Pope Benedict XIII, in the Brief *"Exponi Nobis,"* issued on February 17, 1725, confirmed the exemption of the Congregation of the Mission. In the same Brief the Congregation of the Mission was granted the privilege of issuing dismissorial letters for its subjects.[39]

Exemption is never presumed to be possessed by a society. Any society claiming this privilege of exemption assumes the burden of proving its possession. The only means by which a quasi-religious society can possess the privilege of exemption is through a special concession granted it by the Holy See. This is an application of the principle stated in canon 618: *Religiones votorum simplicium exemptionis privilegio non gaudent, nisi specialiter eisdem fuerit concessum.*[40]

ARTICLE VII. PRECEDENCE OF QUASI-RELIGIOUS SOCIETIES

A certain right of precedence is accorded to quasi-religious societies. As will be seen in the development of this article on prece-

[38] "Statuentes ut dicta Congregatio Missionis exempta sit a subiectione locorum Ordinariorum in omnibus, excepto quod personae quae a Superioribus eiusdem Congregationis deputabuntur ad missiones aliquas subsint ipsis Ordinariis tantum quoad missiones et ea quae illas concernunt."—*Acta,* p. 16.

[39] Superioribus praedictae Cong. Missionis concedendi litteras dimissorias suis subditis . . . in vim Const. fel. reg. Urbani VIII et Alexandri VII . . . per quas dicta Congregatio ab Ordinariorum iurisdictione, exceptis pertinentibus ad Missiones dumtaxat, exempta reperitur."—*Acta,* p. 23.

[40] "Religious institutes of simple vows do not possess the privilege of exemption unless it was specially conceded to them."—can. 618, § 1; cf. Schäfer, *De Religiosis,* p. 794.

dence, the conclusions drawn result to a great extent from an appli cation of the canonical principle, *Odia restringi et favores convenit ampliari.*[41] In other words when in the interpretation of a canon there is a possibility of making a concession favorable or beneficial to a person or an institution, then the canon in question should be given as wide and as generous an interpretation as possible, so that the favor delineated in the canon may be granted to as many recipients as possible. On the other hand, if the canon concerned points to a burden or is in any way adverse to freedom of choice or liberty in action, then it is to be interpreted as strictly and narrowly as possible. In this way the burden is placed upon as few as possible.

In the question of precedence, whenever any sort of preference is granted to religious institutions, the term *religious* is widely interpreted so as to include the members of quasi-religious societies. On the other hand, in cases in which secular groups are given preference over religious institutes in the matter of precedence, the word *religious* is strictly interpreted so as not to include the members of quasi-religious societies. By reason of such an exclusion, the quasi-religious societies are placed among the secular groups and consequently enabled to share in their precedence over the religious institutes. These principles justify the following conclusions.

The members of quasi-religious societies, whether they be considered in their individual personal status or in the status whereby they are formed as a moral personality, precede the laity. However, religious institutes always take precedence over lay quasi-religious societies. Thus a religious institute, even though it be one of merely diocesan approval will precede a lay quasi-religious society which possesses pontifical approval. This is true in spite of the fact that religious institutes of pontifical law always take precedence over religious institutes of diocesan law.

The precedence of the members of a quasi-religious society over laymen follows from the prescription of canon 680, under which quasi-religious societies are entitled to the privileges of clerics. It follows, too, from the fact that the precedence of religious is to be extended to them, as noted above. Lay quasi-religious societies are always preceded by religious institutes, since only in the wide sense of the word are the members of these societies considered as reli-

---

[41] Reg. 15, R. J., in VI°.

gious. Consequently these societies can never share equally in the privileges which are granted to the religious institutes properly so called. This fact is especially true when there is question of determining the relations between lay quasi-religious societies and religious institutes. Among themselves, however, a quasi-religious society of pontifical law takes precedence over a society of diocesan law.[42]

According to the principles as stated in canon 491, § 2, secular clerics always precede laymen, and also religious clerics when they are outside their own churches. They precede lay religious even in their own churches.

In the question of clerical quasi-religious societies the word *religious* is strictly interpreted in relation to burdens, so that the members of clerical quasi-religious societies are not comprised in its meaning. Consequently such members must be considered as secular clerics in relation to onerous matters. Accordingly the members of a clerical quasi-religious society, which actually consists of secular clerics, precede all religious, even regulars.[43]

Moreover, if the religious are laymen, then the members of clerical quasi-religious societies precede them absolutely. This is to say that, whether the clerics of the quasi-religious society are present in a body or individually, they everywhere precede laymen religious even in their own churches. However, if the religious are clerics, then the members of the clerical quasi-religious societies do not precede these in their own churches.[44]

Within quasi-religious societies themselves precedence for their members is determined by the prescriptions of canon 106, n. 5. Accordingly one would determine this precedence by consulting the constitutions of the particular society. If the constitutions do not establish the order of precedence among the members, then legitimate custom becomes the determining factor. If, finally, even custom is lacking, then the provisions of the common law determine it.[45]

---

[42] Larraona, "Commentarium Codicis,"—*CpR,* IV (1923), 210-213; Schäfer, *De Religiosis,* p. 115.

[43] Larraona, "Commentarium Codicis,"—*CpR,* IV (1923), 273.

[44] Larraona, *loc. cit.*

[45] Larraona, "Commentarium Codicis,"—*CpR,* IV (1923), 275.

ARTICLE VIII. QUASI-RELIGIOUS SOCIETIES CONSIDERED AS TERTIARY GROUPS

Tertiaries are generally defined as those who in some way are affiliated with an Order and strive for perfection by living a life in harmony with the spirit of the Order, according to approved constitutions. The Code considers various types of tertiaries. Canon 702 mentions secular tertiaries, i.e., those who remain in the world; canon 492, § 1, refers to tertiaries who live in common. A further distinction may be made between the tertiaries who live in common and the regular tertiaries who pertain to the regular Orders.[46]

There is nothing contradictory in the notion of a quasi-religious society existing as a tertiary group living in common as provided for in canon 492, § 1.[47] Accordingly, if a group of tertiaries wished to form themselves into a society living in common without public vows, they would have to approach the local ordinary, who in turn would refer the matter to the Sacred Congregation for Religious. A decree of approval must be obtained from the Holy See before a community or society may be aggregated, as a tertiary group, to an Order.[48]

When this approval of the Holy See has been received, the ordinary may approve the society which then becomes a society of diocesan law. Upon this follows the act of aggregation by which the society is admitted as a moral member of the regular Order through the authoritative act of the supreme head of the Order. This aggregation to a first Order need not necessarily be made at the very time of the foundation of the society, as has just been described. It may also be made after the society has already existed as a moral person and only thereupon wishes to become aggregated.[49]

As a result of the act of aggregation to a first Order, a society becomes known as a third Order or as a society of tertiaries of the regular Order. However, the first Order obtains no jurisdiction over the society of tertiaries, nor does the latter group receive any

---

[46] Blat, *De Religiosis,* p. 65; Schäfer, *De Religiosis,* p. 135.

[47] Larraona, "Commentarium Codicis,"—*CpR,* V (1924), 82.

[48] Can. 703, § 1.

[49] Schäfer, *De Religiosis,* p. 135; can. 492, § 1.

freedom or exemption from the local ordinary. There merely arises between the tertiaries and the first Order a mutual sharing in the indulgences and spiritual favors conceded to the latter.[50]

This inter-communicated sharing in the indulgences was affirmed by the Sacred Congregation of Indulgences on August 28, 1903, when, in answer to an inquiry whether the members of all institutes of tertiaries living in common share in the indulgences granted to the first and second Order, the Sacred Congregation responded in the affirmative.[51]

The following question may now be proposed: may a member of a quasi-religious society which is not a society of tertiaries join some third Order secular group while he is still a member of the quasi-religious society? Canon 704, § 1, states that while one is bound by vows to a religious institute he cannot at the same time be enrolled in a third Order, even if before his profession he was a member of such a tertiary group.[52] It will be noted that in canon 704, § 1, the specific word *religione* is employed. Consequently there seems to be no doubt that the prescriptions of this canon do not apply with relation to quasi-religious societies. Therefore, unless the constitutions prescribe otherwise, a member of a quasi-religious society may at the same time be juridically constituted also as a member of a third Order secular.

The words *juridically constituted* are used by the writer simply with a view to intimating that according to strict principles of law this double membership is not forbidden. However, the holding of such a double membership should be discouraged, since the good order of a society and the proper discipline in the personal life of a member should certainly suffer if a member of a quasi-religious society was at the same time a member of a third Order secular.

---

[50] Blat, *De religiosis,* pp. 65-66.

[51] *Acta Sancta Sedis* (41 vols., Romae, 1865-1908, XXXVI (1903), 577 (hereafter cited as *ASS*).

[52] Can. 704, § 1—Quid vota nuncupavit vel in perpetuum vel ad tempus in aliqua religione, nequit simul ad ullum tertium Ordinem pertinere, etsi eidem antea fuerit adscriptus.

ARTICLE IX. THE LEGAL PERSONALITY OF QUASI-RELIGIOUS SOCIETIES

According to the provisions of canon 100, § 1, a moral person may achieve juridical existence in the Church either in view of the prescriptions of the common law itself or in consequence of a formal decree issued by a competent ecclesiastical superior for its erection.

A consideration of canons 531 and 536, § 1, reveals that the law itself gives moral personality to religious institutes, to their provinces, and to their houses. Canon 531 states that not only religious institutes but also their provinces and their houses are capable of acquiring and possessing temporal goods. This clearly implies that these various institutions are endowed with juridical personality. Canon 536, § 1, states: *Si persona moralis* (*sive religio, sive provincia, sive domus*) *debita et obligationes contraxerit etiam cum Superiorum licentia, ipsa tenetur de eisdem respondere.*

These institutions are here actually called moral persons and accordingly are endowed with the capacity for certain functions which can be performed only by a moral person. Therefore it cannot be doubted that religious institutes, their provinces and their houses are all moral persons.[53]

Now, canon 675 applies to quasi-religious societies the prescriptions of canon 532-537, included in which is canon 536, § 1, absolutely, and canon 531 by way at least of an implied cross reference. Therefore it is safe to say that quasi-religious societies, their provinces and their houses possess moral personality in virtue of the prescriptions of the Code itself. There is no formal decree required to establish the moral personality of these institutions. This may be deduced from a consideration of canon 100. For this canon states that moral personality may be established either in consequence of the law itself or in virtue of a formal decree issued by a competent superior for its erection.[54]

---

[53] Maroto, "Commentarium Codicis,"—*CpR,* IV (1923), 199.

[54] Cf. Schäfer, *De Religiosis,* pp. 128-129; Vermeersch, "Instituta Iuris Diocesani,"—*Periodica de Re Canonica et Morali utili praesertim Religiosis et Missionariis* (Brugis, 1905-), XI (1923), 178 (hereafter cited *Periodica;* Larraona, "Commentarium Codicis,"—*CpR,* V (1924), 418 note 338; Maroto, "Commentarium Codicis,"—*CpR,* IV (1923), 199.

CHAPTER V

The Erection and the Suppression of Quasi-Religious Societies, their Provinces and Houses

Article I. Introductory Remarks

Canon 674 in a few words treats of the entire question of the erection and suppression not only of quasi-religious societies, but also of their provinces and their houses. Canon 674 states: *Circa erectionem et suppressionem societatis eiusque provinciarum vel domorum, eadem valent quae de Congregationibus religiosis constituta sunt.* Concerning the erection and suppression of these societies and of their provinces and houses the same laws apply which are prescribed for religious congregations. Consequently all the principles of law stated in Title IX (canons 492-498) concerning the erection and suppression of religious institutes, of their provinces and of their houses are to be applied to quasi-religious societies.[1]

It must be noted however that canon 674 specifically mentions that in these matters only the prescriptions of law referring to congregations are to be applied to quasi-religious societies. Therefore any legislation in Title IX which concerns itself with religious Orders is not to be applied to quasi-religious societies. Furthermore, canon 674 states simply that the principles of Title IX which refer to the erection and suppression of congregations, of their provinces and of their houses are to be applied to quasi-religious societies. Therefore whatever Title IX prescribes con-

---

[1] Cf. Wernz-Vidal, *De Religiosis*, n. 458; Cappello, *Summa Iuris Canonici in Usum Scholarum Concinnata* (3 vols., Vol. II, Romae: Apud Aedes Universitatis Gregorianae, 1930), II, n. 641 (hereafter cited as *Summa*); Fanfani, *De Iure Religiosorum ad Normam Codicis Iuris Canonici* (2. ed., Taurini-Romae: Marietti, 1925), p. 527 (hereafter cited as *De Religiosis*); Oesterle, *Praelectiones Iuris Canonici* (Romae: apud Collegium S. Anselmi, 1931), p. 378.

cerning changes involving these institutions is not to be applied to these societies.[2]

The term *erection* as used in this article signifies the notion of instituting, of founding or of formally approving. Legally this term points to an act and a decree of a superior by means of which canonical existence is accorded to a certain society, province or house.[3]

The term *suppression* as used in this article denotes the juridical act of ecclesiastical authority which implies the direct opposite of the notion of erection. Accordingly it signifies the act of cancelling the canonical existence previously enjoyed by the aforesaid moral persons.[4]

The terms *provinces* and *houses* when applied to quasi-religious societies are to be understood in the sense in which these same terms are defined with reference to religious institutes. These terms are defined in canon 488, nn. 5, 6.

The word *house* as a general term denotes an abode at which the members of any society reside permanently. It is referred to as a *domus formata* if at least six professed members are its permanent inhabitants. In quasi-religious societies, in the constitutions of which the term profession is oftentimes not used, a *domus formata* is a house consisting of at least six members who according to the constitutions of the society are legally enrolled in the society.[5] A house is considered to be *a domus non-formata* if there are not at least six professed or quasi-professed members permanently resident thereat.

Canon 488, n. 2, implicitly distinguishes houses into exempt and non-exempt houses. This same distinction can be applied to the houses of quasi-religious societies. If a particular society possesses the privilege of exemption, then the houses of that society are exempt from the jurisdiction of the ordinary in accordance with the prescriptions of the common law. If on the other hand the

---

[2] Cocchi, *De Religiosis*, n. 10; Schäfer, *De Religiosis*, p. 125; Vermeersch-Creusen, *Epitome*, I, n. 460; Blat, *De Religiosis*, p. 54.

[3] Larraona, "Commentarium Codicis,"—*CpR*, V (1924), 43.

[4] Blat, *De Religiosis*, p. 54.

[5] Cf. can. 488, n. 5; Blat, *De Religiosis*, p. 32.

society is not exempt, then the houses are considered as non-exempt.

A *province* consists of a number of religious houses joined under the same superior. In case of quasi-religious societies, some are divided into provinces, while others are divided into *regions*. For example, the Maryknoll, Mill-Hill and St. Columban societies are divided into regions, while the society of the Pallottine Fathers is divided into both provinces and regions. It seems that, unless constitutions approved after the Code prescribe otherwise, any type of division which juridically corresponds to a province will be governed by the legislation which the law of the Code prescribes for the provinces.[6]

ARTICLE II. THE ERECTION OF QUASI-RELIGIOUS SOCIETIES

In the light of the application of the principles of canon 492 to the quasi-religious societies the following conclusions seem justified. A bishop, but not his vicar general, is authorized to found a quasi-religious society. However, before the founding of any society the bishop must first obtain the permission of the Holy See.[7]

The vicar general can found a quasi-religious society only if he is delegated by the bishop. However he cannot found a society either by means of his ordinary power nor by means of a special mandate. The Code gives a taxative list of all the powers entrusted to a vicar general through a special mandate and the power to found a society is not enumerated among them. Accordingly a vicar general can found a society only when he possesses delegated power. He cannot subdelegate this delegated power unless, as would rarely happen, he would be delegated "ad universitatem causarum" or with the added power of subdelegating.[8]

The first prescription of canon 492, § 1, which states that only a bishop and not a vicar general can found a religious institute, has an invalidating effect for any act which violates this prescription.

[6] Blat, *De Religiosis*, p. 32; can. 488, n. 6.

[7] Can. 492, § 1—Episcopi, non autem Vicarius Capitularis vel Vicarius Generalis, condere possunt Congregationes religiosas; sed eas ne condant neve condi sinant, inconsulta Sede Apostolica.

[8] Schäfer, *De Religiosis*, p. 129.

Therefore, if a vicar general, or anyone other than a bishop, should attempt to found a religious institute or a quasi-religious society, the foundation would be invalid.[9]

On the other hand, the prescription which demands the permission of the Holy See before a decree of erection may be issued sets up a simple requirement for the lawfulness of the action. If, therefore, a bishop failed to secure the necessary papal permission, the foundation would be illicit but nevertheless valid. In this case however the Holy See could invalidate the erection of the society, and the offending bishop would be held liable for punishment.[10]

Under the term *Episcopi* in canon 492, § 1, vicars and prefects apostolic have the same rights and faculties in their territories as bishops have in their dioceses, unless the Holy See reserves certain rights and faculties. Likewise included under the term *Episcopi* are apostolic administrators permanently constituted, for canon 315, § 1, states: apostolic administrators who are permanently constituted enjoy the same rights and honors, and are held to the same obligations, as residential bishops.

In line with the prescriptions of canons 323, § 1, and 215, § 2, abbots and prelates *nullius* enjoy the right of erecting religious institutes and quasi-religious societies. Canon 323, § 1, states: abbots and prelates *nullius* have the same ordinary powers and also the same obligations under the same sanctions as belong to the residential bishops. Canon 215, § 2, states: included under the name of bishops are abbots and prelates *nullius,* unless from the context of the words or the nature of the matter they are excluded.

All the above mentioned prelates exercise ordinary power when they found a religious institute or a quasi-religious society. Canon 197, § 1, states that ordinary power of jurisdiction is that which is annexed to an office. These prelates in founding a society or a religious institute are using the power which, as the law states, is annexed to their very offices.

The vicar general is excluded from the right of founding a

---

[9] Blat, *De Religiosis,* p. 58. The power of the abbot and prelate *nullius* must be included within the power of the bishop in this matter, for in accordance with canon 323, § 1, the abbot and prelate *nullius* are equal to residential bishops in all jurisdictional matters.

[10] Blat, *De Religiosis,* p. 59; Vermeersch-Creusen, *Epitome,* I, n. 496.

quasi-religious society or a religious institute, even when by the prescriptions of canon 429, §§ 1-3, he rules a diocese during the incapacity of the bishop. This exclusion extends also to the vicar delegate in missionary countries. The exclusion of the vicar delegate was certified in a letter of the Sacred Congregation for the Propagation of the Faith issued on December 8, 1919.[11]

The consultation with the Holy See, to which a bishop is held before he founds a religious institute or a quasi-religious society, ought to be more than a mere notification or the simple seeking of advice. The consultation consists rather in the procuring of a real permission from the Holy See. Nevertheless the permission of the Holy See as here demanded is not the equivalent of the papal approbation which a society or an institute of diocesan right must receive if it is to be considered as a society or an institute of pontifical law.[12]

The bishop cannot issue a formal decree of erection for any society until he has received the consent of the Holy See, as demanded by canon 492, § 1. In his consultation with the Holy See the bishop must inform the Sacred Congregation of Religious of the following pertinent facts: the name of the founder of the society; the reasons for the foundation; the form, color, and nature of the habit to be used; the number and nature of the works to be undertaken by the society; the names and the number of the other quasi-religious societies or religious institutes which already perform these same works in the diocese. These are the items about which information is required, as it was indicated in the first chapter of the norms published by the Holy See in explanation of the procedure followed by the Sacred Congregation of Religious when called on to give approval to new religious institutes or societies.[13]

The permission of the Holy See is received in the form of a *nihil obstat.* By "the Holy See" in this connection is meant the Sacred Congregation of Religious, or, if the society is being erected in mission territory, both the Sacred Congregation of

---

[11] *AAS,* XII (1920), 120.

[12] Blat, *De Religiosis,* p. 59.

[13] *AAS,* XIII (1921), 313; Larraona, "Commentarium Codicis,"—*CpR,* V (1924), 46.

Religious and the Sacred Congregation for the Propagation of the Faith.[14]

When the bishop has received the required permission of the Holy See he must issue a formal decree of erection for the society. One copy of the decree is to be kept in the archives of the society, while a second is to be kept in the archives of the diocese. A copy of the decree is likewise to be sent to the Sacred Congregation of Religious. Furthermore once the permission of the Holy See has been received, the society can no longer change the form or color of its habit, its name, or any of the other qualities reported to the Holy See when permission was first sought. To effect any change whatsoever in any of these matters there is required the permission of the Holy See.[15]

A grave obligation to study carefully the constitutions of a new society is placed on the bishop before he may issue the formal decree of erection. This obligation was first expressed by Pope Leo XIII in his Constitution *"Conditae a Christo,"* issued on December 8, 1900. This Constitution stated that the bishop was gravely burdened with the obligation of studying and knowing the constitutions of the religious institutes and quasi-religious societies to be established in his diocese. Moreover, it required him to see that the prescriptions of the constitutions were apt to produce the stated end of the institute, and that they were not contrary to Faith or morals or the sacred canons and Pontifical decrees.[16]

Although this Constitution was issued before the promulgation of the Code, nevertheless the obligations which it placed on the bishops flowed from the very nature of a juridical congregation. Though not explicitly mentioned in the Code, these obligations exist in the present as something which lies beyond, but certainly not as something which stands contrary to, the prescriptions of the Code, and hence remain in force today.[17]

---

[14] Bastien, *Directoire canonique a l'usage des congrégations à voeux simples* (3. ed., Bruges: Charles Beyaert, 1923), p. 344.

[15] Schäfer, *De Religiosis,* p. 128.

[16] *Codicis Iuris Canonici Fontes,* cura Emi Petri Card. Gasparri editi (9 vols., Romae [postea Civitate Vaticana]): Typis Polyglottis Vaticanis, 1923-1939; Vols. VII, VIII, IX ed. cura et studio Emi Iustiniani Card. Serédi), n. 644 (hereafter cited as *Fontes*).

[17] Blat, *De Religiosis,* p. 63.

The Sacred Congregation of Religious issued a decree on November 30, 1922, which instructed the bishops of the various dioceses to conduct an investigation concerning the religious institutes and quasi-religious societies in their respective dioceses. The decree explained the manner of procedure, and likewise contained certain regulations which the bishops were to observe when they might have occasion to found an institute or society in the future.

In issuing this decree the Sacred Congregation of Religious was urged by the grave necessity of determining the validity of the establishment of religious institutes and quasi-religious societies of diocesan law as existing in the various dioceses. It had been brought to the attention of the Sacred Congregation of Religious that in several instances there existed religious institutes and quasi-religious societies which had never been approved through a formal decree of the respective bishops. Such institutes and societies could not be considered as moral persons endowed with a valid existence.[18]

The decree contained the following provisions. 1.) Every bishop or prelate of quasi-episcopal jurisdiction was required to make a specified inquiry, in regard to every institute of either sex in his territory, whether the institute be a religious institute or a quasi-religious society. The inquiry however was to be restricted to those institutes or societies which did not possess pontifical approval or at least a pontifical decree or praise, i.e., every religious institute or quasi-religious society of diocesan law. The inquiry's purpose was to ascertain whether or not these institutes or societies were erected through a formal episcopal decree the tenor of which was known, and whether their constitutions were approved by the same authority.

2.) If some of these religious institutes or quasi-religious societies of diocesan law were of doubtful juridical status in view of the doubtful issuance of the decree of erection, but if because of repeated acts throughout the years preceding the publication of the Code they could claim an episcopal quasi-approval, then the bishops were to recognize them through a formal decree of erection, and to declare them a religious institute or a quasi-religious society of diocesan law. The acts which could prove the existence of an

[18] *AAS,* XIV (1922), 644-646.

episcopal quasi-approval were the reception of vows by the bishop, the ordination of the subjects of the religious institute or the quasi-religious society by the proper bishops of the dioceses where the religious houses were located, the canonical visitation undertaken by the bishop, and other similar acts of equal import. However, if the religious institute or the quasi-religious society which claimed episcopal quasi-approval had been established after the Motu Proprio *"Dei Providentis"* of July 16, 1906,[19] then the bishop was required to seek the permission of the Holy See before he was permitted to issue the decree of erection. Furthermore, it was declared that the decree of erection would have a retroactive effect for the sake of validating any defective canonical erection of the past.

3.) If the religious institute or quasi-religious society had spread through several dioceses, then the bishop of the diocese where the mother house of the religious institute or the quasi-religious society was located had the authority to issue the decree of erection for the entire institute or society. However, before the decree could be issued the respective bishop was required first to consult the bishop of all the other dioceses in which the institute or the society had an establishment. The decree could then be issued only if all the bishops were willing.

4.) If, because of the small number of members, or because of the fact that even indirect proof of the erection of an institute or a society could not be produced, or for any other reason the ordinary could hardly judge it opportune to issue a decree of erection, or if finally all the ordinaries mentioned in n. 3 did not approve of the canonical erection of the institute or the society, then the entire case was to be submitted to the Sacred Congregation of Religious for a decision. This prescription was made necessary because of canon 493 of the Code, which denies local ordinaries the right to suppress any religious institute or quasi-religious society, even one of diocesan law.

5.) For each diocesan institute or society legitimately erected or recognized according to the above stated prescriptions of the decree, the ordinary was required to send to the Sacred Congregation of Religious information concerning the founder, the title, the scope,

---

[19] Cf. *Fontes,* n. 675.

the laws of the foundation, and the decree of erection of each institute and society. The names of the various dioceses into which each had spread, together with a mention of the number of its houses and its members, were also to be transmitted to the Sacred Congregation.

6.) If there existed no religious house of diocesan law in his diocese, the ordinary was required to make this fact known in writing to the Holy See.

7.) Whenever in the future a bishop had permission from the Holy See to erect a community he was required to issue a formal decree of erection in writing. One copy of the decree was to be kept in the archives of the religious institute or the quasi-religious society, and another copy was to be preserved in the archives of the diocese. Furthermore, the notice of the erection had to be sent to the Holy See. This notice had to contain information concerning the founder of the institute, its title, scope of activity, the nature of the habit to be worn by the members, and all the other items mentioned above. It was required moreover that the activities of the institute or society be explicitly and exactly defined.

This decree was presented to Pope Pius XI in an audience granted to the Secretary of the Sacred Congregation of Religious on November 25, 1922. A formal approval was issued by the Pontiff and he stated that all to whom the decree was directed were obliged to obey it. A final clause in the decree abrogated any and all contrary law and usage. According to the principles already explained, this general decree by means of the comprehensive clause, "*Contrariis quibuscumque minime obstantibus,*" abrogated all contrary regulations and usages, even the contrary particular law as contained in the respective institute's or society's constitutions. This abrogation was simply the necessary consequence of the invoked norm of canon 22.[20]

The decree was applied not only to residential bishops but also to abbots and prelates *nullius,* to vicars and prefects apostolic, and to permanently constituted apostolic administrators.[21]

It is interesting to note that in n. 6 of the decree mention was

[20] *AAS,* XIV (1922), 646; *supra,* p. 55.

[21] Schäfer, *De Religiosis,* p. 134.

made of religious institutes while in every other article of the decree both religious institutes and quasi-religious societies were mentioned. It seems, then, that the prescription of this particular article was intended to be applicable only in the cases in which no religious institutes existed in a diocese. Consequently the bishops were not obliged to notify the Sacred Congregation of Religious in the cases in which no quasi-religious societies existed in their dioceses. It seems quite logical that the Holy See would excuse the bishops from the necessity of notifying Rome that no such societies existed in their dioceses when one considers the comparatively few such societies in existence. In fact, if the bishops of every diocese in which such societies had no establishments were to notify the Holy See of this fact by a special written report, the result of so many reports coming to the Holy See would probably bring about confusion rather than information.

ARTICLE III. THE SUPPRESSION OF QUASI-RELIGIOUS SOCIETIES

In accordance with the prescription of canon 674 the suppression of quasi-religious societies is regulated by the principles of canon 493. Canon 493 states: Any religious institute, even a diocesan congregation, which has been legally established cannot be dissolved, though it should consist of a single house, except by the Holy See, to which is reserved the disposition of the goods of a suppressed institute, due compliance with the will and the intention of the donors being always of course properly safeguarded.

Through an application of the prescriptions of canon 493 the following conclusions are justified. Once a quasi-religious society has been legitimately founded, even if it should consist of only one house, it can be suppressed only by the Holy See. Furthermore, the disposal of the goods of the suppressed society is likewise reserved to the Holy See.

A quasi-religious society is legitimately erected when it possesses the formal decree of its establishment by the competent ecclesiastical authority. In the case of a society consisting of only one house, the particular house could be either a domus *formata* or a domus *non formata*.

By the Holy See is meant the Sovereign Pontiff himself, who may exercise this power through various pontifical channels. For example, the Order of Penitential Brothers of Jesus of Nazareth was suppressed by means of a document of the Secretariate of Briefs to Princes and of Latin Letters.[22] In 1933 a congregation of women known as the Missionary Adorers of Reparation of the Sacred Eucharistic Blood of Jesus was suppressed by means of a document issued by the Sacred Congregation of the Holy Office.[23]

The right of the Holy See to decide concerning the material goods of suppressed societies is found in canon 1518 which states: the Roman Pontiff is the supreme administrator and dispenser of all ecclesiastical goods.

The ecclesiastical goods considered in canon 1518 includes all possessions both movable and immovable of the suppressed society.[24]

In accordance with the final prescription of canon 493 the Supreme Pontiff, in disposing of the goods of the suppressed society, will observe the norms of charity and canonical equity, always having regard for the will of donors.[25]

After the society has been suppressed it likewise pertains to the Holy See to provide for the future status of the members of the society. It must be decided whether they may transfer to other organizations, or whether they are to be dispensed from their obligations entirely.[26]

In accordance with the prescription of canon 102, § 1, a moral person, and consequently a quasi-religious society, becomes extinguished not only through an act of suppression imposed by legitimate authority, but also through its failure to furnish any outward show of existence for a period of one hundred years. Consequently a quasi-religious society ceases to exist if after the death or expulsion of the society's last member the society itself is not restored within a period of one hundred years.[27]

If a society of diocesan law has been suppressed it can be

---

[22] Blat, *De Religiosis*, p. 71; *AAS*, XXVII (1935), 482.

[23] *AAS*, XXV (1933), 36-37.

[24] Blat, *De Religiosis*, pp. 69-70.

[25] Wernz-Vidal, *De Religiosis*, n. 64; *ASS*, XXII (1889-1890), 693.

[26] Wernz-Vidal, *De Religiosis*, n. 64; Schäfer, *De Religiosis*, p. 148.

[27] Schäfer, *loc. cit.*

restored by the local bishop. But once a society of pontifical law has been suppressed it can be restored only through the intervention of the Holy See. However, if only one member remains in a society it remains radically possible for him to bring about a restoration of the society which, though practically extinct, nevertheless has not lost its juridical existence. Still in such a case the intervention of the bishop or of the Holy See would be needed in view of the lack of any legitimate superior who could accept the admission of the new members, except in the unusual supposition that the one remaining member would himself be such a legitimate superior.[28]

According to the legislation of Leo XIII's Constitution "Conditae a Christo," issued on December 8, 1900, ordinaries could suppress communities of diocesan law, provided that along with grave reasons there had also been obtained the consent of the bishop under whose protection the society originally was founded.[29] However, this previously acquired authorization was abrogated by the prescription of canon 493.

ARTICLE IV. THE PROVINCES OF QUASI-RELIGIOUS SOCIETIES

Section 1. Quasi-Religious Societies of Pontifical Law

By the prescription of canon 674, laws concerning the erection and suppression of provinces of religious institutes are to be applied to the erection and suppression of the provinces of quasi-religious societies. Canon 494 states: It rests with the Holy See to divide a religious institute of pontifical law into provinces, to join provinces which have been established or to change the boundaries of provinces, to establish new provinces, and to suppress established ones, . . .

When a province has become extinct, the right to dispose of its goods belongs to the General Chapter, or, outside the Chapter,

---

[28] Coronata, *Institutiones Iuris Canonici ad Usum Utriusque Cleri et Scholarum* (5 vols., Vol. I, 2. ed., Taurini: Marietti, 1939), I, 608 (hereafter cited as *Institutiones*) ; Larraona, "Commentarium Codicis,"—*CpR,* V (1924), 257; Fanfani, *De Religiosis,* p. 25.

[29] *Fontes,* n. 644.

to the superior general with his council, unless the constitutions provide otherwise; the laws of justice and the will of persons who have made foundations must be duly respected.

With the prescriptions of canon 494 properly applied to the quasi-religious societies, the following conclusions are justified. It rests with the Holy See to divide a quasi-religious society of pontifical law into provinces, to join provinces which have already been established or to change their boundaries, to establish new provinces, and to suppress established ones. Furthermore, when a province has become extinct, the right to dispose of its goods belongs to the General Chapter, or outside the Chapter, to the Superior General with his council, unless the constitutions provide otherwise.

Included in the term "Holy See" are the Sacred Congregation of Religious and the Sacred Congregation for the Propagation of the Faith, according as the societies concerned are established either in dioceses or in territories which still are subject to the jurisdiction of the Sacred Congregation for the Propagation of the Faith.

Under the notion of the erection of a province is not to be included the restoration of provinces which in active operation reflect no existence, but which in juridical status have retained their existence for the reason that as yet there has not been a lapse of one hundred years since the last manifestation of all activity. In the restoration of these memberless provinces there is not required any act of the Holy See, but only the intervention of the Superior General and his council.[80]

The jurisprudence of the Holy See requires that there must be at least four houses for the erection of a new province. Furthermore, the Holy See will not divide a religious institute of pontifical law into provinces unless at least four provinces can be erected.[81]

In accordance with the prescription of canon 494, § 2, even if the extinction of a province has resulted *ab intrinsico,* i.e., from

---

[80] Berutti, *Institutiones Iuris Canonici* (6 vols., Vol. III, *De Religiosis,* Taurini-Romae: Marietti, 1936), III, n. 13 (hereafter cited *De Religiosis*); Wernz-Vidal, *De Religiosis,* nn. 67-68; Cocchi, *De Religiosis,* n. 13.

[81] Coronata, *Institutiones,* I, 611; Schäfer, *De Religiosis,* p. 150.

the fact of the complete inactivity of a province for a continued and unbroken period of one hundred years, the goods of such an extinct province are to be disposed of by the General Chapter, or, outside of the Chapter, by the Superior General with his council, provided always that the constitutions do not establish otherwise.

Although when treating of the action of councillors the Code does not explicitly exclude the sufficiency of only a consultative vote, nevertheless it is the opinion of the authors that a deliberative vote is meant. This seems demanded in view of the grave nature of the business involved, which properly and by way of primary regulation pertains to the competence of the General Chapter, unless the constitutions provide otherwise.[32]

Section 2. Quasi-Religious Societies of Diocesan Law

Canon 494 provides legislation for the erection and suppression of provinces of religious institutes and quasi-religious societies of pontifical law, but not of institutes and societies of diocesan law. It is the opinion of authors that the lack of provision for the status of provinces of institutes and societies of diocesan law was not due to any oversight on the part of the legislator, but rather to the fact that the legislator did not judge it expedient to allow for their division into provinces. However, since the law does not forbid the division of institutes and societies of diocesan law into provinces, they can be so divided.

A society of diocesan law can be divided into provinces without the permission of the Holy See. The division should be provided for in the constitutions of the society. In the event that the prescriptions of the constitutions do not so provide, the prescriptions of canon 20 may be invoked. Accordingly, for the making of the division there is needed only the permission of the bishop in whose diocese the entire society is established. This may be gathered from the general principles which deal with the erection of quasi-religious societies of diocesan law as expressed in canon 492. On the other hand, if the quasi-religious society has foundations in several dioceses, the consent of all the ordinaries, in whose

[32] Schäfer, *De Religiosis*, p. 151; Blat, *De Religiosis*, p. 74; Cocchi, *De Religiosis*, n. 13; Wernz-Vidal, *De Religiosis*, n. 69.

dioceses are located the houses which are to form the new province, must be secured.

Although the authors state these conclusions in exclusive connection with religious institutes of diocesan law, nevertheless the same conclusions may be equally applied to quasi-religious societies of diocesan law. This deduction appears to be valid in virtue of the general principles stated in canon 674, whereby the same laws that determine the erection and the suppression of provinces of religious institutes are to be applied also to the quasi-religious societies.[83]

Larraona states that the consent of the ordinary of the diocese in which the mother house of the institute is located must be secured in addition to the consent of the ordinaries of the various dioceses in whose territory the houses of the proposed province are located.[84]

It must be remembered that these principles are to be applied only if the constitutions do not provide the procedure for the erection of provinces, and, in the absence of a decree from the Holy See for their division.

The principles just enumerated which provide for the erection of provinces in quasi-religious societies of diocesan law likewise apply in the suppression and the modification of the extent of these provinces.

If the constitutions do not provide for the disposal of the goods of a suppressed province of a society of diocesan law, then canon 20 must again be invoked for a proper directive norm. Accordingly, the prescription of canon 492, § 2, which provides for the disposal of the goods of a suppressed province of an institute of pontifical law, is to be applied. This disposal, then, rests with the General Chapter of the society, or, outside the Chapter, with the Superior General together with his council.

---

[83] Chelodi, *Ius de Personis Iuxta Codicem Iuris Canonici* (ed. altera a Sac. Ernesto Bertagnolli recognita et aucta, Tridenti: Libr. Edit. Tridentum, 1927), p. 411 (hereafter cited as *De Personis*); Schäfer, *De Religiosis*, p. 149; Vermeersch-Creusen, *Epitome*, I, n. 464; Wernz-Vidal, *De Religiosis*, n. 69.

[84] "Commentarium Codicis,"—*CpR*, V (1924), 263.

That the disposal of the goods of the suppressed province is reserved to the society itself, and not to the bishop of the diocese within which the province had been located, is further supported by the legal norm contained in canon 1501. Canon 1501 states that the goods of an extinct moral person belong to the immediately superior ecclesiastical moral person.

In the case in question the society, and not the diocese, is the immediately superior ecclesiastical moral person of the suppressed province.[85]

While canon 495 does not explicitly treat of the provinces of religious institutes of diocesan law, it does treat of them indirectly by providing for the expansion into other dioceses of an institute possessing a single province. It is for this reason that canon 495 will now be treated under the article dealing with provinces of societies of diocesan law.

Canon 495, by reason of the general application made in canon 674, governs quasi-religious societies as well as religious institutes. It states that an institute of diocesan law, and consequently also a quasi-religious society cannot establish houses in another diocese except with the consent of both the bishop of the diocese where the mother house is located, and the bishop of the diocese in which it wishes to establish a new house. The ordinary of the diocese of the mother house should not, except for grave reasons, refuse to grant this permission.

From the wording of this canon there can arise a doubt as to whether the permission of the bishop in whose diocese the mother house of the society is located must be secured each time a new house is desired in another diocese, or only when the first house is desired there. Some authors hold that the permission is needed every time a new house is desired in another diocese.[86]

On the other hand, the authors in greater number claim that the permission of the ordinary of the diocese in which the society has its mother house must be secured only for the foundation of the first house in another diocese, and not for any further houses.

---

[85] Schäfer, *De Religiosis,* p. 149.

[86] E.g., Prümmer, *Manuale Iuris Canonici* (3. ed., Friburgi: Herder & Co., 1922), p. 238, q. 181 (hereafter cited as *Manuale*).

These authors point out the fact that in other places in the Code the law uses the plural number when the singlar number might also have been used, i.e., to designate the singular, e.g., in canons 492, 494, § 1. So too in canon 495, § 1, which is the canon in question, the law, in order to signify in a singular sense that the permission of both ordinaries is needed for the foundation of a house (meaning the first house) in a new diocese, was not restricted to the use of the singular number, but could state, as it actually does, in a plural form, that both permissions are required for the founding of houses in a new diocese. Furthermore, these authors contend that in pre-Code law as expressed in the Constitution *"Conditae a Christo,"* issued by Pope Leo XIII on December 8, 1900, it was decreed that *sodalitas quaevis dioecesana ad dioeceses alias ne transgrediatur*" (no society of diocesan law shall in any other way enter another diocese). Now, a diocesan society enters another diocese with the foundation of the first house in that other diocese, and not through the subsequent foundation of houses. Moreover, the very verb *commigrare* as used in canon 495, § 1, expresses, these authors insist, the idea of a first transfer.[37]

That house is the mother house of the society which was its first foundation. If the location of the mother house is changed from the site of its first foundation, then that house is the mother house in which the Superior General and his council reside. If a society wishes to change its mother house from one diocese to another, there must be obtained the permission of both the ordinary of the diocese in which the mother house is located as well as the permission of the ordinary of the diocese to which the mother house is to be transferred. This is necessary because the former is being deprived of a certain right given him in canon 495, while the latter is being burdened with a special obligation of vigilance over the society.[38]

The prescription of canon 495, § 1, which states that the ordinary of the mother house should not refuse the permission for

---

[37] Schäfer, *De Religiosis,* pp. 158-159; Coronata, *Institutiones,* I, 164; Larraona, "Commentarium Codicis,"—*CpR,* V (1924), 326; Blat, *De Religiosis,* p. 78; Vermeersch-Creusen, *Epitome,* I, n. 464; Maroto, "Commentarium Codicis,"—*CpR,* II (1921), 325.

[38] Schäfer, *De Religiosis,* p. 159.

a new house in another diocese without grave reasons, flows from the very nature of the institute or society as a collegiate moral person. For a collegiate moral person is concerned not only with its own conservation, but also with its growth and expansion. If the superiors of a society think that the ordinary of the diocese in which their mother house is located does not have sufficiently grave reasons to refuse the permission for a new house to be founded in another diocese, they may have recourse to the Holy See. Pending an answer, however, the decision of the ordinary in his refusal of the permission must be observed.[39]

Canon 495, § 2, states that, if a congregation of diocesan law spreads into other dioceses, changes in the laws of that congregation cannot be made except with the consent of each and every ordinary of the diocese in which the congregation has a house. However, matters which according to the prescription of canon 492, § 1, have to be submitted to the Holy See before a bishop can establish a congregation of diocesan law may not be changed even with the consent of the bishops concerned.

In accordance with the general prescription of canon 674, the principles of canon 495, § 2, are applicable to quasi-religious societies. Consequently the following conclusions may be drawn. If a quasi-religious society of diocesan law spreads into other dioceses, no changes in the laws of that society may be made except with the consent of every ordinary into whose territory the society has spread. However, the matters which were submitted to the Holy See previous to the foundation of the society may not be changed even if the ordinaries should consent.[40]

The prescription of canon 495, § 2, which demands the consent of the several bishops before any changes may be made in the constitutions of religious institutes and quasi-religious societies which have spread into several dioceses, is a prohibitive prescription. Conseqently, the consent of each and every bishop is required for the validity of any changes. For in accordance with the

---

[39] Blat, *de Religiosis*, p. 78.

[40] The matters which must be submitted to the Holy See prior to the foundation of a society were discussed in an earlier article. Cf. *supra*, p. 77.

prescriptions of canon 101, § 1, n. 2, what touches all must be approved by all.

Any privilege which stands contrary to the prescriptions of canons 494-495 are not abrogated. However the particular constitutions of societies which contravene the prescriptions of these two canons are abrogated, unless the contrary constitutions were approved by the Holy See after the promulgation of the Code.[41]

ARTICLE V. LEGISLATION CONCERNING THE ERECTION OF HOUSES OF QUASI-RELIGIOUS SOCIETIES

Section 1. The Material Element

Canon 496 states that no religious house is to be erected unless it can prudently be judged that the new house will be able to provide for the proper lodging and sustenance of its members. The means of support of the members of a house should be reasonably anticipated from either the usual income of the house, from customary alms, or from some other adequate source.

Canon 674 in its general provision for houses of quasi-religious societies applies the prescription of canon 496 to the erection of the houses of these societies.

The prudent judgment concerning the future support of houses of these societies is to be made according to the ordinary norms of judgment on the part of prudent men. The responsibility for this judgment rests equally upon the superior who must seek the necessary ecclesiastical permission for the erection of the house and upon the person who with proper ecclesiastical authority is empowered to grant the necessary permission.[42]

The necessary support for these houses, as the canon states, may be secured from the income of the house itself, which is reasonably assured either as remuneration for the personal labors of the members of the house, as offerings prompted by the personal kindnesses of benefactors, or as returns on invested capital.

---

[41] Schäfer, *De Religiosis*, p. 151.

[42] Blat, *De Religiosis*, p. 80; Larraona, "Commentarium Codicis," *CpR*, V (1924), 330.

The support may also be procured from customary alms. These, however, must be proved, if given to the society at large, to be sufficient to support the houses already established in addition to the new house. Other adequate and juridically recognized means of support are dowries in societies of women, or patrimony when according to the constitutions the patrimony of the members is to be used for the support of the society.[43]

The prescription of canon 496 does not, however, bind under pain of nullity.[44]

Section 2. The Formal Element

In accordance with the general provisions of canon 674 all the prescriptions contained in canon 497, which are concerned with the erection and modification of houses of religious institutes, are to be applied to quasi-religious societies.[45]

According to the prescriptions of canon 497, § 1, the approval of the Holy See and the written consent of the local ordinary are required for the erection of houses of exempt religious institutes, or whenever the houses are to be erected in a territory subject to the Sacred Congregation for the Propagation of the Faith. In all other cases, that is, for the erection of houses of non-exempt institutes which are not to be located in mission territory, only the permission of the local ordinary is required. Hence for the erection of a house of an exempt quasi-religious society, or of a house of a quasi-religious society in a mission territory, the consent of the Holy See and the written permission of the local ordinary must be secured. In all other cases the permission of the local ordinary is sufficient.

This approval of the Holy See and the written consent of the local ordinary for the erection of a house belonging to an exempt quasi-religious society, or of a house of a non-exempt quasi-religious society which is going to be erected in mission territory, is for the validity of the erection. This may be proved by the very wording of the canon itself. It may likewise be proved from the

---

[43] Chelodi, *De Personis*, p. 412.

[44] Schäfer, *De Religiosis*, p. 162.

[45] Cocchi, *De Religiosis*, n. 14.

fact that the pre-Code law from which this prescription was taken demanded the approval of the Holy See for the validity of the erection in these cases. In accordance with the principles of canon 6, n. 2, when a law is derived from pre-Code law the previously accepted interpretations of the latter are controlling. Furthermore, in canon 497, § 1, no distinction is made between the degree of necessity in the requisite of approval to be obtained from the Holy See and from the local ordinary. Consequently, if the permission of one is required for validity, as the permission of the Holy See is required, then the permission of the other is likewise demanded for validity.[46]

There is some discussion among the authors whether the permission of the local ordinary in these cases must be in writing in order that the permission be considered valid. There is likewise some question whether his permission must be in writing in the case of the erection of houses of non-exempt societies outside mission territory.

As to the first discussion, the following authors hold that the permission of the local ordinary must be in writing in order that it might be considered as valid: Chelodi (1880-1922),[47] Larraona,[48] Oesterle[49] and Schäfer.[50] Vermeersch-Creusen[51] and Coronata, on the other hand,[52] hold that the permission of the local ordinary need not be in writing for its validity.

It is the opinion of the writer that the permission must be in writing for validity in the cases involved. This conclusion was reached not only because of the extrinsic weight of the opinion of the authors holding this view, but also because of the fact that the text of the canon relates the writing of the decree to the substance of the consent, and finally, because the two concepts in the text, namely the consent and the writing of this consent, seem to be equalized in their juridical import.[53]

---

[46] Blat, *De Religiosis*, pp. 84-85; Schäfer, *De Religiosis*, pp. 153-154.

[47] *De Personis*, p. 413.

[48] "Consultationes,"—*CpR*, I (1920), 112.

[49] *Praelectiones Iuris Canonici*, I, 246.

[50] *De Religiosis*, p. 154.

[51] *Epitome*, I, n. 465.

[52] *Institutiones*, I, 615, note 4.

[53] Cf. can. 497, § 1; Blat, *De Religiosis*, p. 85.

As regards the second discussion, namely, whether the consent of the local ordinary must also be in writing for the valid erection of the houses of non-exempt societies outside mission territory, Larraona,[54] Chelodi,[55] Schäfer[56] and Blat[57] all contend that, although the words of the canon do not state that the permission of the local ordinary must be in writing, nevertheless it is their opinion that it too must be in writing for a valid erection of the houses concerned. This is likewise the opinion of the writer, since the canon is speaking of the same act, the permission of the local ordinary, which must be performed under two different sets of circumstances. Now since the necessity of writing is expressed in the one clause which requires this permission, it is also intended in the second clause which similarly requires this permission.[58]

There is some further discussion among the authors as to the extent of the term *Ordinarii loci,* as used in the first paragraph of canon 497. It is the opinion of Schäfer that the vicar general would need a special mandate to found a house of a religious institute or of a quasi-religious society, or to give permission for the erection of such a house. He likewise claims that the vicar capitular or the diocesan administrator could grant this permission only if this act did not import an innovation in the diocese.[59]

However, according to canon 198, § 1, both the vicar general and the vicar capitular are equivalently considered as sharing the status of a local ordinary. At most it could be said that the vicar general would act illicitly in granting permission or in actually founding a house of a religious institute or of a quasi-religious society. For according to the prescriptions of canon 369 the vicar general is to refer the more important acts of the curia to the bishop. He is likewise forbidden to use his power contrary to the mind and will of the bishop. Similarly, the vicar capitular or the diocesan administrator could at most be said to act illicitly in

---

[54] "Consultationes,"—*CpR,* I (1920), 113; "Commentarium Codicis,"—*CpR,* V (1924), 426.

[55] *De Personis,* p. 413.

[56] *De Religiosis,* p. 155.

[57] *De Religiosis,* pp. 85-86.

[58] Cf. can. 497; Schäfer, *De Religiosis,* p. 155.

[59] *De Religiosis,* p. 154.

founding or in granting permission to find a house of a religious institute or a quasi-religious society. For according to the prescription of canon 436 they are forbidden to perform any action which might be considered an innovation.[60]

Section 3. Churches and Oratories Annexed to Houses of Quasi-Religious Societies

According to the second paragraph of canon 497, when a clerical religious institute has obtained the necessary permission to erect a house, there is included in this permission the further right to annex a church or a public oratory to the new foundation. However, the prescription of canon 1162, § 4, must be observed. This demands that the permission of the local ordinary be secured before a religious institute may build either a church or a public oratory in a certain and determined location. Moreover, the religious institute may perform the functions of the sacred ministry in these places, observing the specific laws enacted in the Code in regulation of these sacred functions. According to the principles of canon 497, § 2, permission is likewise implied for a nonclerical religious institute to carry on in the houses, for the erection of which permission has been received, all the pious works proper to the particular institute, unless certain conditions concerning the exercise of these works were incorporated in the permission given by the ordinary.

In accordance with the general prescription of canon 674, all the prescriptions of canon 497, § 2, just mentioned with regard to religious institutes, are to be similarly applied to quasi-religious societies.

Canon 1162, § 4, prescribes that a separate permission to build a church or a public oratory must be secured from the local ordinary, even though the right to erect it is given a clerical religious institute in the concession which canon 497, § 2, connects with the earlier granted permission for the erection of the house. This same regulation is applicable to clerical quasi-religious societies. The local ordinary is not to grant this separate permission until he has consulted with the rectors of the churches in the vicinity of

[60] Blat, *De Religiosis*, p. 92; Coronata, *Institutiones*, I, 615.

the location selected by the religious institute or quasi-religious society. He must receive from these rectors their opinion as to whether another church or public oratory in the locality would be beneficial or harmful.[61]

It is within the right of the local ordinary to forbid the erection of a church in a particular location. However, Larraona,[62] and Schäfer[63] contend that the local ordinary cannot forbid the building of at least a private oratory. This is the minimum which the law allows.

A lay religious society which has received the necessary permission to erect a house needs a special permission of the local ordinary if it desires a church or even a semi-public oratory annexed to its foundation.[64]

Furthermore, the expression *domui adnexum* means that the church or the public oratory of a clerical society is either materially joined with the new house, or, if it be materially separated from the house, at least not located at any notable and appreciable distance from it.[65]

Section 4. Other Establishments Annexed to Houses of Quasi-Religious Societies

In the third paragraph of canon 497 it is stated that if a religious institute, and therefore also a quasi-religious society, wishes to erect a school, a hospice or similar buildings separated from the house, then the permission of the local ordinary is indeed necessary but also suffices. The prescription of this paragraph applies even in the erection of such buildings as distinct from an exempt house.

The local ordinary mentioned is the same local ordinary contemplated in the first two paragraphs of this canon.[66]

If the additional buildings mentioned in canon 497, § 3, are not

---

[61] Schäfer, *De Religiosis*, pp. 162-163.
[62] "Commentarium Codicis,"—*CpR*, V (1924), 427.
[63] *De Religiosis*, p. 164.
[64] Can. 1192, § 1.
[65] Fanfani, *De Religiosis*, p. 385.
[66] Schäfer, *De Religiosis*, p. 166.

separated from the religious house, so that either materially or morally they are to be considered as one with the house, then no new permission is needed for the exercise of the functions proper to these types of buildings unless, according to the second paragraph of this canon, certain conditions concerning the exercise of these works were included in the permission for the erection of the house. Here again the notion of separation from the religious house is not verified if the location of the newly erected building is nearby, for it is only if the buildings are at a great distance from the house that they should be considered as new houses.[67]

Section 5. Change of Function in Houses of Quasi-Religious Societies

The conversion from the original work of a house of a quasi-religious society to another work is, in accordance with the general principle established in canon 674, to be effected in the same manner as the conversion from the original to another kind of work when the house of a religious institute is in question. The norms determining the conversion of the functions of houses of religious institutes are found in canon 497, § 4. Consequently, with the application of the prescription of canon 497, § 4, to the houses of quasi-religious societies, there results the following norms which determine the procedure to be followed in the conversion of the functions of a house.

If a house of a quasi-religious society is to be converted to serve other than its original functions, all the formalities prescribed in the first paragraph of canon 497 must be observed. An exception is made for the conversion to a work affecting only the internal discipline of the society.[68]

In the application of canon 497, § 4, it must be ascertained whether or not the new use of the house pertains to the internal government or discipline of the society. The addition to the house made with the view to converting it into an apostolic school for the young members of the society is considered as a matter that

---

[67] Schäfer, *De Religiosis*, p. 166; Larraona, "Commentarium Codicis,"—*CpR*, V (1924), 427.

[68] Cf. can. 497, § 4, in relation with can. 674.

pertains to the house's internal affairs. But the addition of a college to which externs are admitted is not to be considered as pertaining merely to an internal change and consequently the permission of the bishop is required.[69]

When the change affects both the internal and the external relations of the society the solemnities of a new foundation are required and that by reason of the word *duntaxat* in canon 497, § 4, which dispenses from this obligation only when the change affects the internal order alone.[70]

The transfer of the location of a house from one site to another is equivalent to a new foundation.[71] However, if the change of location of the house is made within the same town or city, then the only permission needed is that of the local ordinary. This opinion is held by Schäfer, who cites Piat (1815-1904) as having held the same opinion.[72]

ARTICLE VI. THE SUPPRESSION OF HOUSES OF QUASI-RELIGIOUS SOCIETIES

In accordance with the general principle established in canon 674, the suppression of the houses belonging to quasi-religious societies is to be effected in the same manner as the suppression of the houses of religious institutes. The norms determining the suppression of the houses of religious institutes are found in canon 498. Consequently, through the application of the prescriptions of canon 498 to the houses of quasi-religious societies, there result the following norms which determine the procedure to be followed in their suppression.

If the houses (*formatae* and *non-formatae* alike) of quasi-religious societies pertain to exempt societies, they cannot be suppressed without the approval of the Holy See. If the houses pertain not to exempt societies, but to societies of pontifical law, they must be suppressed by the Superior General of the society with

---

[69] Larraona, "Commentarium Codicis,"—*CpR,* V (1924), 436; Coronata, *Institutiones,* I, 618.

[70] Schäfer, *De Religiosis,* p. 168.

[71] Chelodi, *De Personis,* p. 414; Fanfani, *De Religiosis,* p. 32.

[72] *De Religiosis,* p. 169.

the consent of the local ordinary. Finally, if the houses belong to a society of diocesan law, they can be suppressed only through the authority of the local ordinary after he has consulted the Superior General of the society. If the suppression is made by the local ordinary contrary to the mind of the Superior General, the Superior General has the right of recourse to the Holy See. This recourse has a suspensive effect. Consequently any such act of suppression by the ordinary remains without effect until ratification is had from the Holy See.[73]

The concluding sentence of canon 498 refers to the prescription of canon 493, according to which the Holy See alone can suppress a house if it be the only house of the society, for in such a situation the suppression of the particular house would entail the suppression of the society itself.

It will be noticed that there is no special legislation for the suppression of houses existing in territories subject to the Sacred Congregation for the Propagation of the Faith. However, the permission of the Holy See is required for their erection.[74]

The permission of the Holy See needed for the suppression of houses of exempt societies is required for the validity of the act. This permission partakes of the same nature as the permission of the Holy See required in canon 497, § 1, for the valid erection of these houses. The reasons given for stating that the permission which receives mention in canon 497, § 1, is a requirement for validity apply also for claiming that the papal permission which receives mention in canon 498 is likewise necessary for the validity of the act.[75]

In legislation for the suppression of houses of non-exempt societies, the Code does not require the Superior General of the society to consult with his council. Rather it leaves the act of suppression entirely in the hands of the Superior General and the local ordinary. However, the constitutions of each society are to be consulted for determining whether or not the Superior General must seek the advice of his council. If the constitutions

[73] Cans. 674; 498.

[74] Cf. can. 497, § 1.

[75] Cf. *supra*, p. 93.

demand this consultation, though it is not demanded by the Code, then the prescription of the constitutions retains its force, for such a demand is not contrary to the Code but rather beyond (*praeter*) the Code.[76]

The consent of the local ordinary which must be obtained by the Superior General before the suppression of a house of a non-exempt society of pontifical law is necessary for the valid suppression of that house. The reasons which were stated to prove that the consent of the local ordinary is a requirement for validity in the circumstances contemplated in canon 497, § 1 and 3, apply likewise in this case.[77]

In the suppression of houses of quasi-religious societies of diocesan law the prescription of canon 498 which imposes on the local ordinary the obligation of consulting with the Superior General of the society, does not demand the *consent* of the Superior General for the validity of the suppression of the house.[78]

Schäfer bases his opinion on the law contained in canon 105, n. 1. This canon states that, when the law demands of a superior that he seek the advice of another, it is necessary for the validity of the act that the superior at least listen to the other person. The superior, however, is not bound to follow the advice of the other party.[79]

By reason of the suspensive nature of the recourse to the Holy See which is allowed the Superior General against the local ordinary's intention to suppress a house of a society of diocesan law, the local ordinary would act invalidly if he proceeded to suppress the house before receiving a concurring reply from the Holy See.

It will be noted that the law is silent concerning the disposal of the property of a suppressed house. The constitutions of each society determine the proper method for this disposal. However,

---

[76] Cf. *supra*, p. 53; Blat, *De Religiosis*, pp. 93-95.

[77] Cf. *supra*, p. 93; Cocchi, *De Religiosis*, n. 17; Vermeersch-Creusen, *Epitome*, I, n. 467.

[78] Schäfer, *De Religiosis*, p. 171, note, 232.

[79] Can. 105, n. 1.—Cum ius statuit Superiorem ad agendum indigere consensu vel consilio aliquarum personarum . . . si consilium tantum . . . satis est ad valide agendum ut Superior illas personas audiat.

if the constitutions are silent on this point then the norm of canon 20 is to be applied. As a result of this application, the prescription of canon 1501, which constitutes law that governs similar cases, will determine the method for this disposal. According to the prescription of canon 1501 the property of a suppressed or extinct moral person belongs to the immediately superior ecclesiastical moral person. In this case that person is the province of which the suppressed house was a part. If the society has only one province, the society itself will determine the disposal of the property.[80]

It must be kept in mind that in the case of the suppression of houses of non-exempt societies the permission of the Holy See must be secured whenever there is question of an alienation exceeding the sum of 30,000 francs.[81]

Finally, according to the prescription of canon 102, § 1, if a house of a quasi-religious society is deserted for over one hundred years, it becomes extinct by the prescription of the law itself. The disposal of the property of the house is then effected as in the case of the property of any suppressed house.[82]

---

[80] Berutti, *De Religiosis,* p. 43.

[81] Cf. can. 1532, § 2, n. 2; Schäfer, *De Religiosis,* p. 170.

[82] Coronata, Institutiones, I, 260.

CHAPTER VI

The Juridical Organization of Quasi-Religious Societies

Article I. The Relations of Quasi-Religious Societies to Ecclesiastical Authority

Section 1. Introduction

Canon 675 in a comprehensive statement codifies as it were the constitutions of quasi-religious societies with regard to the determination of the juridical organization of these societies. However, this first general statement of canon 675 is considerably modified by its concluding clause. This clause states that all the canons of the Code which determine the juridical organization of religious institutes are to be applied whenever possible to quasi-religious societies. This includes the prescriptions of canons 499-530.[1]

Included in the general term *regimen* is the element of the external government of the societies, comprising the juridical relations between the society and ecclesiastical authority, as well as the element of its internal government, comprising the juridical relations between the superiors and their subjects.

As was previously stated, it would be impossible in a work of this nature to discuss in detail the implications of every canon which requires consideration. This is especially true of the canons involved here. An attempt must be made, however, to point out precisely what laws of the Code comprised under the general heading of *regimen* apply to quasi-religious societies. Consequently any accepted interpretations of the canons so selected, should be presented here because of their application to quasi-religious societies.

---

[1] Can. 675.—Regimen determinatur in unius cuiusque societatis constitutionibus; sed in omnibus serventur, congrua congruis referendo, can. 499-530.

Section 2. Subjection to the Roman Pontiff

All members of quasi-religious societies are subject to the authority of the Roman Pontiff and are obliged to consider him as their supreme superior. They likewise are obliged to obey him by reason of the bond which makes them subjects of the authority of their own superiors.[2] This is an application of the principle expressed in canon 499, § 1, to the quasi-religious societies. This application is justified in virtue of the prescriptions of canon 675.

The subjection to the Pope binds not only the individual members of the society, but also its individual aggregate units, such as its chapter and its bodies of councillors. The term *"Roman Pontiff"* as used in canon 499, § 1, refers not to the various agencies of the Roman Curia but to the very person of the Roman Pontiff. This power of government and rule may of course be delegated by the Roman Pontiff to whomsoever he may choose.[3]

Inasmuch as no public vow of obedience is pronounced by the members of quasi-religious societies, the Roman Pontiff could not impose an obligation on any such members by reason of the *vow* of obedience. Nevertheless he could impose on them a grave obligation under the *virtue* of obedience. While it is true to say that the Roman Pontiff is not subject to the constitutions of a quasi-religious society whenever he wishes to command the obedience of its members, still he may not require of them, in virtue of their membership, anything that they did not implicitly or explicitly promise at the time of their incorporation into the society, i.e., through the promises that were based on the provisions of the constitutions.[4]

Section 3. Obedience Owed the Sacred Congregations

Quasi-religious societies are bound by the virtue of obedience to respect the legislation of the Sacred Congregation of Religious

---

[2] Cf. can. 499, § 1.

[3] Schäfer, *De Religiosis*, pp. 177-179.

[4] *Raus, De Sacrae Obedientiae Virtute et Voto secundum Doctrinam divi Thomae et S. Alphonsi, iuxta Normas ac Codicem Iuris Canonici* (Lugduni-Parisiis: E. Vitte, 1923), pp. 203-206; Blat, *De Religiosis*, p. 103-106.

concerning matters pertaining to the government, the discipline, the studies, the property, and the privileges of the society. The Sacred Congregation is also exclusively competent in the matter of dispensations from the common law when such are granted to their subjects. Canon 247, § 5, makes an exception to this competence whereby it reserves to the Holy Office the enacting of legislation and the granting of dispensations relative to the Eucharistic fast to be observed by priests in the celebration of Mass. Judgment on certain crimes is also reserved to the Holy Office.[5]

Societies erected in a territory subject to the Sacred Congregation for the Propagation of the Faith are likewise subject to the legislation of this Sacred Congregation.[6]

As regards the several other Sacred Congregations to which the quasi-religious societies owe obedience, most notable are the Sacred Congregation of Rites and the Sacred Congregation of Studies. A similar obedience is of course likewise due the Sacred Penitentiary.[7]

In the case of relations between quasi-religious societies and the Oriental Church, the Sacred Congregation for the Oriental Church is competent to settle the matter.[8]

Section 4. Cardinal Protectors

Generally considered, quasi-religious societies do not have a Cardinal Protector. In those cases in which a quasi-religious society does have a Cardinal Protector the prescriptions of canon 499, § 2, are applicable.

Canon 499, § 2, prescribes the necessary legislation for Cardinal Protectors of religious institutes. These prescriptions, by virtue of the general prescription of canon 675, are also applicable to quasi-religious societies. Accordingly, there is conceded to the Cardinal Protector of a quasi-religious society a right of honor, but no power of jurisdiction or authority in the internal affairs or in the administration of the property of the society. In a particular case,

[5] *AAS*, I (1909), 11-12.

[6] Can. 252, § 5.

[7] Cf. cans. 256; 250, §§ 2, 3; 247, § 5.

[8] Larraona, "Commentarium Codicis," *CpR*, VI (1925), 80.

with the approval of the Holy See, the Cardinal Protector could be given real power over the society, but this would be exceptional.[9]

Section 5. Subjection to the Local Ordinary

From an application of the prescriptions of canon 500, which application is justified by canon 675, quasi-religious societies which do not possess the privilege of exemption are subject to the rule of the local ordinary in the same way as non-exempt religious institutes. The general authority exercised by the local ordinary over non-exempt religious institutes, and, consequently, likewise over non-exempt quasi-religious societies, derives from his jurisdiction and not from the possession of dominative power. This follows from the definition of exemption, as contained in canon 488, n. 2, as the authoritatively implemented withdrawal of a religious institute, and consequently also of a quasi-religious society, from the jurisdiction of the local ordinary. Consequently when in canon 500 the Code considers an exempt institute as not subject to the jurisdiction of the local ordinary, it implies that the only subjection affecting a non-exempt institute is that which flows from the power of jurisdiction.

Canon 499, § 1, states that religious are subject (*subduntur*) to the Roman Pontiff and are bound to obey him by virtue of their vow of obedience. This clearly signifies a double source of authority in the Roman Pontiff: one, that of jurisdiction, and the other, that of dominative power based on the vow of obedience. Now in the first paragraph of canon 500 the term *subduntur* is again used for the purpose of expressing the subjection of non-exempt religious institutes to the local ordinary. However, no mention is made of any subjection to dominative power as flowing from the vow of obedience. Nor is there the use of any term which might indicate the possession by the local ordinary of a power similar to that of the dominative power of the Roman Pontiff.[10]

---

[9] Can. 499, § 2; Larraona, "Commentarium Codicis,"—*CpR,* VI (1925), 133.

[10] Larraona, "Commentarium Codicis,"—*CpR,* V (1924), 144, note 93; "Commentarium Codicis,"—*CpR,* VI (1925), 183; Coronata, *Institutiones,* I, p. 624; Bastien, *Directoire Canonique,* p. 344.

The conclusions just stated are equally applicable to quasi-religious societies and to religious institutes. This is said in virtue of canon 675, which applies the prescriptions of canon 500 to quasi-religious societies.

The only exception to this rule is had when in accordance with the constitutions, a local ordinary is considered a legitimate superior of a quasi-religious society and thus is accorded the right to command by virtue of the incorporation of the member into the society, just as any other superior of the society might command.[11]

It must be remembered, however, that even exempt quasi-religious societies, just as exempt religious institutes, are subject to the local ordinary in certain matters specified in the prescriptions of the common law.[12]

Moreover, even though exempt, religious institutes are subject to certain acts of jurisdiction on the part of the local ordinary to the extent determined in the common law and the constitutions.[13]

The local ordinary's right and duty of visitation are warranted by canon 512, § 1, n. 2 and § 2, n. 2, 3.

According to the general principle stated in canon 675 the prescriptions of these paragraphs of canon 512 are applicable to quasi-religious societies. Consequently the following conclusions are justified.

The local ordinary has the right and duty to visit at least once every five years each house of men and women of quasi-religious societies of diocesan law. Since no limits are placed by the Code as to the extent of this visitation, the local ordinary is to inquire into all things subjected to his inspection by the common law and the constitutions of the societies themselves.

In general the scope of the local ordinary's inquiry includes the observance of the internal and external discipline, and the state of the society's economic and financial affairs. More specifically, the local ordinary inquires into the condition of the church and the observance of the laws as regards the altar, the sacristy, etc.[14]

---

[11] Cocchi, *De Religiosis,* n. 22.

[12] Cf. can. 500, § 1; Schäfer, *De Religiosis,* p. 192.

[13] Schäfer, *De Religiosis,* p. 197.

[14] Cans. 1261; 1382.

Included in the inquiry are the proper structure of the confessionals;[15] the frequency of the reception of the sacraments;[16] the conformity of religious discipline with the constitutions, particularly as regards the promises, spiritual exercises and other daily duties;[17] the existence of harmonious relations among the members as well as with outsiders;[18] the observance of the law of enclosure,[19] and the efficiency of the administration of the society's property.[20]

Likewise by reason of the prescriptions of canon 512, § 2, n. 2, the local ordinary is obliged to visit every house of clerical quasi-religious societies of pontifical law, even though exempt. This visitation should concern itself with the church, the sacristy, the public oratory and the confessionals. Finally, every five years he must visit every house of lay quasi-religious societies of pontifical law, even if exempt, and inquire not only into the matters just mentioned, but also into the observance of discipline in a manner conformable to the constitutions; the preservation of sound doctrine and good morals; the observance of the law of enclosure; the frequency of the reception of the sacraments; the efficient administration of property.[21]

The rights of the bishop concerning the administration of the property of these societies will be considered in a later chapter, which will treat precisely of the administration of that property.

Furthermore, in regard to all quasi-religious societies, even though they be exempt, the local ordinary has the right to visit their hospitals, orphanages, schools and similar institutions destined for works of charity both spiritual and temporal.[22]

If these institutions are conducted by quasi-religious societies of diocesan law, the local ordinary has complete jurisdiction over them. They likewise are subject to the full visitation of the local ordinary as expressed above.[23]

---

[15] Cans. 909-910.
[16] Cans. 125; 592; 595.
[17] Cans. 610; 618, § 2, n. 2.
[18] Cans. 512, § 2, n. 3; 690, § 2.
[19] Cans. 604, § 3; 605; 679, § 2.
[20] Can. 535, § 3.
[21] Cf. can. 512, § 2, n. 2, 3; 618, § 2, n. 2; Blat, *De Religiosis*, pp. 168-170
[22] Cans. 1489; 1491, § 1.
[23] Cf. *supra*, p. 106.

On the other hand if these institutions belong to quasi-religious societies of pontifical law, the local ordinary has the right of visitation with regard to the teaching of religion, the status of moral conduct, the exercises of piety and the administration of the sacraments.[24]

According to the prescription of canon 513, § 1, the local ordinary has the right to interrogate the members of these societies who he thinks should be questioned, and thus to obtain knowledge of those matters which are within the scope of the visitation. All the members are bound to answer truthfully, and the superiors are forbidden to dissuade them from this obligation or in any way to hamper the purpose of the visitation. Furthermore, against the decrees of the local ordinary there is granted the possibility of a recourse which, however, remains devoid of all suspensive effect, unless the local ordinary has proceeded with his investigation by means of a judicial trial. This means that his orders are to be obeyed pending the results of the recourse, except in the case of a canonical trial when the sentence of the local ordinary remains suspended until the court of appeal has rendered a conformable sentence.[25]

The local ordinary is bound by the prescriptions of canon 1261, § 1, to safeguard divine worship in his diocese and to prevent all forms of superstition among the faithful. If in the fulfillment of this obligation the local ordinary has enacted special laws for his territory, all quasi-religious societies, even those which are exempt, are obliged to obey them.[26]

The superiors of quasi-religious societies are likewise liable to the penalties determined by the Code if they interfere with the visitation in the ways prohibited by the law.[27] This was expressly declared by the Pontifical Commission for the Authentic Interpretation of the Code on June 3, 1918.[28]

Consequently, if a superioress, after a visitation has been an-

---

[24] Cf. can. 1491, § 2; Schäfer, *De Religiosis*, p. 200.

[25] Cf. cans. 513, §§ 1, 2; 1889, § 2; Cocchi, *De Religiosis*, n. 27, B.

[26] Can. 1261, §§ 1, 2; Schäfer, *De Religiosis*, p, 201.

[27] Can. 2413, §§ 1, 2.

[28] *AAS*, X (1918), 347; Gallik, *The Rights and Duties of Bishops Regarding Diocesan Sisterhoods* (St. Paul, Minnesota; Wanderer Printing Co.; 1939), pp. 83-86.

nounced, should transfer a member to another house without the consent of the visitor, she is to be declared by the visitor as disqualified for the obtaining of any and all offices which entail the government of others, and moreover she is to be deprived of the office which she holds. This same penalty is to be imposed on all members of a quasi-religious society of women, whether superioress or not, who personally or through others, directly or indirectly, induce a member to remain silent when questioned by the visitor, or to conceal the truth in any manner, or to answer otherwise than with sincerity, or who under any pretext molest the member because of the answers she has given to the visitor.[29]

The precepts outlined in the preceding paragraph are likewise applicable to quasi-religious societies of men.[30]

Section 6. Exemption

Concerning the question of exemption of clerical quasi-religious societies, Goyeneche makes mention of a certain clerical quasi-religious society to whom a rescript was given for the sake of allowing them to share in the privileges which regulars and clerical exempt religious institutes enjoy in the Church. In a further decree this society was exempted from the jurisdiction, correction and visitation of the local ordinaries, except in the cases in which the law made particular exceptions also for Regulars, e.g., as in canon 521, § 2, n. 2.

When the society inquired as to the exact extent of its exemption it was told to consult approved authors and the practice of the religious institutes which enjoyed the privilege of exemption. Still in doubt, the society inquired of the *Commentarium pro Religiosis* whether this exemption gave to their superiors ecclesiastical jurisdiction both for the internal and the external forum according to the norm of canon 501 for clerical exempt religious.

The society was told that it enjoyed all the privileges of religious in general, and that it had the exemption of clerical religious as expressed in canon 501, inasmuch as it was indeed a clerical institute

---

[29] Can. 2413, § 1.

[30] Can. 2413, § 2.

and of its nature, that is as a clerical institute, enjoyed that exemption which is had by clerical exempt religious.

Goyeneche points out that it is disputed whether or not an exempt quasi-religious society should be regarded as subject to the same limitations of exemption as are placed on exempt religious congregations. He states it as his opinion that such a society should be considered as subject to the same limitations of exemption, since it does not seem fitting that the exemption of a quasi-religious society should exceed the exemption of religious congregations. If this were not so, then an exempt quasi-religious society would enjoy the complete exemption of Regulars with but the exception of those few cases in which the Code makes a particular exception even for Regulars, while exempt clerical congregations would be subject to every exception to exemption that is mentioned in the Code.[31]

ARTICLE II. DIRECTION OF QUASI-RELIGIOUS SOCIETIES OF WOMEN

In canon 500, § 3, the Code states that no religious institute of men can, without a special papal indult, have under its jurisdiction a religious congregation of women, nor can it claim any special right to the care and direction of such congregations of women.

Some of the authors argue that, inasmuch as the Code in this canon expressly mentions religious congregations of women, quasi-religious societies of women are not affected by it.[32] However, although it is true that only congregations of women are mentioned in canon 500, § 3, nevertheless in the general prescriptions of canon 675 it is stated that whenever possible the prescriptions of canons 499-530 are to be followed, which obviously includes the legislation of canon 500, § 3. Accordingly, even though quasi-religious societies of women are not expressly considered in canon 500, § 3, it certainly must be declared that at least they are implicitly included according to the mind of the legislator. Moreover, if one were to hold that in every canon where quasi-religious societies are not expressly mentioned they are not included, then all

---

[31] "Consultationes,"—*CpR,* I (1920), 144-145.

[32] E.g., Larraona, "Commentarium Codicis," *CpR,* VI (1925), 293-294.

the general canons of Title XVII which make comprehensive references to several canons in other parts of the Code wherein quasi-religious societies are not mentioned would be useless and unexplainable.

The opinion that quasi-religious societies of women are included under the restrictions set in canon 500, § 3, may be substantiated from the purpose of the law, which seeks to forestall as much as possible any unnecessary relations between men and women religious, for the sake of averting both scandal and interference in the religious progress of all concerned.[33]

Furthermore, the practice of the Church seems to be in accordance with the view that the quasi-religious societies of women as well as the congregations of women religious are treated in canon 500, § 3. The Congregation of the Mission was granted the special privilege of directing the Daughters of Charity of Saint Vincent de Paul, a quasi-religious society. In making such a concession, the Holy See implied that not only are quasi-religious societies of women included under the prohibition of canon 500, § 3, but also that even quasi-religious societies of men are forbidden to undertake any direction of quasi-religious societies of women without a special privilege granted by the Holy See. Although this privilege was granted before the Code, it nevertheless expresses the constant mind of the Church on this matter.[34] Its renewal after the Code and its existence up to the present day fortifies this opinion.

As a result of including quasi-religious societies under the restriction enacted in canon 500, § 3, one may draw the following conclusions. Quasi-religious societies of men are not allowed to have under their jurisdiction any community of women, or to claim any special right to its direction or care. This is true whether it be a religious institute of women or a quasi-religious society of women. Quasi-religious societies of women may not subject themselves to the jurisdiction or the direction of any community of men, whether the latter be a religious institute or a quasi-religious society.[35]

---

[33] Blat, *De Religiosis,* p. 114; Berutti, *De Religiosis,* p. 367.

[34] *Bull. Rom. Taur.,* XV, 53.

[35] Blat, *De Religiosis,* p. 114.

ARTICLE III. SUPERIORS OF QUASI-RELIGIOUS SOCIETIES

Section 1. Preliminary Remarks

The authority of the superiors of quasi-religious societies must be determined in great part by the prescriptions of the Code regulating the office of the superiors of religious institutes. These regulations are contained in canons 501-517, which according to the general prescription of canon 675 are to be applied whenever possible to quasi-religious societies. Various aspects of the office of superior are brought within the scope of these canons, such as their power, their election, their qualifications, their duties and similar matters.

The major superiors mentioned in the present article with reference to a quasi-religious society include the Supreme Moderator, the Provincial Superior, and all Vicars who by law are acknowledged as possessing equal powers with the provincial. Delegated power over a society or over a province does not constitute its possessor a major superior. In order to be considered a major superior, one must possess ordinary power at least vicariously.

Local superiors exercising dominative power over the members of a house of the society are considered minor superiors.

If the Code does not specify exactly what class of superiors is contemplated in a particular instance, then even local superiors are to be included, unless from the very text or context it is evident that only major superiors are contemplated. Novice Masters and directors of study are not considered superiors according to the prescriptions of the Code, since they do not exercise even dominative power over their respective charges.[36]

By the power of *jurisdiction* the present article contemplates the public power of ruling over subjects with the view of achieving a supernatural end. This power is called public for the reason that it emanates from the public authority of the Church. It extends to the executive, the legislative, the judicial and the coercive functions of the government, including the internal forum, both the sacramental and the non-sacramental, as well as the external forum.

---

[36] Schäfer, *De Religiosis*, pp. 216-217.

The *dominative* power mentioned in the present article denotes a less perfect form of rule than the power of jurisdiction. It is a private power by which superiors direct their subjects to the proper end of the society. It is based on the quasi-contract executed between the society and its members at the time of incorporation into the society. Dominative power contains a power analogous to legislative power. By means of it the superiors may establish ordinances to be observed by their subjects concerning those obligations which are at least implicitly mentioned in the constitutions. There is present also a power analogous to judicial power, since the possession of dominative power enables superiors to inquire into the acts of transgressions against the constitutions, and extra-judicially to settle controversies arising among the members. Finally, dominative power contains a power analogous to coercive power, inasmuch as superiors may impose paternal penalties and corrections in accordance with the prescriptions of the constitutions. The administrative rights of superiors also fall under their dominative power, for there is given to superiors the right of appointing subjects to definite duties, of changing these appointments, of receiving and of dismissing members in accordance with the prescriptions of the constitutions, of founding houses, and of performing similar acts including the administration of property.[37]

Section 2. The Power of Superiors of Quasi-Religious Societies

Through the application of canon 501, § 1, to quasi-religious societies, which application is justified by canon 675, the common law concedes to the superiors and chapters of these societies, in accordance with their constitutions, dominative power over their subjects, and, in clerical exempt societies, jurisdiction in both the internal and the external forum. The superiors possessing these powers must be determined by the constitutions. No distinction need be made here between societies of diocesan right and societies of pontifical law. Consequently, dominative power can be predicated of superiors of both groups according to the prescriptions of their constitutions.

---

[37] Schäfer, *De Religiosis,* pp. 221-222; Blat, *De Religiosis,* pp. 97-99.

It cannot be argued that the clause, *congrua congruis referendo,* of canon 675 forbids the application of the law of canon 501 to quasi-religious societies. This clause refers not to the substance of the canonical provision involved, but rather to the manner of its application in the concrete. On the other hand, it has been explained in a previous chapter that, even if no private vows, or oaths, or promises are taken in a quasi-religious society, there nevertheless arises, from the quasi-contract of public incorporation, the possession of dominative power by the superiors over the members of the society.[38]

Accordingly the superiors of quasi-religious societies may, in accordance with the prescription of canon 1312, § 1, completely annul the private vows of a subject made after his incorporation in the society, so that the obligations of these vows will never again arise. Likewise, in accordance with canon 1313, n. 2, the superiors of clerical exempt societies may for a just cause dispense a member from a non-reserved vow, as well as a novice or a person living night and day in the house of the society, as mentioned in canon 514, § 1.[39]

All superiors can suspend all non-reserved private vows inconsistent with the duties of their subjects.[40] Moreover, by reason of their dominative power the superiors of quasi-religious societies may in individual cases and for a just cause excuse their subjects from the obligations of the constitutions.[41]

Both the jurisdictional and the dominative powers of superiors are restricted by the second paragraph of canon 501, whereby superiors are forbidden to concern themselves with matters which, in accordance with canon 247, are reserved to the jurisdiction of the Holy Office.

The Supreme Moderator of a quasi-religious society exercises either dominative power or, if it be a clerical exempt society, jurisdiction over all the provinces, houses and members of the society in accordance with the respective constitutions of each society. The

---

[38] Cf. *supra,* pp. 60-64.

[39] Goyeneche, "Consultationes,"—*CpR,* I (1920), 144; Maroto, *Institutiones,* I, n. 459; Schäfer, *De Religiosis,* p. 239.

[40] Can. 1312, § 2.

[41] Schäfer, *De Religiosis,* p. 240.

other superiors exercise their power within the limits of their office as specified in the constitutions.[42]

The constitutions may determine, in so far as the common law does not anticipate them, whether or not the advice or the consent of the chapter or of the council is needed for the exercise of certain powers on the part of the superior.

In clerical exempt societies the major superiors may appoint notaries, but only for the ecclesiastical business of the society. The acts of these notaries are public acts, and serve accordingly as trustworthy evidence in ecclesiastical tribunals.[43]

Section 3. The Necessary Qualifications of Superiors of Quasi-Religious Societies

If the constitutions of a quasi-religious society do not demand a more advanced age or other further requirements, its Supreme Moderator must have spent at least ten years in the society since his incorporation in it. He must have been born of legitimate wedlock and be at least forty years of age. Other major superiors of the society must be at least thirty years old.[44] The application of canon 504 to quasi-religious societies is justified by reason of the general prescription of canon 675, which applies to these societies all the prescriptions of canons 499-530.[45]

The qualifications of the superiors as just mentioned are required for the valid appointment of the superiors involved. The ten years of membership as required must be years that have been spent under the bond of union with the society. Consequently, if some interval is spent in military service with a release from that bond, it cannot be counted as a part of the necessary period of ten years. If a member was quasi-secularized and then later received again into the society, the period of ten years must be counted from the renewed incorporation. Likewise the ten years must be years that have been spent in the same society. If a member transferred from one society to another, the period of ten years must be counted from the time of incorporation into the new society.

---

[42] Can. 502.

[43] Cf. cans. 503; 374.

[44] Can. 504.

[45] Cf. can. 675.

This computation of time follows the prescription of canon 34, § 3, n. 3, whereby the day of first incorporation is not counted, so that the lapse of the ten year period comes only at the conclusion of the day that marks the tenth anniversary.[46]

If a member of a quasi-religious society has been legitimated by a subsequent marriage in accordance with the prescription of canon 1116, he is considered by the common law juridically in the category of those born of a legitimate marriage. Consequently, he is eligible for the office of major superior.[47] Canon 1117 establishes this general principle with regard to those legitimated by a subsequent marriage, a principle which it affirms as controlling unless an exception is expressly mentioned in the constitutions or the law. No such exception to this principle is mentioned in canon 504. Therefore those legitimated by their parents' subsequent marriage are to be considered eligible for the office of major superiors. On the other hand, exceptions are expressly mentioned in canons 331, § 1, n. 1, and 232, § 2, n. 1, concerning appointments to the dignities of the episcopate and the cardinalate.[48] The completion of the fortieth or respectively the thirtieth year is likewise to be computed according to the prescriptions of canon 34, § 3, n. 3, whereby the day of birth is not counted, so that the necessary period of time is completed at the conclusion of the day that marks the fortieth or respectively the thirtieth anniversary of the candidate's life.[49]

Section 4. The Term of Office of Superiors of Quasi-Religious Societies

The appointment of major superiors of religious institutes and of quasi-religious societies is to be of a temporary nature unless the constitutions prescribe otherwise. The local superiors are not to be appointed for more than a three-year term, though upon the completion of this term, if the constitutions permit it, they may be reappointed for a second term of three years. There may not be any further appointments of the same local superior in the same

---

[46] Schäfer, *De Religiosis,* pp. 243-245.

[47] Can. 1116 in connection with can. 1117.

[48] Schäfer, *De Religiosis,* pp. 242-243; Blat, *De Religiosis,* p. 131.

[49] Schäfer, *De Religiosis,* p. 243, notes 126, 128.

house immediately following the completion of the second term of three years.[50]

The exception which permits constitutions to allow a life term or an indefinite term to major superiors is intended only for constitutions approved before the Code. All later constitutions must follow the legislation of the Code, and thus may permit only temporary appointments for major superiors.[51]

Local superiors may be appointed for a period of less than three years. In this case individual local superiors may be reappointed oftener than twice, provided they do not remain in office more than six consecutive years in the same house.[52]

Blat holds a contrary opinion, he maintains that canon 505 aims at precluding more than two consecutive appointments of the same local superior in the same house. He concludes, therefore, that three consecutive appointments for two years or also four consecutive appointments for one year would be contrary to the mind of canon 505.[53]

However, his doctrine does not seem to be well founded, for it appears rather that the legislator simply aimed at forestalling a situation in which a local superior would be in charge of the same house for too long a period of time. The legislator realized that this could tend, on the part of the superior, to a certain complaisance and to a certain attitude of domination and ownership over the matters entrusted to his charge. A period of more than six years, and not simply a multiple number of reappointments, was regarded by the legislator as furnishing occasion for the emergence of the afore-intimated evils and as correspondingly calling for a due restriction.

Canon 505 does not, however, contain any invalidating clause with reference to the third consecutive appointment. Therefore a third reappointment to the same house would indeed be illicit, but not invalid.[54]

---

[50] Can. 505.

[51] Blat, *De Religiosis,* p. 133.

[52] Schäfer, *De Religiosis,* p. 250; Wernz-Vidal, *De Religiosis,* n. 102, note 27; Berutti, *De Religiosis,* p. 64.

[53] *De Religiosis,* p. 137.

[54] Schäfer, *De Religiosis,* p. 248; Larraona, "Commentarium Codicis,"—*CpR,* VII (1926), 380, note 289; cf. can. 11, which rules that no law is to be considered as invalidating what is done in contravention of it unless the penalty of invalidity is expressly or at least equivalently stated in the law.

Section 5. Responses of the Sacred Congregation Concerning Canon 505

The Sacred Congregation of Religious was asked on March 6, 1922, whether it is permissible for founders of religious institutes and quasi-religious societies to be allowed to retain the office of Supreme Moderator for life, in contradiction to the prescriptions of the constitutions of the institute or of the society which demand a definite term of office for the Supreme Moderator and forbid a re-election. The Sacred Congregation replied in the negative. A life-time tenure of office on the part of the founder was admissible only with the possession of an apostolic indult which granted it.[55]

The Sacred Congregation was asked on February 1, 1924, whether a member is to be regarded as a true superior when he directs a *filial* house of a religious institute or of a quasi-religious society. A filial house does not in a proper sense constitute an independent unit or possess property of its own, but is rather a quasi-member of a nearby house. It is directed by the aforesaid member who is appointed by the superior of the larger house.

The reply of the Sacred Congregation of Religious was in the negative, and the following explanation was added. In the revision of the constitutions of a community in accordance with the Code this condition should be provided for through an application of those canons which determine the relations between a superior and his subjects, so that in the future the superior would visit these filial houses regularly, abstain from hearing the confessions of the members of these houses, and in general observe the norms regulating the relations between a superior and his subjects.[56]

The Pontifical Commission for the Authentic Interpretation of the Code was asked on June 2-3, 1918, whether the three year limit of the term of office of a local superior, as demanded by the prescription of canon 505, should be applied to directors of schools, hospitals and other pious houses. The Commission replied that if the latter had under their direction other religious of the same community and were considered their superiors with regard to religious discipline, then the prescriptions of canon 505 were to prevail.[57]

---

[55] *AAS,* XIV (1922), 163.

[56] *AAS,* XVI (1924), 95.

[57] *AAS,* IX (1918), 344.

In discussing this last mentioned decision, Maroto suggests that, if great inconvenience should arise from the limitation because of the particular ability of the superior whose reappointment is forbidden, and if his unusual familiarity with the particular work is considered as a qualification essential to its success, the superior could be appointed to a position imposing on him the direction of the work, while another religious should be appointed as the superior charged with the direction of the religious discipline of the members of the community. Maroto further states that greater inconvenience would arise from the reappointment of the same superior for a third term than from the sacrifice of the continued employment of the particular ability of the retiring superior.[58]

The Pontifical Commission for the Authentic Interpretation of the Canons of the Code was asked on July 25, 1926, whether canon 505 was to be applied to superiors of houses of religious institutes, when the houses whose superiors were involved were not properly and truly houses of the institute, but rather houses devoted to externs, e.g., seminaries, hospices and colleges. In these institutions a few members of the institute reside for the purpose of direction and administration.

The Commission responded in the affirmative in accordance with the response of June 3, 1918, cited above, i.e., if the superior in question is charged with the direction of the religious discipline of the members of the institute, he is subject to the prescription of canon 505.[59]

The responses to these inquiries are applicable to quasi-religious societies, since they constitute interpretations and explanations of canons which by reason of canon 675 are likewise applicable to quasi-religious societies.

In an inquiry submitted to the *Commentarium pro Religiosis* it was asked whether the superiors of quasi-religious societies appointed *ad nutum* are obliged to observe the prescription of canon 505. In his reply, Goyeneche states that all quasi-religious societies, by reason of the general prescription of canon 675, are obliged to follow the provisions of canon 505. Consequently, the superiors of these societies cannot be appointed *ad nutum,* but must be appointed

[58] "Annotationes,"—*CpR,* I (1920), 99-100.

[59] *AAS,* XVIII (1926), 393.

for a three-year term or less. Therefore if a provision of their constitutions is contrary to the prescription of canon 505, it must be corrected and accommodated to the requirements of the Code. Goyeneche also states that if the words *ad nutum* are understood to mean an appointment for a period of three years or less, but for a definite term, then the constitutions are not to be considered as contrary to the Code.[60]

Section 6. The Election of Superiors of Quasi-Religious Societies

Canons 506 and 507 in a general way treat of the election of superiors in religious institutes. However, the prescriptions of these canons are applicable to quasi-religious societies by reason of the prescription of canon 675. Consequently the following norms determine the election of superiors of quasi-religious societies.

Canon 507 considers the election of superiors by a chapter, and states that in the process of election the chapter is to follow not only the general norms for election as delineated in the Second Book of the Code (Canons 160-182), but also the particular prescriptions of each institute which are not contrary to these canons.[61]

If the society has an indult which contains prescriptions contrary to the regulations of the Code as governing elections, the indult retains its force and its provisions may be observed. Furthermore, if the constitutions which contain norms for election contrary to the Code have after the publication of the Code received the necessary approval of the Holy See, they likewise retain their force.[62]

In view of the probability that the majority of societies have particular valid legislation governing the matter of election of superiors, Larraona wisely states that in the election of superiors the common law governs not absolutely but only in the case wherein a juridically valid particular law is lacking. The common law is, therefore, not an imperative, but rather a dispositive or supplementary norm.[63]

The opinion of Larranoa is further enhanced by the prescription of canon 160, which states that in ecclesiastical elections other than

[60] "Consultationes,"—*CpR,* VII (1926), 103.

[61] Can. 507, § 1.

[62] Cf. can. 4; Schäfer, *De Religiosis,* p. 258.

[63] "Studia Canonica,"—*CpR,* VIII (1927), 178.

the election of the Pontiff the special provisions provided for each particular office are to be followed.

Canons 160-182, will be treated in a general way in subsequent pages. However, it should be stated here that these canons provide general norms for the proper time within which elections must be held, but at the same time leave intact the prescriptions of the particular constitutions. These canons likewise make provision for the proper manner of convoking the electors; for the necessary qualifications of the voters; for the essential characteristics of a valid ballot; for an election undertaken by a limited number of duly deputed and accredited electors and for the conditions attendant upon their proper authorization; for the proper notification of the result of an election; for the necessary confirmation of an election; and, finally, for the appointment in consequence of a previous electoral postulation.[64]

It must be noted that canon 507 legislates only for elections which are made by chapters. However, in a broader sense elections may occur outside chapters. An election or a nomination may be made by a major superior with either the advice or the consent of his councillors. In such cases the prescriptions of canons 507 and 506, § 1, would not apply.[65]

Furthermore, appointments may be made to the office of superior by the Pope, or by the local ordinary in societies of diocesan law under constitutions granting him such a right, or, finally by major superiors when an election is not held within the proper time, or when a body of electors has by penalty lost its right of election.[66]

The second paragraph of canon 507 forbids any soliciting of votes either directly or indirectly by any of the electors either for themselves or for others.

The third paragraph of canon 507 permits an electoral postulation only in extraordinary cases and as long as it is not forbidden by the constitutions. Postulation occurs whenever the electors prefer for office a particular candidate who labors under an impediment from which a dispensation is possible, and accordingly by their

---

[64] Cf. *infra*, pp. 123-127.
[65] Schäfer, *De Religiosis*, p. 258; Wernz-Vidal, *De Religiosis*, n. 114.
[66] Cf. cans. 181, § 2; 178; 507; Schäfer, *De Religiosis*, pp. 255-256.

votes request the competent superior to admit their candidate to office.[67]

The first paragraph of canon 506 concerns only such elections as are carried out by a chapter of an institute or a society of men. Before the election the members of the chapter must take an oath through which they promise that they will vote only for those whom before God they judge worthy of the office of superior.

Section 7. The Election of Superioresses of Quasi-Religious Societies

Canon 506, § 4, prescribes certain regulations which determine the election of a Supreme Moderator in religious institutes of women. By virtue of the general prescription of canon 675, these regulations are applicable to the election of the Supreme Moderator in a quasi-religious society of women. Consequently, the following conclusions are justified.

The election of the Supreme Moderator of a quasi-religious society of women is to be presided over by the ordinary of the place where the election occurs. If the society is one of diocesan law, the ordinary has the right either of confirming the election or of rescinding it completely, as in conscience he sees fit.[68]

The Sacred Congregation of Religious on July 2, 1921, stated that the right to preside at the election of a Supreme Moderator of a religious institute of women belongs not to the local ordinary of the diocese in which the mother house is located, but to the local ordinary of the diocese in which the election is held.[69]

Since this response is an explanation of canon 506, § 4, its prescription is applicable to quasi-religious societies of women.

In the elections of major superioresses other than the Supreme Moderator the local ordinary has no right of attending or presiding unless this right is granted him by the constitutions of the respective institute or society.[70]

---

[67] Cans. 179-182; 507, § 3; *infra*, p. 126.

[68] Can. 506, § 4.

[69] *AAS*, XIII (1921), 481.

[70] Cocchi, *De Religiosis*, n. 26.

Section 8. True Election by Chapters

A quasi-religious society which has no particular laws that govern the elections of superiors, and in which the superiors are appointed by means of a true election by a chapter of the society, must observe the norms given below. Furthermore, for other forms of election held outside of chapters in accordance with the legitimate prescriptions of the particular constitutions, and consisting in the nomination made by a major superior or effected by the vote of several members of the society, the following norms offer directive and guiding rules. It will be apparent that some of these norms must be observed in any form of election.

Canon 160 in a general prescription canonizes the special regulations of constitutions which provide for election to individual offices. This general provision, as has already been seen, is somewhat modified by the more restrictive provision of canon 507, § 1, which states that, in elections by a chapter, only those particular prescriptions are valid which are not contrary to the provisions of the common law. It seems then, that if so-called elections are held outside a chapter, the particular constitutions would be valid even though their prescriptions governing these so-called elections might be contrary to the prescriptions of the Code regulating a strictly so-called election by a chapter. However, the norms of these particular constitutions cannot be contrary to the prescriptions of the common law which are based on the natural law.

The right to elect to a vacant office cannot be deferred more than three months from the day on which notice of the vacancy is received. The period of three months is considered as a *tempus utile*, and if this period elapses without an election, the right to appoint to the vacant office rests with the superior who has the right of confirming the election, or the superior who has the right of appointment after a default on the part of the electoral college.[71]

The convocation of the electors is to be made by the president of the electoral college, provided that particular legislation does not provide otherwise for the manner of convocation. If one of the voters is not invited and misses the election, the election is valid, but the neglected voter may petition that the election be rescinded,

[71] Can. 161.

provided that he can prove that no notification of the election was sent him. If more than one third of the voters qualified to cast a ballot at the election were culpably left unnotified, the election is automatically (*ipso jure*) invalid. No elector may vote by letter or proxy unless particular law rules otherwise.[72]

Each elector is allowed one vote. Only the members of the electoral college may vote, otherwise the election is automatically invalid. The interference of laymen invalidates an ecclesiastical election.

The following may not cast a vote: 1) persons incapable of a human act; 2) those under the age of puberty; 3) those under censure or infamy of law after such infamy or censure has been determined by means of a declaratory sentence or inflicted by a condemnatory sentence; 4) persons who have joined a heretical or a schismatical sect, or who publicly adhere to such a sect; and 5) persons deprived of a vote either in consequence of a juridical sentence or by the prescriptions of the common or the particular law.

If any disqualified person casts a vote, the vote is invalid, but the election is valid, unless it is certain that the person would not have been elected without the invalid vote. If an excommunicated person upon a declaratory or a condemnatory sentence is knowingly admitted to an election, the election is invalid.

A sick elector who is present at the place of election may vote through a teller, unless particular law provides otherwise.[73]

A vote must be free, secret, certain, absolute and determinate. It can not be cast by the voter in favor of himself. A vote cast under the influence of grave fear or deceit, or by an elector who votes for himself, is invalid.[74]

Two tellers of the electoral college, are to be appointed before the election by secret ballot, unless the particular constitutions decree otherwise. The tellers having previously, together with the president of the electoral college, taken the oath of duty and secrecy, are to collect the votes and to report the number of votes cast for

---

[72] Cans. 162; 163.

[73] Cans. 164-168.

[74] Cans. 169; 170.

each candidate. If the number of votes collected is larger than the number of voters present, the election is invalid.[75]

Election by means of a common commitment of trust (*per compromissum*) occurs when the electors by unanimous and written consent agree on a given occasion to transfer the use of their electoral right to one or several qualified persons. An electoral college of clerics must choose priests for this function; a non-observance of this requirement would leave the election invalid. All conditions attached to the compact of the committed trust, as long as they are not contrary to the common law, must be observed for the validity of the election. If but one person is selected to vote in the name of the electoral college, he cannot cast his vote in his own favor, nor may any one of the several appointed vote for himself. The commitment of the electoral trust ceases and the right of election returns to the electors if the latter recall their commitment before their representatives begin to exercise their right, or if a condition as set in the compact is left unfulfilled, or, finally, if the executed election as undertaken by the authorized representatives has resulted in nullity.[76]

A person is elected when he has received an absolute majority of the votes cast; or, in the absence of an absolute majority on the first or the second ballot when he has received a relative majority on the third ballot. If the votes are equally divided on the third ballot so that no relative majority of votes has been obtained by any of the candidates, then the presiding officer of the electoral college may break the tie election by casting a second vote. If the president does not wish to decide the issue in this fashion then that person is elected who is the senior in ordination, or, if there be equality in that respect, the person who is longest professed, or, finally, if there be equality likewise in this latter respect, the person who is the oldest in age. However, it must be observed that these prescriptions need to be followed only if the common law or the particular constitutions do not provide a different course of action.[77]

The norms determining the manner of election are not followed

---

[75] Can. 171.

[76] Cans. 172-173.

[77] Can. 101, § 1.

in the case of an electoral postulation. In order that the postulation may be valid, the majority of the voters must be in its favor. If the postulation is concurrent with an election, there must be at least two thirds of the votes in its favor.[78]

The Pontifical Commission for the Authentic Interpretation of the Canons of the Code on July 1, 1922, decided that, if on the third ballot (when it is final) some voters should vote by postulation for one person, while others should vote in election for another, and the one postulated does not have the required two thirds majority, then the other is elected on a relative majority of the votes. If votes are cast by postulation for one person and by election for two or more persons, then on the third ballot, if the one postulated does not have the required two thirds majority of the votes, that one of the others is elected who has a relative majority of the votes exclusive of the votes given the one postulated.[79]

The person who is elected according to the above mentioned norms is to be declared elected by the presiding officer of the electoral college. The person elected, within eight days from the reception of the notice of the election, must declare whether or not he accepts the election; otherwise he loses all right acquired by the election. If he refuses the election, he forfeits all those rights. However, he may be re-elected. The electoral college must proceed to a new election within one month from the notice of the renunciation of the election. If no confirmation of an election is needed, then the elected person receives the full rights of office immediately on his act of acceptance. If confirmation is required, he obtains merely a claim to the office by his act of acceptance, and any acts of office performed by him before he receives notice of the confirmation are null and void.[80]

If an election needs confirmation, then the person elected must seek the required confirmation within eight days after his act of acceptance. If he neglects this and cannot prove that he was justly impeded from doing so, he loses his right to the office of superior. The proper superior may not refuse to grant confirmation, once he

---

[78] Can. 180.

[79] *AAS*, XIV (1922), 406.

[80] Cans. 174-176.

knows that the elected person is qualified and that the election was validly conducted.

If the election was not completed within the prescribed time, or if the voters were deprived of their right of voting, the appointment to the elective office devolves on the superior who would have the right of confirming the election or on him who succeeds to the right of the voters to fill the office.[81]

The superior upon whom the right of free appointment devolves under canon 178 is the superior immediately higher in rank. In the case of the failure of a general chapter of a religious institute or of a quasi-religious society of women of diocesan law to elect a Supreme Moderator, the right of appointment devolves upon the ordinary of the place in which the chapter was held, or was to be held.[82]

By reason of analogy it seems that the same is true with reference to every failure to elect in religious institutes or in quasi-religious societies of women of diocesan law. The same conclusions seem to be applicable, likewise, in failure to elect on the part of all chapters of diocesan religious institutes or quasi-religious societies of men.

In the case in which the chapter of an institute or a society of pontifical law loses its active right of election, it appears that the right of free appointment devolves on the provincial superior, or, if the election was held to fill the office of provincial superior, on the Superior General. If the office of Superior General is involved, the appointment would have to be made by the Sacred Congregation of Religious.[83]

Section 9. Rights and Duties of Superiors of Quasi-Religious Societies

A. Residence

The prescription of canon 508 considers the question of residence on the part of superiors of religious institutes. By reason of the

[81] Cans. 177-178.
[82] Cans. 178; 506, § 4.
[83] Schäfer, *De Religiosis*, p. 291.

prescription of canon 675 the law contained in canon 508 becomes applicable to quasi-religious societies. Consequently the following conclusions are justified.

Superiors of quasi-religious societies are obliged to dwell in their proper houses, and may leave them only on those occasions when the constitutions require a departure, e.g., to make a visitation or to transact community business.[84]

B. Execution of Decrees of the Holy See

Again, by virtue of canon 675, all superiors of quasi-religious societies are bound by the specified obligations which the law of canon 509 places upon superiors of religious institutes. Consequently, they must promote among their subjects the knowledge and the execution of all the decrees of the Holy See concerned with the affairs and interests of the society. This flows from the obligation resting on superiors of insuring that their subjects satisfy all their obligations, among which the most important and most rigorously binding are those arising from the pronouncements of the Holy See. It must be remembered, however, that the notice of a decree given by a superior is not the promulgation for the members of the society, but rather a mere divulgence of a decree already binding upon them. The manner of divulging a decree is not determined by the common law. Consequently, if it is not determined by the constitutions, the selection of the manner is left to the superior himself. An implicit obligation is thus placed on superiors of a lay society to read these decrees in the vernacular and of urging their execution by pious exhortations and recommendations.[85]

C. Reading of Constitutions and of Papal Decrees

The obligation placed on superiors of religious institutes of reading the constitutions and papal decrees to their subjects is likewise binding on superiors of quasi-religious societies. This application of canon 509, § 2, n. 1, to quasi-religious societies is justified in view of the prescription of canon 675.

---

[84] Cf. can. 508; Blat, *De Religiosis*, p. 154.

[85] Wernz-Vidal, *De Religiosis*, n. 143, IV.

Superiors of quasi-religious societies are charged with the obligation of insuring, at stated times, the public reading of the constitutions. The particular times designated for the reading of the constitutions may be determined from the constitutions. If not, the local superior determines them.

The local superior is further charged with the obligation of procuring the public reading each year of the decrees which the Holy See orders to be publicly read. Only those decrees the reading of which has been ordered since the promulgation of the Code are comprised under the prescription of the law.[86]

The instruction of the Sacred Congregation of Religious, "*Quantum religiones,*" issued on December 1, 1931, stated clearly, in n. 21, that this instruction was to be read each year not only to the members of clerical religious institutes but also to the members of clerical quasi-religious societies. Furthermore, the superiors of clerical religious institutes and of quasi-religious societies were to incorporate in their quinquennial report a statement as to their observance of this instruction.[87]

D. Christian Doctrine and Pious Exhortations

According to the general prescription of canon 675, superiors of quasi-religious societies are bound by the enactment contained in canon 509, § 2, n. 2, which places on superiors of religious institutes the obligation of providing Christian Doctrine instructions and pious exhortations for their subjects. Accordingly, superiors of quasi-religious societies are charged with the obligation of providing twice a month an instruction on Christian Doctrine for the lay members of the society as well as the working people who remain night and day in the house of the society. Those who reside in the house of the society for reasons of health, study or lodging are not included within the scope of this obligation.

The instruction may be given by the superior himself or by one appointed to this task by the superior. It must always be suited to the mental capacity of the listeners.

---

[86] Can. 509, § 2, n. 1; Schäfer, *De Religiosis,* p. 294.

[87] *AAS,* XXIV (1932), 74; Blat, *De Religiosis,* pp. 159-160.

Local superiors of lay societies are charged with the obligation of providing pious exhortations for all of the society under their charge. Both the instructions and the pious exhortations must be given twice a month. The working people need not be called to the pious exhortations.[88]

E. Pious Exercises

By reason of the prescription of canon 679, superiors of quasi-religious societies are charged with the duties indicated in canon 595. This canon places the obligation on superiors of religious institutes of providing regular pious exercises for their subjects. Accordingly, the superiors of quasi-religious societies must make sure that their subjects attend a yearly retreat, practice daily mental prayer, and devote themselves to the other pious exercises prescribed by the constitutions. The superiors must likewise see to it that their subjects present themselves at least every week for the reception of the sacrament of penance, and they must likewise promote the frequent, and even daily reception of the Holy Eucharist.[89]

The common law places no strict obligation upon local superiors of quasi-religious clerical societies to enforce the prescription of canon 565, § 2, which indicates a weekly instruction in Christian Doctrine for the novices who aspire to the lay brotherhood in the community. For even though a particular society might, according to its constitutions, require a novitiate, nevertheless the common law which deals with the institution of the novitiate does not strictly apply to quasi-religious societies. However, in such societies which require a novitiate the constitutions should certainly make provision for this instruction.

F. Report on the Religious State of the Society to the Holy See

By a continued application of canon 675, superiors of quasi-religious societies are bound by the enactment contained in canon

---

[88] Can. 509, § 2, n. 2; Schäfer, *De Religiosis*, p. 265; Coronata, *Institutiones.* I, 645.

[89] Can. 595, §§ 1-2.

510, which obliges superiors of religious institutes to report on the religious state of their institute to the Holy See. In view of this application, the following conclusions may be drawn.

The Supreme Moderators of quasi-religious societies of pontifical law are obliged to submit at least every five years to the Holy See a report on the religious state of their societies. This report must be signed by the Superior General together with his council. In pontifically approved societies whose membership consists of women, the report must also be signed by the ordinary of the diocese in which the Superioress General and her council reside. The report must include complete information concerning the material and economic state of the society, the observance of religious discipline, and the general status of the society's membership. There is no necessity of inserting details concerning particular houses or members, or even regarding particular provinces.[90]

If the constitutions demand a more frequent report, the constitutions must be observed. However, as Larraona remarks, this more frequent report will generally be made only by such societies whose constitutions were written before the advent of the Code. Since the promulgation of the Code, the constitutions generally require that the reports be made every five years.[91]

The years specified for religious and quasi-religious institutes in the sending of their reports began with January 1, 1923. Every fifth year, commencing with 1927, quasi-religious societies whether of men or of women were to make their report. The decree stated, in n. 11, that if the first report had been submitted before the year in which it was actually to come due, that is before the year 1927 for quasi-religious societies, it would not have to be submitted again until the second report was due that is, in the year 1932 for the quasi-religious societies.[92]

The fourth article of the decree *"Sancitum est"* stated that societies which had not submitted reports before the Code were to submit with their first report a complete and truthful résumé of the state of their society, so that the Holy See might fully under-

[90] Blat, *De Religiosis,* p. 161; can. 510.

[91] "Commentarium Codicis,"—*CpR,* VIII (1927), 280.

[92] S. C. de Religiosis, decr. *"Sancitum est,"* 8 mart. 1922,—*AAS,* XIV (1922), 162-163.

stand its material, moral and disciplinary state. This first report was required to contain in addition an account of the historical foundation of the society and its constitutions. It was also to relate all that concerned the papal approbation of the society and its constitutions. Moreover it was to describe the internal government of the society and the nature of its bond of union. Any change that had been made in regard to them since the foundation of the society had to be reported. Finally, the report was required to note any relaxation in the observance of the constitutions, and to state by what authority permission for this relaxation had been granted.[93]

The legislation of this fourth article of the decree *"Sancitum est"* affected practically all quasi-religious societies, since before the advent of the Code they had not been obliged by the Common Law to send any such report.

The Holy See, as named in canon 510, is the Sacred Congregation of Religious, or, for such societies as are subject to its jurisdiction, the Sacred Congregation for the Propagation of the Faith.

It is to be noted that, in addition to their sending of this report, the superiors of religious institutes or of quasi-religious societies have no obligations, such as bishops have, to submit the report to Rome in connection with an *ad limina* visit to the Holy City.[94]

The signature of the local ordinary is required in authentication of the reports made by pontifically approved institutes or societies whose membership consists of women. The purpose of his signature is to furnish proof, not regarding the truth of the matter stated in the report, but merely regarding the fact that the report was written and signed by the superioress and her council.[95]

G. The Act of Profession of Faith

According to the prescription of canon 1406, § 1, n. 9, superiors of clerical religious institutes are bound to make an act of profession of faith, according to a formula approved by the Holy See, in the presence of the chapter or of the superior by whom

[93] *AAS,* XIV (1922), 163.
[94] Larraona, "Commentarium Codicis,"—*CpR,* VIII (1927), 282-283.
[95] Blat, *De Religiosis,* p. 162.

they were elevated to their office, or before the deputy of either of these.

Nowhere in Title XVII (canons 673-681) is there any direct reference to the necessity of an act of profession of faith on the part of superiors of quasi-religious societies when appointed to their office. It was therefore generally believed that they were not bound by this prescription. However, the Pontifical Commission for the Authentic Interpretation of the Canons of the Code on July 25, 1926, replied that they also are held to the prescription of canon 1406, § 1, n. 9. Consequently they must make an act of profession of faith as therein prescribed.[96]

Maroto, in discussing the decision of the Commission, declares that the members of the Commission applied the principles of canon 18 and thus gave a comprehensive interpretation to canon 675 whereby it comprised the prescription of canon 1406, § 1, n. 9, within its scope. Furthermore, the Cardinals of the Commission, he says, considered that the end of the law, the circumstances of the law and the mind of the legislator all tend to foster the opinion that the prescription of this canon is to be regarded as comprised within the general application made by canon 675.[97]

Together with the profession of the faith, the superiors of religious clerical institutes must also pronounce an oath against Modernism. This was prescribed by the Holy Office on March 22, 1918.[98]

Although the Holy Office did not explicitly include mention of the superiors of clerical quasi-religious societies in its decree, nevertheless it appears to the writer that such mention must be considered as implicitly included. This may be argued from the fact that the taking of the oath against Modernism was added as a supplement to the act of profession of faith. It appears from this combination that it was the mind of the legislator to take every precaution lest superiors of clerical religious by means of their position do anything that might prove a danger to the faith of those under their charge. Superiors of clerical quasi-religious societies hold the same position of influence over the clerics sub-

---

[96] *AAS,* XVIII (1926), 393.

[97] "Annotationes," *CpR,* VII (1926), 435; Schäfer, *De Religiosis,* p. 1034.

[98] *AAS,* X (1918), 136.

ject to them, and consequently could be an equal source of danger to their faith. The very fact that the Commission replied that they were to pronounce a profession of faith seems to bear this out. Consequently, it appears that by an application of canon 18, and from a consideration of the end of the law and the mind of the legislator, superiors of clerical quasi-religious societies must take the oath against Modernism for the same reason that it is required of them to make an act of profession of faith.

The failure to make the act of profession of faith does not affect the validity of the installation of the superior in office. However the penalties mentioned in canon 2403, as affecting those who fail to make it, when obliged by the common law to do so, do apply to the superiors of clerical quasi-religious societies. The superiors of quasi-religious clerical societies, by reason of the response of the Pontifical Commission for the Authentic Interpretation of the Code, are obliged by the common law to pronounce the act of profession of faith; consequently they are made liable to the penalties established by the common law for those who fail to comply with this requirement.[99]

H. Visitation by Superiors of Quasi-Religious Societies

Visitation implies the making of a general inquiry in the house of a society by a legitimate superior concerning the general state of the house, its government and the particular lives of the members. A visitation is to be conducted in a paternal manner. Its object is to discover and correct faults or abuses.

Canon 511 places an obligation on superiors of religious institutes to conduct regular visitations. The prescription of this canon is likewise applicable, in virtue of canon 675, to the superiors

---

[99] Goyeneche, "Quaestio Canonica,"—*CpR,* XVIII (1937), 96; Schäfer, *De Religiosis,* p. 292; Can. 2403.—A person who, in violation of canon 1406, neglects without a legitimate impediment or excuse to make the profession of faith, shall be admonished to do so within a specified time; if he stubbornly persists in his refusal beyond the term fixed, he shall be punished even with deprivation of office, benefice, dignity, or position, and he forfeits the revenue of his benefice, office, dignity, or position, during the time he refuses to make the profession of faith.

of quasi-religious societies. Hence the following conclusions may be drawn.

A visitation is to be made by that major superior of a quasi-religious society who is designated by the constitutions for this function. He may delegate the exercise of this office to another. The time for the visitation should be specified in the constitutions; otherwise it is left to the discretion of the proper major superior to select the time. Every house which is subject to the visitor, whether it be perfected or only formative in its organization must submit to the act of visitation.[100]

The obligations binding both the visitor and the subject of a visitation, as also the penalties to be imposed upon local superiors who interfere with the success of a visitation, have already been discussed above in the study of the duties and the rights of the local ordinary over quasi-religious societies.[101]

ARTICLE IV. THE ADMINISTRATION OF THE SACRAMENTS

Canon 514 provides for the right of superiors of clerical religious institutes to administer certain sacraments to their subjects under particular circumstances. The prescriptions of this canon, in virtue of canon 675, are applicable to the superiors of clerical quasi-religious societies. Consequently the following conclusions may be stated.

In all clerical quasi-religious societies whether exempt or non-exempt, the superiors, even the local superiors, have the right and the obligation of administering Holy Viaticum and Extreme Unction, either personally or through another, to the sick members of their society, whether these members be already incorporated or are still on probation as novices, and to all who reside in the houses of the society night and day, whether this residence be for reasons of health, of study, of lodging or of engaged labor. Moreover, there is no obligation on the part of the superior to notify the local pastor of these administrations of the last rites.[102]

---

[100] Can. 511; Blat, *De Religiosis*, pp. 165-166.
[101] Cf. *supra*, pp. 119-120.
[102] Cf. can. 514, § 1.

If any of the persons to whom clerical superiors may thus minister the sacraments should enter a house of a quasi-religious society with the intention of remaining at least one day and night, but actually are in the house only one day when they become ill, they nevertheless are to receive the last rites from the superior of the house.[103]

The Pontifical Commission for the Authentic Interpretation of the Canons of the Code on July 16, 1931, replied that this right belonged to the superior of an institute even if a member of the institute or a novice was sick and actually away from the house. However, the use of this right does not extend to the lay people mentioned in canon 514, § 1, if they are sick and away from the house.[104] The reply of the Commission is applicable to quasi-religious societies for the simple reason that it is an interpretation of canon 514, § 1. Since this canon, by the norm of canon 675, extends to quasi-religious societies, any authentic interpretation of it likewise applies to these societies.

In lay quasi-religious societies whether of men or of women, the right of administering the last sacraments to the members of the society, and to novices and to the lay people mentioned in canon 514, § 1, belongs to the chaplain to whom the local ordinary has given full parochial powers in accordance with the option which canon 464, § 2, grants. If a chaplain has not been appointed, or if parochial powers have not been given him, then the right of the administration of these sacraments belongs to the pastor in whose parish the particular house is located.[105]

ARTICLE V. HONORARY TITLES

Canon 515 prohibits to all religious, aspiration to merely honorary titles of dignities and offices. If the constitutions permit it, then the use of titles of major offices which religious actually held in their own organization is made allowable. In virtue of canon 675, these provisions are applicable also to quasi-religious.[106]

---

[103] Cocchi, *De Religiosis,* n. 28; Vermeersch-Creusen, *Epitome,* I, n. 485, 4.
[104] *AAS,* XXIII (1931), 353.
[105] Cf. cans. 464, § 2; and 514, § 3.
[106] Berutti, *De Religiosis,* pp. 367-368.

The prescriptions of these two canons forbid such titles as *ex-general* or *ex-provincial* to be used by a religious or a quasi-religious who actually never was either a general or a provincial respectively. If the constitutions permit it, these titles may be used, however, by a religious or a quasi-religious who at one time actually held these offices. Academic titles granted on the completion of secular or ecclesiastical studies are not forbidden by these canons, for such titles are not merely honorary, since they are the reward of study.

Blat maintains that the prescription of canon 515 does not apply to the members of quasi-religious societies, since in the strict sense of the term they are actually secular clerics or laymen, depending on the nature of the society.[107]

However, it is the opinion of the writer that the conclusions of Blat are not valid, since the entire aim of the general prescription of canon 675 is precisely to apply to quasi-religious the prescriptions of certain canons which primarily are intended for the religious life properly so called. Moreover, canon 675 states that canons 499-530 *"congrua congruis referendo"* are to be applied to quasi-religious. Furthermore, nowhere in the treatment of quasi-religious does the Code exclude canon 515 from having its proper application to quasi-religious. As has been previously explained, the clause *"congrua congruis referendo"* does not refer to the substantial legal provision which is to be applied, but rather to the manner of the application.[108]

Finally, the very spirit of the religious life is the source and foundation of the prohibition contained in canon 515. Now, it is precisely the spirit of the religious life which quasi-religious societies wish to imitate. Consequently, any prescription so intimately connected with the religious life as that of canon 515 should be, according to the very end of the law, applicable to quasi-religious societies, whose main characteristic is this very imitation of the spirit of the religious life.

---

[107] *De Religiosis,* p. 180.

[108] Goyeneche, "Consultationes,"—*CpR,* I (1920), 144; *supra,* p. 114.

ARTICLE VI. THE DIGNITY OF THE BISHOPRIC AND QUASI-RELIGIOUS SOCIETIES

Canon 627 states that a religious who is raised to the Cardinalate or to the episcopate remains a religious. He likewise continues to enjoy the privileges of his organization and he is bound by his vows and the other obligations of his profession, except as provided in canon 628 and with respect to those things which, according to his own prudent judgment, are not compatible with his dignity. He is, likewise, exempt from the authority of his superiors, and by his vow of obedience owes obedience only to the Roman Pontiff.[109]

The Code, in the treatment of quasi-religious societies, does not determine the legal regulations which must be observed in the event of a quasi-religious being raised to the dignity of the Cardinalate or of the episcopate. It is the opinion of the writer that, since such a situation is not explicitly provided for in the Code, the prescription of canon 20 may be applied. Consequently, the regulations of canons 627 and 628, insofar as they determine the legal consequences which are involved in the appointment of a religious to the dignity of the cardinalate or to the episcopate, are applicable to quasi-religious. This application results in the following conclusions. A quasi-religious who is raised to the cardinalate or to the episcopate remains a member of his society. He likewise continues to enjoy the privileges of his organization and he is bound by his oaths or promises or whatever bonds he may have pronounced at his entrance into the society, except as provided in canon 628 and with respect to those things which, according to his own prudent judgment, are not compatible with his dignity.[110] The question of the proper administration of the property which comes to a quasi-religious who has been raised to the cardinalate or the episcopate must be determined by the prescriptions of canon 628 considered in conjunction with the particular constitutions of the society.

Canon 629 states that when a religious abdicates the cardinalate or the episcopate, or has finished the office committed to him by

---

[109] Canon 628 provides regulations which determine the administration of the property of a religious who has been raised to the episcopate.

[110] Cf. can. 627.

the Holy See, he is bound to return to his religious organization. He has the right to choose any house of his organization for his residence, but he has neither an active nor a passive vote. It is the opinion of the writer that by a continued application of canon 20, the prescriptions of canon 629 are applicable to a quasi-religious who abdicates the cardinalate or the episcopacy. Consequently, the quasi-religious cardinal or bishop, too, is bound to return to his society whenever he abdicates his office or completes the work committed to him by the Holy See. He, like the religious bishop or cardinal, may choose any house of the society for his residence, but he loses both his active and his passive vote.

ARTICLE VII. COUNCILS OF SUPERIORS OF QUASI-RELIGIOUS SOCIETIES

Canon 516, § 1, prescribes certain regulations concerning the councils of superiors of religious institutes. The prescriptions of this canon are applicable to quasi-religious societies by virtue of canon 675.

The Supreme Moderator, the provincial superior and the local superior of a formally organized house of quasi-religious societies must have councillors whose consent they must secure or whose advice they must explore whenever the constitutions or the prescriptions of the common law so demand.[111]

The superior of a house which is but formatively organized (*non formata*) may also have a council to assist him in the execution of his duties, if the constitutions so prescribe.

In every case the number of councillors, their appointment and their term of office, must all be determined according to the norms of the particular constitutions.

If the constitutions or the common law demand the consent of the council with regard to a particular act of a superior, the act would be invalid if the superior did not act according to the mind of the council. On the other hand, if only the advice of the council is required, the superior acts validly provided that he at least listened to the views of his councillors, although he actually acted contrary to them.[112]

---

[111] Can. 516, § 1.

[112] Can. 105, n. 1; Schäfer, *De Religiosis*, pp. 324-325.

If the particular norms concerning the manner of securing the consent or of exploring the advice of the council are not determined by the constitutions, then the prescriptions of canon 101, § 1, concerning voting in ecclesiastical meetings in general, are required to be followed.[113]

ARTICLE VIII. THE ECONOMES OF QUASI-RELIGIOUS SOCIETIES

Canon 516, §§ 2-4, regulates the matter regarding the various economes needed in a religious institute. By reason of canon 675, the prescriptions of this canon are equally applicable to quasi-religious societies. Consequently the following conclusions are justified.

Quasi-religious societies should have various types of economes to provide for the administration of the property of the society. A general econome should be appointed to administer the property of the society in general; a provincial econome, for the property of the province; and finally a local econome, for the property of any dependent house in the province. All these officers are required to perform their duties under the direction of proper superiors as prescribed in the constitutions. Generally the constitutions provide for the manner of appointment of economes. However, if the constitutions should not prescribe it, then the economes are to be appointed by a major superior with the consent of his council. The office of general or provincial econome cannot be joined to the office of superior, but the office of local econome may be joined with the office of local superior, although the intent of the Code is that even these two offices should if possible be separated.[114]

In canon 516, § 3, the unqualified word *"superior"* is used. It seems accordingly that all superiors, even local superiors, are precluded from holding simultaneously the office of general or provincial econome. Larraona, however, maintains that the term *"superior"* is here used in a relative meaning, so that the Superior General or the provincial superior of a religious institute or of a quasi-religious society cannot at the same time be the general or the provincial econome. Hence, since the local superior may also

[113] Can. 101, § 1; *supra,* p. 125.

[114] Can. 516, §§ 2, 3, 4.

be the local econome, it does not appear prohibited for a local superior to be at the same time a general or a provincial econome, or for a major superior to be a local econome. Nevertheless, such combinations of offices do seem contrary to the mind of the Code.[115]

ARTICLE IX. THE PROCURATOR GENERAL

Canon 517 provides for the office of procurator general in religious institutes. By a continued application of canon 675, the prescriptions of this canon are applicable to quasi-religious societies, thereby justifying the following conclusions.

It is the office of the procurator general to administer the affairs of the whole society, of a province, of a house, or of a subject when these affairs require the intervention of the Holy See. The prescription concerning the removal of the procurator general as mentioned in canon 517, § 2, is enacted not as condition for the validity, but simply for the liceity of his removal from office.[116]

Quasi-religious pontifically approved societies of women as also diocesan law quasi-religious societies are not included within the prescriptions of canon 517. Accordingly, they may use other agencies in transacting their affairs with the Holy See. Such other agencies could be the curia of the local ordinary, the Cardinal Protector, or any person enjoying ecclesiastical authority or dignity.[117]

ARTICLE X. CONFESSORS

Section 1. Introduction

According to the general norm of canon 675, all the canons which from canon 499 to canon 530 inclusive refer to religious institutes properly so called are applicable to quasi-religious societies whenever the application in the concrete is possible. Con-

---

[115] Schäfer, *De Religiosis*, pp. 330-331; Larraona, "Commentarium Codicis," —*CpR*, X (1929), 35; Cocchi, *De Religiosis*, n. 31, b.

[116] Schäfer, *De Religiosis*, p. 333.

[117] Schäfer, *loc. cit.*

sequently canons 518-528 which regulate the sacramental confessions of religious are also to be applied to these societies in the matter of sacramental confessions.

Section 2. Confessors of Quasi-Religious Societies of Men

In every house of a clerical society several confessors, lawfully approved, should be appointed to hear the confessions of its members. The number of confessors should be in proportion to the number of members in the house.[118]

The notion of lawful approval as required in canon 518, § 1, includes the following elements. In accordance with the prescription of canon 872, in order to hear confessions validly, the minister, in addition to the power of orders, must also possess jurisdiction for the hearing of confessions. In accordance with the prescription of canon 874, § 1, this jurisdiction is granted by the ordinary of the place where the confessions are to be heard. Furthermore, religious, in addition to the power of orders and of jurisdiction, should also possess at least the presumed permission of their superiors.

By an application of canon 20, the members of quasi-religious societies also need at least the presumed permission of their superiors, in addition to the powers of orders and of jurisdiction, for the licit hearing of confessions. The very end of this law, as contained in canon 874, § 1, and aimed directly at religious properly so called, is to preserve the proper order between superiors and subjects and the good order of the institute in general. These very same reasons seem to justify the application of this prescription to quasi-religious societies.

The notion of lawful approbation as just explained requires modification in the case of the exempt clerical societies. In accordance with the prescription of canon 501, § 1, applicable to quasi-religious societies in virtue of canon 675, the superiors of clerical exempt societies have jurisdiction over their subjects in both the internal and the external forum. The particular superiors having this jurisdiction must be determined according to the prescriptions of the constitutions of each exempt society.

[118] Can. 518, § 1.

These superiors may hear the confessions of their subjects without any special jurisdiction obtained from other superiors or from the local ordinary.[119] Moreover, in accordance with the norm of canon 875, these superiors of exempt societies may grant the necessary power of jurisdiction for the hearing of the confessions of their subjects to any priest, secular or religious, even to a priest of another quasi-religious society. Furthermore, when this jurisdiction is granted with general reference to the subjects of these superiors, its use is available not only for the confessions of the members incorporated in the society, and of the novices, but also of those who for reasons of employment, of study, of health, or of lodging, remain night and day in the house of the society.[120]

In accordance with the prescription of canon 518, § 1, applicable to quasi-religious societies in virtue of canon 675, the proper superiors of clerical exempt quasi-religious societies must grant to the confessors, when these have been given the necessary jurisdiction by the proper superiors to hear the confessions of the subjects of the society, the power of absolving from the cases reserved in the society.[121]

The right to reserve cases in an exempt clerical religious institute is by the prescription of canon 896 granted to the Supreme Moderator, or in independent abbeys, to the abbot, each of these acting in conjunction with his council.

As has already been shown in a previous chapter, exemption enjoyed in a quasi-religious society rests on the same juridical basis as that which is enjoyed in a religious institute. Consequently, whatever prerogatives or rights are extended by the Code to a religious institute by reason of its exemption are likewise applicable to exempt quasi-religious societies. Therefore the Supreme Moderator of an exempt clerical quasi-religious society together with his council is empowered to reserve certain sins in the society.[122]

Although, as has already been stated, the superiors who according to the constitutions of exempt clerical societies possess jurisdiction in the internal forum may hear the confessions of their

[119] Can. 501, § 1.
[120] Cf. can. 875, § 1.
[121] Cf. can. 518, § 1.
[122] Cf. *supra*, pp. 109-110.

subjects, nevertheless, according to canon 518, § 2, they may avail themselves of this power only when their subjects of their own free will and choice seek them out for the purpose of confession. Even then, unless grave reasons are present, the superiors may not habitually hear their confessions.

Finally, canon 518, § 3, likewise applicable to quasi-religious societies by virtue of canon 675, warns superiors, major and minor, not to induce any of their subjects to come to them for confession, whether they do this personally or through others, and whether the urging consists of force, fear or any other means.

In an exempt lay institute the proper superiors may propose to the ordinary of the place where the house of the religious institute is located the priests they desire as confessors. However, these confessors must obtain the jurisdiction for the hearing of these confessions from the local ordinary. The ordinary ought to grant the necessary jurisdiction to these proposed confessors unless he has adequate cause for a refusal.[123]

As was just stated, exemption in a quasi-religious society is equal in all respects to exemption in a religious institute. Consequently the right given to exempt lay religious institutes by canon 875, § 2, is applicable to exempt lay quasi-religious societies.[124]

With the application of the norm of canon 519 to quasi-religious societies, which application is justified by canon 675, the following conclusions are reached. Without any prejudice to constitutions which may require or urge the members of a society to make their confessions at stated times and to certain specified confessors, a member of a quasi-religious society, even if it be exempt, may for the peace of his conscience make his confession to any priest approved by the ordinary of the place where the confession is made, even though the priest be not appointed, in the case of an exempt clerical society, by the religious superior. Furthermore, the particular priest approached for the purpose of confession can absolve from the sins and censures reserved specially in the society. Any contrary privilege or custom must be considered as revoked.

With reference to the case just mentioned it should be noted that a priest who has obtained his jurisdiction from the local ordi-

---

[123] Can. 875, § 2.

[124] Cf. *supra*, pp. 109-110; 143.

nary cannot validly absolve a member of an exempt society from any sin that the local ordinary has reserved to himself. For, although the exempt member is not directly subject to the local ordinary who has reserved the sin, nevertheless he is indirectly subject inasmuch as the reservation of the sin restricts the confessor's power of absolution with regard to that particular reservation. However, if the confessor in the same case held jurisdiction which was granted to him by the religious superior, he could absolve from the sins reserved by the ordinary of that place.[125]

The expression, *tranquility of conscience,* as used in the canons which deal with the confessions of religious, is generally interpreted by the authors as inserted rather in explanation than as a strict condition, for every confession, seriously and earnestly made, is undertaken for the sake of obtaining peace of conscience.[126]

Canon 528 considers the question of confessors for lay religious institutes of men. The prescriptions of this canon, in virtue of the general application of canon 675, are likewise applicable to quasi-religious male societies. Accordingly, in lay quasi-religious societies of men there should be approved ordinary confessors who regularly hear the confessions of the subjects of the society on stated days and at regular hours. There should likewise be extraordinary confessors, who at least four times every year hear their confessions. Moreover, if some members should desire a special confessor, the superior should not in any way inquire into the reason for such a request or show any signs of disapproval or reluctance in regard to it.

Section 3. Confessors of Quasi-Religious Societies of Women

In accordance with the prescription of canon 876, §§ 1 and 2, all contrary privileges and particular law being revoked, priests both

---

[125] Kelly, *Jurisdiction of the Confessor According to the Code of Canon Law* (New York; Benziger Bros., 1928), pp. 190-191.

[126] Woywod, *A Practical Commentary on the New Code of Canon Law* (7. ed., 2 vols., New York; Wagner, 1943), I, 195-196; Cocchi, *De Religiosis,* n. 36; Fanfani, *De Religiosis,* p. 141; Goyeneche, "Quaestio Canonica,"—*CpR,* II (1921), 16; Larraona, "Commentarium Codicis,"—*CpR,* XI (1930), 156; Chelodi, *De Personis,* n. 256; Augustine, *Commentary on the New Code,* IV, 269; Beste, *Introductio in Codicem* (Editio altera, Collegeville, Minn.: St. John's Abbey Press, 1944), p. 519.

secular and religious of any rank or office, in order licitly and validly to hear the confessions of women religious and their novices, must possess a special jurisdiction from the ordinary of the place where the confessions are heard.

Exceptions to this general rule are contained in canons 239, § 1, n. 1, whereby cardinals are given the power of hearing these confessions without this special jurisdiction; and in canons 522, 523, § 2, to be treated in the later sections of this article. Implicitly, exceptions are likewise contained in canon 882, whereby jurisdiction is given to all priests whenever a penitent is in danger of death; and likewise in canon 883, in accordance with which faculties for the hearing of confessions are given to priests aboard a ship with reference to the confessions of all on board the vessel, provided the priest possesses faculties for the hearing of confessions from at least one of the several ordinaries enumerated in the canon.

There is some question whether or not the prescription of canon 876, § 1, applies to quasi-religious societies of women. The main reason for denying it arises from the fact that canon 675 in its general application refers only to canons 499-530 as being applicable to quasi-religious societies. Thus canon 876 is not specifically mentioned. Furthermore, quasi-religious societies of women are not religious institutes. Now, the restrictive canons applicable to the latter, are generally not applied to quasi-religious societies unless the necessity of application is indisputable. It would follow from these arguments that any priest approved for women's confessions in a particular territory could hear in that territory the confessions of the members of quasi-religious societies of women without the special jurisdiction demanded in canon 876, § 1.[127]

However, the majority of the authors are of the opinion that the prescription of canon 876, § 1, is applicable to quasi-religious societies of women, and that consequently confessors need special jurisdiction from the local ordinary to hear the confessions of their members.[128]

---

[127] Cocchi, *De Religiosis,* n. 45 (d); Berutti, *De Religiosis,* p. 368.

[128] Schäfer, *De Religiosis,* p. 364; McCormick, *Confessors of Religious,* The Catholic University of America Canon Law Studies, n. 33 (Washington, D. C.: The Catholic University of America, 1926), p. 181; Cance, *Le Code de Droit Canonique,* Vol. II, *Des Religieux* (5. ed., Paris: Librairie Lecoffre,

This same opinion is held by de Oliveira, who states that, for the valid and licit granting of absolution to a member of a quasi-religious society of women, the confessor needs the special jurisdiction of the local ordinary as specified in canon 876, § 1. He quotes from the decrees of the Plenary Council of Brazil which indirectly substantiate his claim, in so far as they show the mind of the Fathers of the Council in this matter to be similar to his own. The inspection and revision accorded by the Holy See to these decrees may be regarded as lending additional weight to his opinion. The 230th decree of this Council states that by virtue of canon 876, § 1, special faculties of the local ordinaries are required for the hearing of the confessions of all the members of institutes of women living in common after the manner of religious.[129]

It is likewise the opinion of the writer, that the special jurisdiction of the local ordinary as specified in canon 876, § 1, is required for the valid and licit hearing of the confessions of women who belong to quasi-religious societies. This opinion was reached not solely in consequence of the superior weight it enjoys by reason of the authors who advance it, but also in the light of the very purpose of the law in question.

The whole legislation of canon 876, § 1, seems to be founded on the necessity of the particular care which must be taken in the appointing of priests for the delicate and difficult task of hearing the confessions of women who are living the life of a religious. Certainly quasi-religious societies of women, who so closely imitate the lives of women religious, especially in their spirit and methods of advancing in spiritual perfection, are in a similar need of carefully selected confessors. The same precautions used to guarantee

---

J. Gabalda, 1939), II, 167; Larraona, "Commentarium Codicis,"—*CpR,* X 1929), 447; Chelodi, *De Personis,* n. 258; Vermeersch-Creusen, *Epitome,* I, n. 676; Wernz-Vidal, *De Religiosis,* n. 458, II, note 4; Ferreres, *Institutiones Canonicae* (2 vols., Barcinone, 1918), I, 327, note 1; Noldin-Schmitt, *Summa Theologiae Moralis,* III, n. 350, 2, note 1; Goyeneche, "Questio Canonica,"—*CpR,* II (1921), 15.

[129] "Para Ouvir de Confessão as Filhas de Caridade ou Vincentinas Requer se Peculiar Jurisdicão,"—*Revista Ecclesiastica Brasileira,* IV (1944), 397-400.

women religious suitable confessors ought to be employed to assure women members of quasi-religious societies suitable confessors.

The application of canon 520 to quasi-religious societies of women justifies the following conclusions. In each house of a quasi-religious society of women there should be appointed one ordinary confessor for the entire house, unless on account of the large number of members attached to the house, or because of the diversity of languages spoken by the members, two or more ordinary confessors are needed. Moreover, if any member, for the peace of her conscience, according to her own judgment, or for the greater progress of her spiritual life, asks for a special confessor or director, the local ordinary should readily grant her request, but he should guard against any misuse of this concession which may upset the peace or discipline of the house. If any abuse should creep in, the ordinary should eliminate it cautiously and prudently without any prejudice to the freedom of conscience.[180]

The Pontifical Commission for the Authentic Interpretation of the Canons of the Code was asked on January 16, 1921, whether the obligation of appointing ordinary confessors for every house of women religious applied also to the formative houses (*domus non formatae*) where fewer than six professed sisters were living. The Commission replied that the prescriptions of canon 520 and canon 521 were to be observed. This was a private response, and was never authentically promulgated.[181] Nevertheless this response does show the mind of the Sacred Congregation for religious to favor the opinion that all houses, whether or not they have gained a full juridical stature, are included under the prescriptions of canon 520 and 521.[182]

Since this response of the Commission was an interpretation of canon 520, all those obliged by the prescriptions of canon 520 are likewise bound by the interpretation of that canon. Consequently, quasi-religious societies of women, while not specifically mentioned in the response, nevertheless were implicitly included because of their obligation to submit to the prescriptions of canon 520.

---

[180] Can. 520.

[181] Schäfer, *De Religiosis*, p. 367, note 95.

[182] Blat, *De Religiosis*, pp. 202-203; Larraona, "Commentarium Codicis,"—*CpR*, X (1929), 455.

The application of canon 521, through the prescription of canon 675, to quasi-religious societies of women results in the following conclusions of law. Every house of a quasi-religious society of women should have an extraordinary confessor who will visit it at least four times a year to hear the confessions of the members residing there. Every member should go to him, at least to receive his blessing.[133]

Whether or not the extraordinary confessor is to visit the house more than four times a year must be determined by the particular laws of the diocese and the nature of the particular society concerned. Sufficient reasons could demand the appointment of more than one extraordinary confessor, e.g., a large number of sisters or their diversity of language.[134]

The local ordinary should furthermore appoint several priests in the vicinity of each house, so that in particular cases the members residing in the house may freely have recourse to them as confessors.[135]

The same supplementary confessors may be appointed by the local ordinary for several houses of a society. The scope of their authority is determined from the faculties granted to them.[136]

The special cases which would warrant the calling of a supplementary confessor could be the absence or the illness of the ordinary confessor, the special necessity of an individual member for peace of conscience, and other similar reasons. However, if without special cause the supplementary confessor is called, he should notify the superior that he is not authorized to act. Otherwise the office of the ordinary confessor would be rendered nugatory. If some quasi-religious woman wishes to use the services of the supplementary confessor regularly, the special permission required for a special confessor as prescribed in canon 520, § 2, should be sought from the ordinary.[137]

If the member of a quasi-religious society of women should desire the ministration of one of these confessors, no superioress

---

[133] Can. 521, § 1.

[134] Larraona, "Commentarium Codicis,"—*CpR,* XI (1930), 22, note 127.

[135] Can. 521, § 2.

[136] Blat, *De Religiosis,* p. 208.

[137] Schäfer, *De Religiosis,* pp. 373-374.

is allowed either personally or through another, directly or indirectly, to inquire into the reason for or to refuse the grant of the request, or in any way, either by word or action, to show any displeasure at the making of the request.[138]

The words *"ex iis"* of canon 521, § 3, certainly refer to paragraphs 1 and 2 of canon 521, including both the supplementary and the extraordinary confessors. Larraona goes further. He states that these words refer to canon 520 as well as to canon 521, thereby including within their scope both the ordinary and the special confessors. He bases his opinion on the analogy inherent in the acts of selection, inasmuch as the concession of freedom granted in canon 521, § 3, seems to require that it be extended to the ordinary and special confessors with even more reason than to the extraordinary and supplementary confessors.[139]

The application of canon 522 to quasi-religious societies of women, justified by the norm of canon 675, results in the following conclusions. If notwithstanding the concessions of the two foregoing canons, a member of a quasi-religious society of women, for the peace of her conscience, goes to any confessor approved by the local ordinary for the hearing of the confessions of women generally, in any church, public or semi-public oratory, the confessor may licitly and validly hear her confession. Any privilege to the contrary is revoked, and the superioress cannot forbid the use of this concession or inquire even indirectly into the reason for it, nor are her subjects bound to offer her any explanation.

The penitent mentioned in canon 522 must approach the confessor for the purpose of confessing. This condition is necessary for the validity of the act of absolution. The word *"approach"* (*adeat*) allows various interpretations. The Pontifical Commission for the Authentic Interpretation of the Canons of the Code on December 28, 1927, decided that it not be so restrictively understood that it is not permitted to summon the confessor to the place legitimately designated for the confession of women or of women religious.[140] It seems therefore that as long as the woman

---

[138] Can. 521, § 3.

[139] "Commentarium Codicis,"—*CpR,* XI (1930), 75-76.

[140] *AAS,* XX (1928), 61.

religious takes the initiative in calling the confessor, such a request juridically constitutes an *"approach,"* no matter what means are used.[141]

The reply of the Commission is applicable to quasi-religious societies of women in virtue of the principle already stated, namely, that the interpretations of a canon are applicable to all those who are bound by the canon itself.

The possession of faculties for the hearing of women's confessions in the place where the confession is heard is likewise demanded for the validity of the absolution. Furthermore, the confession must be made in a church, a public or a semi-public oratory, or a place designated for the hearing of the confessions of women.[142]

On November 24, 1920, the Commission for the Authentic Interpretation of the Canons of the Code declared, concerning the place for the hearing of confessions as prescribed by canon 522, that it includes besides the church, or also the public and the semi-public oratory, any place designated for the hearing of the confessions of women.[143]

On December 28, 1927, the Commission further stated that the confessions of women religious heard outside one of the places designated either in canon 522 or in the reply of the Commission on November 24, 1920, would not only be illicit but also invalid.[144]

The place designated for the hearing of the confessions of women religious as already noted in the replies of the Commission of November 24, 1920 and December 28, 1927, was further described by a third response of the Commission on February 12, 1935, when it declared that the place designated in the interpretation of November 24, 1920, is to be understood not only of a place habitually designated for the confessions of women, but also of a place so designated in a particular case (*per modum actus*) or selected according to the norms of canon 910, § 1.[145]

Consequently, the confessions of women religious can be heard

---

[141] Vermeersch-Creusen, *Epitome,* I, n. 498; Choupin, *Nature et Obligations de l'Etat Religieux* (Paris: Beauchesne, 1923), p. 228.

[142] Blat, *De Religiosis,* pp. 213-215.

[143] *AAS,* XII (1920), 575.

[144] *AAS,* XX (1928), 61.

[145] *AAS,* XXVII (1935), 92.

in accordance with canon 522 in a place which is habitually designated for the hearing of the confessions of women by an ecclesiastical superior competent to make this designation, such as the local ordinary, or even a superior of lower rank, such as the pastor or the rector of a church, as long as the place selected corresponds to the law of the Code and the statutes of the ordinary. The confessions may also be heard in a place which has become designated in a particular case (*per modum actus*) by a confessor in some extraordinary circumstance, such as sickness, as considered in canon 910, § 1, grave inconvenience, an exceptionally large number of confessions to be heard, the celebration of a great feast, or other considerations of a similar nature.[146]

All the foregoing authentic interpretations of canon 522 are applicable to quasi-religious societies of women in view of the principle stated above, so that, if a canon is applicable to a particular person or group, the authentic interpretations, being in reality a part of the canon itself, are also applicable.

The application of canon 523 to quasi-religious societies of women, likewise warranted by the prescription of canon 675, results in the following legal conclusions. Whenever a member of a quasi-religious society of women is seriously ill, even though there be no danger of death, she may call any priest approved for the hearing of the confessions of women, though he be not approved for the confessions of women religious, and she may confess to him during the illness as often as she desires. Moreover, the superioress may not directly or indirectly prohibit her from making use of this concession.

The grave illness mentioned in this canon need not mean that the penitent woman is in danger of death. Schäfer states that, when it is judged necessary to call a doctor, a woman religious may be considered as gravely ill. For ordinarily a doctor is not called for a woman religious when she suffers but a light illness.[147] Vermeersch-Creusen claim that an illness requiring a woman religious to remain in bed for at least a week may be considered grave.[148]

---

[146] Schäfer, *De Religiosis,* p. 383; Blat, *De Religiosis,* pp. 215-216; can. 910. § 1.

[147] *De Religiosis,* p. 384; Coronata, *Institutiones,* I, 663, note 5.

[148] *Epitome,* I, n. 499.

These opinions, although directed to women religious may be equally applied to women quasi-religious, for both classes are equally bound by the prescriptions of the canon in question.

It seems safe to mention that in general a grave illness is an illness whereby probably, or at least possibly, a person may become confronted with the danger of death. This condition may best be judged by the doctor or some other prudent person, who from experience with the sick can prudently judge whether or not the patient may easily come to be in danger of death.[149]

In canons 521, § 3, 522 and 523, all of which are applicable to quasi-religious societies of women in view of the norm of canon 675, there are contained special warnings which forbid superioresses, either personally or through others, directly or indirectly, to inquire into the reasons prompting their subjects to seek the ministrations of the confessors mentioned in these canons, or to show any signs of displeasure at such a desire by either their words or their actions. If a superioress has acted contrary to these prescriptions, she should be warned by the local ordinary. If the warning proves unsuccessful, the local ordinary should punish her with removal from office. Notice of this authoritative act should immediately be sent to the Holy See.[150]

The application of canon 2414 to superioresses of quasi-religious societies of women is not contrary to the prescription of canon 2219, § 3, which forbids the extension of penalties from one class of persons to another. For the penalties of canon 2414 are applicable to all superiors contemplated in canons 521, 522, and 523. Now, according to the general application of these canons to quasi-religious societies of women, justified by the norm of canon 675, the superioresses of the latter are subject to the penalties imposed on those who violate these canons.[151]

However, if a superioress prudently thinks that a subject is abusing the rights given to her by the Code with reference to the matter of making her confession, she should inform the local ordinary.[152]

---

[149] Blat, *De Religiosis,* p. 219.

[150] Cf. can. 2414.

[151] Schäfer, *De Religiosis,* p. 385, note 206; Blat, *De Religiosis,* p. 211.

[152] Cf. can. 520, § 2; Schäfer, *De Religiosis,* p. 386.

With the application of the provisions of canon 524 to quasi-religious societies of women as warranted by canon 675, the following conclusions result. The local ordinary, in appointing ordinary and extraordinary confessors for houses of quasi-religious societies of women, may select priests either from the secular clergy or from a religious clerical institute, provided that the latter have the permission of their superiors to accept the appointment. The priests thus appointed should have no power over the women quasi-religious in the external forum. They should possess the virtues of prudence and integrity. Furthermore, the ordinary and the extraordinary confessor should be at least forty years of age, unless for a just reason the local ordinary thinks it proper to dispense with this particular qualification.[153]

A just reason for dispensing from the qualification of the requisite age is the lack of suitable priests of the required age. The power in the external forum to which the canon refers can be either dominative resulting from incorporation in the society or that of jurisdiction whether ordinary or delegated.[154]

Canon 524, § 1, governs the qualifications of only the ordinary and the extraordinary confessors. Consequently, it is left to the wisdom of the ordinary to select the other confessors according to his own judgment.[155]

The term of office of the ordinary confessor in houses of quasi-religious societies of women is governed by canon 526, which is applied to these societies through canon 675. The ordinary confessor should not hold office in the same house for more than a single term of three years. The local ordinary may reappoint him for a second term and a third, if, on account of the scarcity of priests qualified for this work, he cannot provide new confessors every three years, or if the majority of the women quasi-religious has by a secret ballot petitioned the local ordinary to reappoint him in the capacity of the ordinary confessor. Even those who otherwise would not have an active voice in the affairs of the society,

---

[153] Can. 524, § 1.
[154] Blat, *De Religiosis*, pp. 223-224.
[155] Schäfer, *De Religiosis*, p. 386.

should participate in this vote. Those who dissent must be given another confessor if they request one.[156]

The ordinary does not have to reappoint a confessor when he has been requested by a vote of the women quasi-religious in accordance with the prescription of canon 526. He is given the right to reappoint him, but he is free in the manner in which he sees fit, to invoke or to forego the use of this right.

Schäfer mentions the fact that, according to a faculty given to local ordinaries in the quinquennial faculties by the Sacred Congregation of Religious, they may reäppoint ordinary confessors for the houses of women religious even a fourth and a fifth term of three years as long as the greater number of the religious attached to the house consent to the reappointment, and provided that other confessors are supplied for the dissenters if they wish it.[157]

It seems safe to conclude that by reason of this faculty local ordinaries may likewise reappoint ordinary confessors for the houses of quasi-religious societies of women for a fourth and even a fifth term. The faculty is an extension of the grant incorporated in canon 526. This canon governs the appointment of ordinary confessors for both religious institutes and quasi-religious societies of women, and it seems that the extension of the canon's application should affect all whom it includes. Furthermore, a consideration of the end of the law seems to justify the extension of the faculty with reference to quasi-religious societies of women. The granting of the faculty was intended, in all probability, to forestall the difficulty which would arise from a shortage of priests suitable for the office of ordinary confessor. This difficulty can exist equally as well in regard to quasi-religious societies as with reference to religious institutes.

By virtue of the prescription of canon 675, the further norms governing the confessors of women religious as contained in canon 524 are likewise applied to the confessors of quasi-religious societies of women. Accordingly, the ordinary confessor of a house of a quasi-religious society of women cannot immediately be made the extraordinary confessor for the same house until at least one year has elapsed from the expiration of his term, except of course in the

[156] Can. 526.

[157] *De Religiosis,* p. 389.

case mentioned in canon 526. However, the extraordinary confessor may immediately be appointed the ordinary confessor of the same house on the expiration of his term of office in the capacity of extraordinary confessor. Both the ordinary and the extraordinary confessors are forbidden to interfere in any way with the external or internal government of the society.[158]

The term of office for the extraordinary confessor is not specified in the law. It must receive its determination from the local ordinary.

Although the prohibition which in canon 524, § 3, forbids confessors to intervene in the government of the society is specifically directed to only the ordinary and the extraordinary confessors, nevertheless, from the very nature of the law it can safely be said that the prohibition applies equally to all confessors of women religious and quasi-religious. Moreover the prohibition as contained in canon 524, § 3, was derived from the decree *"Cum de sacramentalibus,"* issued on February 3, 1913. In number 10 of that decree, those for whom this prohibition of interference existed were specified as *"confessarii omnes."*[159] In accordance with the prescription of canon 6, n. 4, the scope of the prohibition of the earlier law should be retained.[160]

Further legislation concerning the confessors appointed for religious institutes of women is contained in canon 527. The prescriptions of this canon are likewise applicable to quasi-religious societies of women in virtue of canon 675. Consequently, the following conclusions may be drawn. The local ordinary may remove both the ordinary and the extraordinary confessors of a quasi-religious society of women. He is not bound to give any reason for the removal to anyone except the Holy See, should the Holy See request an explanation. In accordance with the prescription of canon 880, § 1, the ordinary may not exercise this right without a grave cause.

Schäfer includes in the prescriptions of canon 527 the right of the local ordinary to remove also the special and the supplementary confessors.[161]

---

[158] Can. 524, §§ 2, 3.
[159] *AAS,* V (1913), 63.
[160] Blat, *De Religiosis,* p. 225.
[161] *De Religiosis,* p. 391.

The grave cause necessitating the removal of these confessors is to be based entirely upon the consideration which looks to the fruitful administration of the sacrament. It does not matter whether or not the confessor is at fault.[162]

Canon 527 implicitly gives a right to religious institutes and quasi-religious societies and also to the confessors to have recourse to the Holy See against the act of removal from office. Otherwise the Holy See would hardly have an occasion to ask for an explanation of the removal of a confessor.[163]

It is incorrect to apply to houses of religious institutes or quasi-religious societies of women the prescription of canon 880, § 3, in view of which the ordinary, without consulting the Holy See, cannot simultaneously deprive a religious house which has full juridical status (*domus formata*), of all its confessors. It is clear from the context of the canon, wherein no reference is made to the houses of women religious and from the text of the pre-Code law, from which this prescription was taken, that canon 880, § 3, refers only to the confessors of a clerical religious institute delegated to hear the confessions of the members of the house to which they are attached. The Constitution *"Superna"* of Pope Clement X, issued on January 21, 1670, contained this prescription in the earlier law.[164]

ARTICLE XI. THE MANIFESTATION OF CONSCIENCE

Canon 530 legislates concerning the manifestation of conscience by religious properly so called. The prescriptions of this canon are likewise applicable to quasi-religious societies by reason of the application mentioned in canon 675. Consequently the following conclusions are justified.

All superiors of quasi-religious societies are strictly forbidden to induce their subjects in any manner whatsoever, whether by threats or praise or in any other way, to manifest to them their state of conscience. The subjects in a quasi-religious society however, are not forbidden, of their own free will and choice, to

---

[162] Blat, *De Religiosis,* pp. 231-232.

[163] Cf. can. 527.

[164] *Fontes,* n. 246; Schäfer, *De Religiosis,* p. 829; Blat, *De Religiosis,* p. 232.

manifest their conscience to their superiors. On the contrary, it is proper that the subjects should approach their superiors with filial confidence, and, if the superiors be priests, reveal to them any doubts of their conscience.[165]

Only superiors properly so called are included in the prohibitions of this canon. Consequently novice masters and prefects of discipline and study and spiritual directors are not included.

The general revelation of conscience allowed to be made to non-clerical superiors concerns the acquisition of virtue, progress in spiritual perfection, the performance of duties attached to offices, and other questions not involving sin or cases of conscience.

The prohibition of canon 530 is imposed on all superiors as a grave obligation, although it does admit slightness of matter. However, it must be noted that the canon does not forbid superiors to demand that their subjects make a manifestation of conscience to others. Subjects certainly can be exhorted, if not actually commanded, to do this.[166]

ARTICLE XII. CHAPLAINS OF QUASI-RELIGIOUS SOCIETIES

Canon 675 extends the provisions of canon 529 to quasi-religious societies. As thus applied there results the following legal conclusion. In non-exempt lay societies the local ordinary has the right to designate the priests for the sacred ministry and for the office of preaching. In exempt lay societies the superior has the right to designate priests, but in case of default on the part of the superior the right devolves on the local ordinary.[167]

No obligation rests on the local ordinary which requires that he make the appointment of these priests for non-exempt societies. The making of the appointment simply connotes a right that is accorded to him. If the local ordinary does not avail himself of this right, the pastor in whose territory the house is located must perform these functions or at least provide for their performance.[168]

---

[165] Can. 530.

[166] Schäfer, *De Religiosis*, pp. 403-404; Vermeersch-Creusen, *Epitome*, I, n. 502; Wernz-Vidal, *De Religiosis*, n. 213.

[167] Can. 529.

[168] Schäfer, *De Religiosis*, p. 397.

In general, the chaplain of a lay society has the right and the obligations of a rector of a church. However, strictly parochial functions are reserved to the pastor, unless the local ordinary, in virtue of the prescription of canon 464, § 2, has removed the house of the society either totally or partially from the jurisdiction of the pastor. The rights and the obligations given a chaplain of a lay society are to be determined from the norms which obtain in the common law and especially from the letter of his appointment and the particular law of the diocese. Essentially his duties are the celebration of Mass, the distribution of Holy Communion, the performance of the acts of worship in the chapel, or the oratory, and due compliance with the laws of the sacred liturgy.

Strictly, the local ordinary has even the right of appointing the retreat masters for the non-exempt lay societies. However, free choice in this matter is generally given to the societies.[169]

In a non-exempt clerical society the superior appoints a priest of his own household for the performance of these functions. However, the faculty for preaching must be secured from the local ordinary. This may be gathered from the general prescription of canon 1337, which states that only the local ordinary can grant the faculty of preaching within his territory to the secular clergy and to the non-exempt religious. Consequently, only exempt clerical religious are excluded, within certain limits, from the prescription of this canon. Therefore, all members of non-exempt clerical quasi-religious societies, whether they be considered as part of the general group of those who are not members of an exempt clerical religious institute, or whether they be considered not as religious and consequently as secular clerics, must in any case receive the faculty for preaching from the local ordinary.[170]

As has already been stated, the privilege of exemption for quasi-religious societies extends to all the favors given by the law to exempt religious institutes.[171] Consequently, in accordance with the application of canon 529, the superior of an exempt lay society has the right of designating the chaplain for the society from among

[169] Vermeersch-Creusen, *Epitome,* I, n. 501.

[170] Cf. cans. 1337, 1338.

[171] Cf. *supra,* pp. 109-110.

those priests who are approved for these functions by the local ordinary.

Although, in accordance with the prescriptions of canon 529, the superior of an exempt lay society may designate the priest for the ministry of preaching, nevertheless, in accordance with the prescription of canon 1338, § 3, the faculty for preaching must be secured from the local ordinary. However, the preacher cannot make use of this faculty without the permission of the superior.

Scholion I. The Burial of Members of Quasi-Religious Societies

In order to determine the place of burial of the members of quasi-religious societies, it must first be decided whether or not they are to be considered analogous in this matter to religious institutes and subject to the legislation determining this question for the latter.

Canon 1223 gives to all the faithful, unless they are explicitly forbidden by law, the right of choosing a church as well as a cemetery for their burial. Canon 1224 explicitly excludes from the use of this right boys who are under fourteen years of age, girls who are under twelve years of age, and all professed religious, unless they are bishops.

Nowhere in the Code is there any indication that the members of quasi-religious societies are to be comprised under the term *religious* as used in canon 1224, § 2. Furthermore, since canon 1223 states that one must be expressly excluded if one is not to enjoy the right of a free choice, it seems correct to say that the members of quasi-religious societies possess the right of choosing their own church and cemetery of burial. However, it also seems correct to say that, if the constitutions which have been approved after the Code contain prescriptions contrary to this right, then the constitutions control. Any particular rescripts given to any society by the Holy See also retain their force.

In canon 514, § 4, however, a canon which by reason of the general prescription of canon 675 applies to quasi-religious societies, it is stated that with regard to funerals the prescriptions of canons 1221 and 1230, § 5, are to be observed. Consequently, since quasi-religious societies are held to all the prescriptions of canon 514, it seems that they are likewise held to any prescription of that canon which makes reference to other canons. Therefore, quasi-religious societies in so far as it is possible are likewise subject to the prescriptions of canons 1221 and 1230, § 5, to which reference is thus made. It seems that the only reason that mention of canons 1221 and 1230, § 5, was incorporated in canon 514, § 4, was the avoidance of the inconvenience of repeating the legislation already contained in those canons. The reference to the canons by their number has thus the same effect as if the very prescriptions were themselves repeated in the canon.

The burial of the members of these societies is consequently determined as follows:

A. The Burial of Members of Quasi-Religious Societies of Men

When the members of a quasi-religious society of men have not freely chosen a church for their burial, then in accordance with the prescriptions of canon 1221, the bodies of the professed members and of the novices are to be transferred for funeral services in the church or the oratory proper to the house, or at least to some other house of the society. The right to conduct the funeral procession from the place of the person's death to the church of the funeral belongs to the superior of the proper house of the member or the novice. If, however, the person died far away from his proper house, and his body cannot be conveniently taken to his proper house or to any house of the society, he is to be buried from the church of the parish in which he died. The proper superior has, in accordance with the prescription of canon 1218, § 3, the right to transfer the body any distance if he so wishes, provided that the expenses can be met by the proper house of the deceased.

The regulations of canon 1221, §§ 1-2, apply likewise to servants who are in the actual service of the society and live steadily within the precincts of the house of the society. If, however, they die outside the house of the society, they are to be buried according to the common law determining the burial of the laity.[172]

Persons who have stayed at a house of a quasi-religious society for the purpose of health, or of study, or as guests, and persons who die in hospitals conducted by the members of such a society,

---

[172] Can. 1221, § 3; cf. cans. 1218, § 3; 1224, § 1.

are to be buried in compliance with the norms of the common law determining the burial of the laity.[173]

In all clerical societies the superior of the house has the right of conducting the funeral services in their churches and oratories. In lay societies, if they be not exempted from the jurisdiction of the pastor according to the norm of canon 464, § 2, the funeral services are to be conducted by the pastor of the territory where the church of burial is located.[174]

In lay societies, if they be exempted from the jurisdiction of the pastor, the funeral services of the members are conducted by the chaplain, in the church or the oratory of the society.[175]

Finally, if the members or novices of a society of quasi-religious have lawfully chosen a definite church for burial, the pastor of that church has the right to bestow the burial service.

B. The Burial of Members of Quasi-Religious Societies of Women

When the members of a quasi-religious society of women have not freely chosen a church for their burial, then in accordance with the prescriptions of canon 1230, § 5, as applied by canons 675 and 514, § 4, the members of the society and the novices who die within its houses are to have their bodies brought to the threshold of the enclosure, where, if the society is exempted from the jurisdiction of the pastor, the chaplain is to receive the body, to conduct it to the proper church or oratory of the house, and to perform the funeral services.[176]

If the society is not exempted from the jurisdiction of the pastor, the latter has the right of conducting the body to the proper church and of there performing the funeral services.[177]

If women members of quasi-religious societies die outside their houses, they are to be buried according to the norms of burial for the laity.

Finally, if the members or the novices of the society have chosen

---

[173] Can. 1222.

[174] Schäfer, *De Religiosis,* p. 861.

[175] Schäfer, *loc. cit.;* Fanfani, *De Religiosis,* p. 167.

[176] Cans. 464, § 2; 1230, § 5; Schäfer, *De Religiosis,* p. 861.

[177] Can. 1230, § 5.

a church for their burial, the pastor of that church has the right to conduct the burial services.

Exempt lay quasi-religious, whether men or women, follow the same norms that obtain for the burial of members of quasi-religious societies which have been exempted from the jurisdiction of the pastor, saving always their right to freely choose their church of burial.[178]

Scholion II. Celebrets for Priest Members of Quasi-Religious Societies

Canon 804, § 1, states that a priest who desires to say Mass in a church other than that to which he is attached must show to the priest in charge of the church an authentic letter of recommendation of unexpired validity. A secular priest must obtain this letter from his ordinary, and a religious priest from his superior.

In accordance with canon 678, quasi-religious societies with regard to those things which pertain to ordination are to be considered as seculars. Consequently, in the securing of a celebret the members of these societies must follow the norms enacted in law for the secular clergy. For the case in question this implies the securing of the celebret from the local ordinary who as their proper bishop ordained them or issued dimissorials for their ordination.[179]

However, as will be stated in a later chapter, most clerical quasi-religious societies have obtained from the Holy See the privilege of allowing their superiors to issue dimissorials for the ordinations of their own subjects. By virtue of this privilege a society becomes subject to the legislation determining the ordinations of religious. Consequently, these societies which possess the privilege of issuing dimissorial letters may also issue celebrets for their members who wish to say Mass in churches where they are not known.[180]

The special regulations made by the local ordinary on the matter of celebrets must be observed by all, even exempt societies, unless

[178] Fanfani, *De Religiosis,* p. 433.

[179] Augustine, *A Commentary of Canon Law,* IV, 131; Stanton, *De Societatibus,* p. 117.

[180] Cf. *infra,* pp. 198; 205.

there is question of allowing subjects to say Mass in a church belonging to the society of which the priest is a member, and provided that it is a society in which the superiors may issue dimissorial letters.[181]

Scholion III. Confessors for the Daughters of Charity of Saint Vincent de Paul

For some time there have been lengthy discussions and varied opinions concerning the question of the confessions of the Daughters of Charity of Saint Vincent de Paul. The main concern in all of these discussions has centered principally about the question whether or not the confessors of these women are in need of the special jurisdiction which is indicated as necessary for the valid hearing of the confessions of women religious, which jurisdiction must be granted by the local ordinary in accordance with the prescription of canon 876, § 1.

The writer is firmly convinced that the confessors of the Daughters of Charity of Saint Vincent de Paul are not in need of the special jurisdiction which is essential for the hearing of the confessions of women religious, as stated in canon 876, § 1. The writer holds this opinion for the following reasons.

In the *"Monita ad Confessarios,"* published for the confessors of these women and approved by the Sacred Congregation of Religious on August 27, 1923, the following regulation is specified. According to the rules given by Saint Vincent de Paul, by force of the constitution *"Pastoralis curae"* of Benedict XIV, and in virtue of the rescript of Leo XIII, the Superior General of the Congregation of the Mission, either himself or through the provincial directors of these quasi-religious women, is to designate their ordinary and extraordinary confessors, wherever these women may be. However, the choice must be made from among the priests approved by the various local ordinaries for the hearing of the confessions of women. Moreover, this designation or election of confessors confers no jurisdiction. Likewise the sisters, for the consolation and peace of their conscience, are not prohibited from

---

[181] Can. 804, § 3.

going to any confessor approved for women's confessions other than those designated by the Superior General or the provincial director.[182]

While it is true that the text of this prescription of the *"Monita"* does not exclude the necessity of the granting of jurisdiction by the local ordinary for the hearing of the confessions of women religious, still the notion of the word *"designate"* excludes the idea of the special jurisdiction to which canon 876, § 1, adverts. As the *"Monita"* states, the word is to be understood in relation to the various pronouncements of the Pontiffs, especially the rescript of Leo XIII.

In the book of the privileges of the Daughters of Charity of Saint Vincent de Paul, under the heading of privilege XXIII, is contained a letter written by the Superior General of the Congregation of the Mission to Leo XIII. This letter in its contents was read and approved by Leo XIII on July 8, 1882. In his approval the Pontiff stated that the prescriptions contained in the letter and regulating the government of these women by the Superior General of the Congregation of the Mission were not to be changed, and that they had his papal approval. From the prescriptions of this letter there can very clearly be seen the exact meaning of the right given to the Superior General of designating confessors for the Daughters of Charity. The following statements are translations of various sections of this letter.

> . . . Now, certain Ordinaries, led into error by false ideas, think they have the right to exercise over the houses of the Daughters of Charity an authority which appertains to the Superior General; . . . to designate special confessors chosen not only from among the secular priests, but even from among the regular clergy, contrary to the Statutes drawn up by Saint Vincent de Paul, and to the constant practice of two and a half centuries. . . .
>
> And indeed the Holy Founder desired that the said Institute should be absolutely secular, or as they say laic, while he assigned to it for a cloister, hospitals, prisons and the homes of the poor; for a veil, modesty; for their

[182] *Monita ad Confessarios Puellarum Charitatis* (Paris, 1923), p. 5.

confessors, pastors or secular priests approved by the Bishop of the diocese. . . .

In this manner they have lived from the time of their institution and thus they live at present. This is well known by the Ordinaries, and even at Rome under the eyes of the Holy See, without any thought of subjecting the company to the canonical laws which, with such firmness, the S.C. of Bishops and Regulars have applied to recent Institutes. . . .

To the Superior General belongs the presenting of confessors; not that he assumes to confer on them any jurisdiction whatsoever; but, he is obliged in virtue of the Statutes, to select them from among the secular priests approved by the Ordinary, most generally, the pastor being designated; neither the Superior General nor the Missionaries can hear the confessions of the Daughters of Charity without said approbation. . . . It is not evident upon what principle the Most Rev. Ordinaries could impose a special confessor upon secular persons; now, the Daughters of Charity are such, as above explained. It suffices, therefore, that the Superior General present, as confessors of the said sisters, priests approved by the Most Rev. Ordinaries to hear the confessions of the female sex.[183]

Under privilege XXII of the same collection is contained the following: "The Daughters of Saint Vincent de Paul have since their institution a special existence, independent, as to interior affairs, of the Ordinaries, and are entirely subject to the Superior General of the Missionaries or Lazarists . . . they have no deputation of ordinary and extraordinary confessors. The character of this Association has always been, and is ever regarded, by the consent of the Sovereign Pontiffs, as altogether lay and secular; hence, laws relative to other pious Institutes are not applicable to it."[184]

Under the same privilege is contained the following rescript from the Sacred Congregation of Bishops and Regulars. "With

---

[183] *Collection of Privileges and Indulgences for the use of the Daughters of Charity* (new edition, Paris, 1909), pp. 47-59.

[184] *Op. cit.*, p. 45.

the exception of the houses of the Daughters of Charity instituted by Saint Vincent de Paul, all other houses of sisters, colleges, and other pious institutes of women, are subject to the law of change of confessors every three years."[185]

After a consideration of the above mentioned excerpts there seems to be no possible doubt concerning the jurisdiction needed before the advent of the present Code by the confessors of the Daughters of Charity of Saint Vincent de Paul.

They most certainly needed no special jurisdiction other than the general jurisdiction granted by the local ordinary to hear women's confessions. The Daughters of Charity were canonically considered as lay women subject only to the canonical regulations which were intended for the women members of the laity.

Furthermore, there does not seem to be any doubt that the same principle must be regarded as effective after the enactment of the present Code. The *"Monita"* specifically state that the right of the Superior General of the Congregation of the Mission and of the provincial directors to designate confessors is the same right as that possessed by earlier Superiors General, and explained in the rescript of Leo XIII. As has already been shown, this right excluded the further need of additional jurisdiction granted by the local ordinary for the hearing of women religious. In addition, the *"Monita"* were approved by the Sacred Congregation of Religious on August 27, 1923, well after the enactment of the present Code.

It may also be stated that none of the extraordinary privileges which exempt the Daughters of Charity of Saint Vincent de Paul from the jurisdiction of the local ordinaries have been revoked. Consequently, in accordance with the prescriptions of canon 4, they retain their force. This particular conclusion was expressly stated by Bastien (1866-1940), who was a consultor of the Sacred Congregation of Religious and of the Pontifical Commission for the Authentic Interpretation of the Canons of the Code.

After making the statement that the Daughters of Charity, by reason of the norm of canon 4, retain all their privileges which exempt them from the jurisdiction of the local ordinary, Bastien proposed the following conclusions concerning the confessions of

---

[185] *Op. cit.*, p. 47.

the Daughters of Charity under the present legislation of the Code. The Superior General of the Congregation of the Mission has the right of presenting their confessors as selected from priests approved by the local ordinary for the hearing of the confessions of women. The local ordinary has no right to impose special confessors on the sisters, just as he has no right to impose special confessors on lay people. It suffices that the confessors selected by the Superior General be approved for the hearing of women's confessions. The ordinary has the right of approving the confessors presented by the Superior General or by the provincial directors.[186]

Concerning the question of the obligation placed on the Superior General of presenting his list of the confessors to the local ordinary for the latter's approval, there seems to be no doubt that this presentation is necessary only for the liceity of the absolution; for the fulfillment of the obligation is not one that looks to the securing of further jurisdiction. The obligation is imposed simply in the interest of good order, so that the local ordinary may know exactly what is occurring in his territory. This conclusion is stated by de Oliveira in his article which has already been cited. He expressly states that this presentation is not intended in any way with a view to securing additional jurisdiction, but is intended only for the purpose of obtaining the proper permission. The presence or the absence of the act of presentation in no way affects the validity of the sacrament.[187]

It may be stated here that this manner of procedure concerning the appointment of the confessors of the Daughters of Charity has been constantly followed in Spain and in South America without any restrictions or revocations of the practice, or any censure on the part of the Holy See.

The opinion as above presented is also held by Cocchi and Martínez who state that by reason of a special privilege given to the Daughters of Charity of Saint Vincent de Paul, as mentioned in the *"Monita,"* the confessors of this institute do not need any

---

[186] *Directoire Canonique,* pp. 351-353.

[187] "Para Ouvir de Confessão as Filhas de Caridade ou Vincentinas Requer se Peculiar Jurisdicao,"—*Revista Ecclesiastica Brasileira,* IV (1944), 398.

special jurisdiction for the confessions of the members other than the general jurisdiction to hear women's confessions. They also mention the already quoted privilege whereby the confessors of these women are not held to a three-year term of office. They both conclude that the confessions of these women are to be regulated entirely according to the prescriptions of the *"Monita."*[188]

In conclusion, observe that any confessor approved for the hearing of women's confessions may validly hear the confession of a Daughter of Charity, unless the local ordinary has explicitly excluded this when he granted the priest his faculties for the hearing of women's confessions. However, unless the priest was designated either by the Superior General of the Congregation of the Mission or by the provincial director of the Daughters of Charity, and then was approved as their ordinary or extraordinary confessor by the local ordinary, he would act illicitly in hearing their confessions, save in cases wherein they freely approach him or request his ministration for the consolation of their conscience, and provided, of course, that he possesses the necessary jurisdiction for the hearing of women's confessions.

---

[188] *De Religiosis,* n. 45 d; Martínez, *Privilegios e Indulgencias de las Hijas de la Caridad de S. Vincente de Paul* (Madrid, 1945), pp. 15-18.

CHAPTER VII

The Administration of Temporal Goods

ARTICLE I. INTRODUCTION

The entire legislation for the administering of the property of quasi-religious societies is contained in canon 676. Canon 676, §§ 1 and 2, considers the administration of property on the part of the society, the province or the house, while canon 676, § 3, concerns itself with the administration of property on the part of the individual subject of these societies.[1]

The temporal goods here considered are in contradistinction to the spiritual goods such as the Sacraments, indulgences and relics. The temporal goods involved may be movable or immovable, corporeal or incorporeal.[2]

The administration of these goods includes all those acts which, as duly approved by law, are concerned with the acquisition, conservation, improvement, distribution, transfer and use of the temporal goods either by the society, the province, the house or any of the society's members.

Administration is ordinary if it extends only to the transactions carried on for the daily or the periodical uses of the society itself. To ordinary administration, therefore, pertain the ordinary purchases and expenditures occurring daily in the interests of the members of the society through the use of money which is not permanently invested. They correspond to the ordinary acts performed by a good and prudent father in his house and for his household.[3]

---

[1] Can. 676, § 1—Societas eiusque provinciae et domus capaces sunt acquirendi et possidendi bona temporalia. § 2—Administratio bonorum regitur praescripto can. 532-537. § 3—Quidquid sodalibus obvenit intuitu societatis, eidem acquiritur; cetera bona sodales secundum constitutiones retinent, acquirunt et administrant.

[2] Cf. can. 1497, § 1.

[3] Blat, *De Religiosis*, pp. 240-242; Schäfer, *De Religiosis*, p. 418.

ARTICLE II. THE ADMINISTRATION OF TEMPORAL GOODS BY A SOCIETY, A PROVINCE OR A HOUSE

According to paragraph one of canon 676 quasi-religious societies, their provinces and their houses are capable of acquiring and possessing temporal goods. The prescription of this paragraph of canon 676 is a natural consequence of the norm of canon 1495, § 2, which states that all moral persons have the right of acquiring, retaining and administering temporal goods. Consequently, since quasi-religious societies, their provinces and their houses are moral persons, as has already been explained in a previous chapter, they too possess this right of acquiring, retaining and possessing temporal goods.[4]

It is to be noted that the canon parallel to canon 676, namely canon 531, which treats of the right of the administration of temporal goods by religious institutes, accords to the rules and constitutions of these institutes the right of excluding and restricting the privileges of acquiring and possessing temporal goods as given by the Code to these various moral bodies.

However, canon 676, §§ 2-3, does not give a similar right to the constitutions of quasi-religious societies. Therefore, unless a special rescript has been given to these societies, or unless their constitutions have been approved after the promulgation of the Code, the constitutions of quasi-religious societies cannot restrict or exclude the right of the society, of its provinces or of its houses to acquire and possess temporal goods. This opinion is further strengthened by the prescription of canon 676, § 2, which applies the norms of canons 532-537 to quasi-religious societies, expressly omitting mention of canon 531, since paragraph § 1, of canon 676 considers as much of canon 531 as was intended to be applied to quasi-religious societies.

The temporal goods of the society, of its provinces and of its houses are to be administered according to the constitutions of each society. However, expenditures and legal acts of ordinary administration may be validly performed, not only by the proper superiors, but also within the limits of their office by the officers

[4] Cf. *supra*, p. 72.

designated for this purpose by the constitutions.[5] The prescriptions of canon 532, §§ 1, 2 relate to quasi-religious societies for the obvious reason that canon 676, § 2, applies the norms of canons 532-537 to quasi-religious societies.

In accordance with the prescriptions just mentioned, the constitutions of a society cannot call into question the validity of the acts of ordinary administration when these are duly performed by the various officers who are designated for these duties by the constitutions. However, the constitutions could demand that the superiors secure the consent or the advice of their council for certain important acts of administration.[6]

Canon 1523 is intended for all those who are charged with the administration of temporal goods of an ecclesiastical nature. Consequently, its prescriptions extend to those who are responsible for the administration of the temporal goods of quasi-religious societies.[7]

In accordance, then, with the prescriptions of canon 1523, those who are charged with the administration of the temporal goods of quasi-religious societies must guard them against any loss or damage. They must observe the regulations of the common law and of the particular constitutions of the society, and also of the special requirements as set by donors or invoked by legitimate authority. They are to collect the revenues of the goods diligently and at the proper times. These revenues, kept in a safe place, must be spent only according to the law and the regulations which determine the proper spending of these revenues. All records of expenditures and receipts must be kept in good order.[8]

Section 1. Investment

In virtue of canon 533, as applied to quasi-religious societies through canon 676, § 2, the following conclusions are justified. In the investment of money the particular constitutions are to be followed. However, in the following cases the consent of the local

---

[5] Cf. can. 532, §§ 1, 2.

[6] Blat, *De Religiosis,* pp. 245-246.

[7] Blat, *op. cit.*

[8] Can. 1532.

ordinary must also be obtained. The superioress of a society of quasi-religious of diocesan law needs the consent of the local ordinary for every investment of money. In a society of papal law the money of the dowry demanded by the constitutions, may not be invested without the consent of the ordinary.[9]

A superior or a superioress of any house of a society, whether the house be exempt or not exempt, cannot without the permission of the local ordinary invest the funds or property which have been donated or bequeathed to a house for the purpose of divine worship or for works of charity to be carried on in the same place.[10]

The worship of God mentioned in canon 533, § 1, n. 3, includes the offering of the Holy Sacrifice of the Mass and other functions and divine services carried on in a church. The works of charity and beneficence, similarly indicated in this canon refer especially to donations for the poor, for the teaching of children and for works of a similar nature. The funds and the property contemplated are those which are donated for use in a definite place as intended by the donor. The word *locus* in the law can signify a state, a town, a city, a parish or also a diocese. Larraona claims that the word *locus* in canon 533, § 1, n. 3, cannot be identified with an entire diocese. He feels that it must be referred to a smaller local unit such as a city or a town.[11]

If, then, the funds and the property were given for the purpose of divine worship or charity, but without any designation of a specific place or purpose, a superior of his own free choice may invest them, even though he use the income for the purpose of divine worship or charity in the place where the donation was made, and the permission of the local ordinary, as specified in canon 533, § 3, would not have to be secured.[12]

Moreover, it must be noted that in requiring the local ordinary's permission, canon 533, § 1, n. 3, mentions the investment made by a local superior. Schäfer, in commenting on this point, states that, if the investment is made by a provincial superior or by the

[9] Cans. 533, § 1, nn. 1, 2; 676, § 2.

[10] Can. 533, § 1, n. 3.

[11] "Commentarium Codicis,"—*CpR*, XIII (1932), 34; Schäfer, *De Religiosis*, p. 424.

[12] Blat, *De Religiosis*, pp. 248-249.

Superior General, the permission of the local ordinary is not required. Furthermore, if the funds and the property are donated to a province or to a society, the permission of the ordinary is not required, since the goods are then not to be considered as diocesan goods.[13]

No member of a quasi-religious society, whether superior or subject, whether exempt or not exempt, may without the permission of the local ordinary invest any money which was given to a parish or a mission, or to the member of the society for the benefit of the parish or mission.[14]

If the money is given to the rector of a church, it is presumed to be given for the church unless the contrary be proved.[15] Moreover, the rector of a church may not, without the permission of the local ordinary, refuse a donation for a church.[16]

Even though the prescriptions of canon 1536 do not explicitly advert to quasi-religious societies, nevertheless the canon seems to refer to all churches, regardless of the persons to whose direction they are subject. The canon states: Unless the contrary be proved, it is to be presumed that donations given to the rectors of churches, even the churches of religious institutes, are given to the church itself. Consequently, whether the status of a clerical quasi-religious society is strictly interpreted in the sense that its members belong to the secular clergy, or widely interpreted with the result that its members are regarded as pertaining to the class of religious, in all cases the prescriptions of this canon are applicable.

The missions which are mentioned in canon 533, § 1, n. 4, as the potential beneficiaries of charitable donations signify places which in concept are opposed to the notion of parishes. These missions are generally called quasi-parishes. A mission is, therefore, the particular territory which in a vicariate or a prefecture apostolic is under the care of a quasi-pastor. The local ordinary considered in canon 533, § 4, is the local ordinary of the place where the parish or the mission is located, and not the ordinary of the place where the money is to be deposited or invested.[17]

---

[13] *De Religiosis*, pp. 421-422.

[14] Can. 533, § 1, n. 4.

[15] Can. 1536, § 1.

[16] Can. 1536, § 2.

[17] Schäfer, *De Religiosis*, p. 426.

The permission of the local ordinary as required in the various situations discussed in canon 533 must be secured not only when the investment is first made, but whenever any change is made in the original investment. Moreover, a change in the place of investment also needs a new permission of the local ordinary.[18]

Larraona claims that the permission of the local ordinary as required in the various sections of canon 533 is postulated only for the lawfulness of the investments, and hence does not affect the validity of the investments.[19]

Section 2. Alienation

In virtue of canon 676, § 2, the provisions of canon 534 are applied to quasi-religious societies in the following manner. When there is question of the disposal of objects of value or of goods exceeding in value the sum of 30,000 francs ($6,000), or of contracting debts and assuming liabilities above the same amount, the contract is invalid unless the approval of the Holy See has first been obtained. For smaller amounts the written permission of the superior authorized by the constitutions is necessary but also suffices, provided that it be given with the consent of the council of the superior, manifested by a secret ballot.[20]

Alienation or the disposal of objects is in the canonical sense a transfer in whole or in part of proprietorship over property from one person to another. This alienation may be accomplished by sale, gift, trade, or other similar means.[21]

In addition to the prescriptions of canon 534, the prescriptions of canon 1531 must also be observed in the alienation of temporal goods. In accordance with the prescriptions of the latter canon, goods may not be disposed of for a lesser price than was stated in the appraisal of the experts; the sale must be made by public auction, or at least be publicly announced, unless the circumstances make a different course advisable; the goods must be sold to the one who, all things considered, offers the better price; and,

---

[18] Cf. can. 533, § 2; Blat, *De Religiosis*, p. 249.

[19] "Commentarium Codicis,"—*CpR*, XII (1931), 440, n. 518.

[20] Can. 534, § 1.

[21] Schäfer, *De Religiosis*, pp. 428-429.

finally, the money obtained must be placed in a safe and productive investment.

In the opinion of the authors an object is constituted as a valuable object in the sense of canon 534, § 1, when it is worth at least a thousand francs.[22]

The permission of the Holy See and of the lesser superiors mentioned in canon 534, § 1, are both required for the validity of the alienation. This is evident from the prescription of canon 1530, § 1, n. 3, wherein it is stated that the permission of the legitimate superiors must be had in acts of alienation; otherwise the acts are invalid.[23]

Furthermore, the consent of the council of the superior is required, otherwise the permission of the superior is invalid. Moreover, the consent of the council is to be secured by means of a secret ballot. This, in the opinion of Schäfer, is also a condition for validity. He claims that from the very context of the canon the manner of securing the consent of the council pertains to the essence of the consent. However, that the consent be given in writing is not required for the validity of the permission.[24]

For the alienation of temporal goods valued at less than 30,000 francs, when the alienation is to be effected by a diocesan quasi-religious society of women, there must also be secured the permission of the local ordinary, in addition to the permission of the superior designated by the constitutions.[25]

In the petition for consent to contract debts or to assume obligations, there must be mentioned the amount of the debts or obligations already resting on the society, the province, or the house for which the permission is requested. If this information is not furnished then the permission is invalid.[26]

Although alienation is not explicitly mentioned in canon 534, § 2, it likewise comes under the prescriptions of this canon, for in the parallel canon, 1532, § 4, it is stated that in the alienation

---

[22] Blat, *De Religiosis*, p. 254; Schäfer, *De Religiosis*, p. 431; Fanfani, *De Religiosis*, p. 177.

[23] Can. 1530, § 1, n. 3; Blat, *De Religiosis*, p. 255.

[24] *De Religiosis*, pp. 434-435; can. 105.

[25] Can. 534, § 1.

[26] Can. 534, § 2.

of divisible goods the parts which have been previously alienated must be mentioned, under pain of nullity, in the petition for the permission or consent.[27]

By reason of canon 2347 the following penalties are incurred by superiors of quasi-religious societies who violate the prescriptions of the commn law in the matter of the alienation of the temporal goods of these societies. In addition to the nullity of the act and the resulting obligation to make restitution of the goods unlawfully acquired, which is to be enforced even with censures, and over and above the obligations of also repairing whatever damage has been caused, the law enacts penalties for a person who presumes to alienate ecclesiastical goods or to give his consent thereto in violation of the prescripts of canons 534, § 1, and 1532. The following penal enactments obtain: if goods of not over 1,000 francs in value have been alienated, the offender shall be punished with appropriate penalties by the legitimate superior; if the goods are valued at more than 1,000 francs, then a religious superior, and by reason of the application of canon 534 to quasi-religious, also the latter's superior or econome, shall be deprived of his office and of eligibility to acquire any other office, in addition to other appropriate penalties; if the permission of the Holy See was knowingly omitted, all who are in any way guilty, either as givers or receivers of the goods, automatically incur an unreserved excommunication.[28]

The penalties of canon 2347 are certainly applicable to superiors and subjects of the societies of quasi-religious if they be guilty of the offenses penalized in the canon, for canon 2347 expressly mentions that its prescriptions extend to all those who violate the prescriptions of canon 534, § 1. By reason of the general norm set up in canon 676, § 2, canon 534, § 1, becomes applicable to the societies of quasi-religious.

Section 3. The Rendering of an Account of Administration

In virtue of canon 676, § 2, canon 535 applies in the following manner to quasi-religious societies. In all societies of women,

[27] Blat, *De Religiosis,* p. 256.

[28] Can. 2347, nn. 1-3.

whether of pontifical or of diocesan law, an account of the administration of the goods of the dowries must be made to the local ordinary. Obviously, this prescription would not apply to those societies whose constitutions do not demand a dowry. This accounting must be made, when a dowry is demanded by the constitutions, at the time of the episcopal visitation, or even more frequently if the ordinary considers it necessary.[29]

In all diocesan societies of men or women the local ordinary has the right to demand an account of the property administered by their individual houses.[30]

It is to be noted that the word *domus* is used in canon 535, § 3, n. 1. Consequently, the provisions of this canon gives no right of vigilance over the goods of a province, or of the society itself, unless the province or the society is restricted to only one diocese. If the society of diocesan law exists in several dioceses, the various local ordinaries in whose dioceses it has a house have the right of vigilance over the goods of the province and of the society itself, not singly but collectively.[31]

Moreover, the local ordinary has the right of demanding an account of the administration of the property given to any society, whether of men or women, even if it be exempt, for the purpose of divine worship or of charity in the same place, or for the support of a parish or a mission, whether the money was given directly to the parish or the mission itself, or to a member of the society for the support of a parish or a mission.[32]

From these prescriptions it follows that exempt societies and pontifically approved societies of men or women manage their own financial affairs and the property belonging to the society according to their constitutions without the obligation of making a report to the local ordinary, except, of course, for the few instances wherein the Code demands that even these types of societies report to the local ordinary, e.g., regarding dowries, donations for

---

[29] Cans. 535, § 2; 676, § 2.

[30] Can. 535, § 3, n. I.

[31] Larraona, "Commentarium Codicis,"—*CpR,* XIV (1933), 418; Schäfer, *De Religiosis,* p. 441.

[32] Cans. 533, § 1, nn. 3, 4; 535, § 3, n. 2.

worship and charity in a specified place, and donations for a parish or a mission.[33]

Canon 536 has the following application to quasi-religious societies in virtue of canon 676, § 2. If a society or a province or one of its houses has contracted a debt and assumed liabilities, even with the permission of the proper superiors, the respective moral body is liable for their satisfaction, and not the superior giving the permission.[34]

Section 4. Debts and Contracts

If a member of a society makes a debt, he himself is liable, unless he transacted a business of the society with the commission or the command of the proper superiors. If a member makes a contract without this permission, he is personally liable, and neither the society, nor the province, nor the house can be held responsible.[35]

In discussing the permission which is necessary for the making of a contract on the part of an individual religious, canon 536, § 3, indicates that he may not proceed without any permission (*sine ulla licentia*). Consequently, even a tacit or an implicit permission of the proper superior given to a member of a society to contract a debt would make the proper moral body responsible for the fulfillment of the contract, provided, of course, that the debt was contracted for the good of the society and not for the benefit of the individual member.[36] However, the general principle always holds that there is a right of action against him into whose possession something has come through the contract.[37] Therefore, whatever profit or gain either the society or the other contracting party has made by an illegal, but perhaps valid, contract, can be reclaimed by the injured party whenever the contract is repudiated or rescinded.[38]

---

[33] Woywod, *A Practical Commentary on the Code of Canon Law,* I, 205.
[34] Can. 536, § 1.
[35] Can. 536, §§ 2, 3.
[36] Schäfer, *De Religiosis,* p. 443.
[37] Can. 536, § 4.
[38] Blat, *De Religiosis,* p. 265.

In a final prescription, canon 536 warns superiors not to permit the contracting of debts unless it is certain that from the usual revenues the interest on the debt can be paid, and that in not too long a time the debt can be wiped out by legitimate payments.[39] The prescription of canon 1538, § 2, seems to indicate that the payment of debts should be taken care of by means of a sinking fund, that is, by the setting aside of a certain amount of money each year for that specific purpose. Moreover, canon 1529 canonizes the civil law with regard to its decrees on contracts and payments of all kinds, exclusive however of any decree or statute that runs counter to the divine law or the canon law. Consequently, quasi-religious societies are obliged to observe the civil law with regard to the making of contracts and the payment of all kinds of debts, except in cases in which the civil law is contrary to the divine law or the canon law.

Section 5. Donations

Canon 537 is applicable to quasi-religious societies in virtue of canon 676, § 2. Therefore the following conclusions are warranted. The making of donations from the goods of a house, a province or a society is not permitted except in the nature of alms or for other just reasons. Moreover, the permission of the proper superior must be obtained, and all the particular prescriptions of the constitutions concerning the bestowal of donations must be observed.

A donation is a transfer of goods apart from the accrual of any material benefit to the donor. Just causes other than the giving of alms may make it allowable for a society of quasi-religious to give donations. Such causes can arise by reason of the demands inherent in the due and proper exercise of the Christian virtues of benevolence, generosity, liberality, piety and charity.[40]

Section 6. Leases

It is the opinion of Larraona that the leasing of goods which belong to religious institutes is to be considered an act of ordinary

[39] Can. 536, § 5.

[40] Blat, *De Religiosis*, p. 267; can. 1535.

or extraordinary administration according to the lower or higher value of the goods concerned. Furthermore, it rests with the proper superior, as designated by the constitutions, to determine whether or not an act of administration is ordinary or extraordinary. Accordingly, he draws the following conclusions concerning the action of the institute in the leasing of its goods.

If the value of the lease exceeds 30,000 francs and the term of the lease extends for a period of more than nine years, there is required the approval of the Holy See. All other negotiated acts of lease can be considered as either ordinary or extraordinary acts of administration, depending on the lower or the higher value of the goods in question. Consequently, in all such cases the requisite and proper manner of procedure is to be determined by the particular laws of each institute.[41]

ARTICLE III. THE ADMINISTRATION OF GOODS ON THE PART OF THE MEMBERS OF QUASI-RELIGIOUS SOCIETIES

In accordance with the prescriptions of canon 676, § 3, whatever a member of a quasi-religious society acquires as a member (*intuitu societatis*) belongs to the society. With regard to all other goods the members may retain, acquire and administer them in accordance with the prescriptions of the individual constitutions.

The clause *"quidquid sodalibus obvenit intuitu societatis"* refers to the goods which accrue from the labors and administrations of the members of a society, or the goods given by a donor whose will, either expressed in words or deduced from circumstances, is that the goods be devoted to the ends of the society.

It is to be carefully noted that in canon 676, § 3, there is no statement to imply that goods acquired by the members of a society through their private personal activity (*industria sua*) likewise belongs to the society. Such a clause appears in canon 580, § 2, the

[41] "Commentarium Codicis,"—*CpR*, XII (1931), 357, note 482. Since quasi-religious societies by virtue of canon 676, § 2, follow the same general norms as religious institutes in the administration of property, it seems to the writer that this opinion of Larraona may be applied to the former; Schäfer, *De Religiosis*, p. 429, note 111.

parallel canon for religious, wherein it is stated that whatever a religious earns "*industria sua*" pertains to the religious institute.[42]

Consequently, all goods coming to a member of a quasi-religious society, either by heredity, through gifts, through private personal activity, or by any other such means, belong to the member, and he accordingly has a right to the proprietorship, the administration, the use, and the income accruing from these goods, in accordance with the prescriptions of the constitutions of the society. The constitutions may produce a set of regulations more or less in conformity with the practices of the vow of poverty as professed in a religious institute. They may validly demand that all the income derived from the private personal industry of the members be given to the society, or that the subject must dispose of the administration of all his property prior to his incorporation in the society, by ceding this administration either to a third party or to the society itself.[43]

The Sacred Congregation of Religious on March 16, 1922, declared that any pension received by the members of these societies for injuries or disabilities suffered during the war pertained to the members of quasi-religious societies, but that it was to be turned over to the society as long as the members remained in the society.[44]

There is no obligation on the part of quasi-religious societies to have a novitiate for the aspirants to their societies. Consequently, the legislation of the Code concerning the administration of the personal property of novices does not apply to the novices of such societies which actually do possess the institution of a novitiate. Accordingly, the novices of the societies of quasi-religious have no obligation from the Code to dispose by way of a last will or testament, of the goods which they possess or may possess in the future. This obligation is placed upon the novices of religious institutes by the prescription of canon 569, § 3. The particular constitutions of quasi-religious societies must determine this matter for their novices.

Furthermore, novices of quasi-religious societies may, if their constitutions do not deny them the right, administer their goods

[42] Berutti, *De Religiosis*, p. 369.

[43] Cocchi, *De Religiosis*, n. 163; Vermeersch-Creusen, *Epitome*, I, n. 677.

[44] *AAS*, XIV, (1922), 197.

and impose obligations on them during their stay in the novitiate. They are not obliged, except in as far as the constitutions actually demand it, to cede the administration of their temporal goods to anyone, or to dispose of the use and income of these goods prior to their incorporation in the society. These obligations bind, indeed, the novices of religious institutes; but by the law of the Code no similar obligations are binding on the novices in quasi-religious societies.[45]

[45] Cf. cans. 568; 569, § 1; Schäfer, *De Religiosis*, pp. 555-556.

CHAPTER VIII

Profession, Studies and Ordination of Members of Quasi-Religious Societies

Article I. The Admission of Members into Quasi-Religious Societies

Canon 677 in a few general words treats the entire field of the admission of members into quasi-religious societies. In accordance with the prescription of that canon, the admission into quasi-religious societies is governed entirely by the particular constitutions of each society, subject, however, to the laws of canon 542 on the valid and licit admission of candidates.[1]

Anyone who would be invalidly or illicitly received into a religious Order or congregation, in view of any of the impediments enumerated in canon 542, would likewise be invalidly or illicitly received into a quasi-religious society. With the exception of the prescriptions of canon 542, whatever the common law prescribes concerning postulancy, testimonial letters, the novitiate, dowries, or temporary profession before a perpetual profession, is to be observed only if and insofar as these regulations are contained in the individual constitutions of each society. Therefore it follows that if the constitutions do not demand a period of probation, one may be immediately admitted to a quasi-religious society without undergoing any probation whatsoever.[2]

It cannot be argued that, by reason of the norm enacted in canon 20, the prescriptions of the common law regulating the novitiate, the postulancy and the admission of candidates as specified for religious institutes, should be applied to quasi-religious societies. The fact is that in these points there is no lack of laws that needs to be supplied. Indeed the extant laws are present in

---

[1] Canon 677: In admittendis candidatis serventur constitutiones, salvo praescripto can. 542.

[2] Berutti, *De Religiosis,* p. 369.

the various constitutions of each society, for in a very definite manner canon 677 points to these particular laws as the exclusive norms apart from the law contained in canon 542.[3]

As Cocchi notes, the candidates for admission to quasi-religious societies are not required by the common law to make an eight day retreat before their admission, as is demanded of aspirants to the religious life by canon 541. Nor are the prescriptions of canon 544, concerning the testimonial letters to be furnished by aspirants to the religious life, binding on persons who seek membership in quasi-religious societies. The duration and the type of the novitiate are to be governed entirely by the constitutions of each society, unless in this respect the Holy See has issued particular regulations for a certain society.[4]

In accordance with the prescriptions of canon 542, as applied to quasi-religious societies in virtue of canon 677, the following are *invalidly* received into a quasi-religious society.

A). Those who have adhered to a non-Catholic sect. Maroto claims that even though the term "non-Catholic" generally refers only to apostates, heretics and schismatics, nevertheless in canon 542 it seems rather to be used in a wide sense as including all those who profess not to be Catholics, regardless of the reception or non-reception of baptism in their lives.[5]

The Pontifical Commission for the Authentic Interpretation of the Canons of the Code on October 6, 1919, declared that the words "qui sectae acatholicae adhaeserunt" of canon 542 do not include those who were converted from heresy or schism in which they had been born, but only those who had fallen away from the faith and had joined a non-Catholic sect.[6]

B). Those who have not completed their fifteenth year, computed according to the norms of canon 34, § 3, n. 3, whereby, if the hour of birth was not coincident with the beginning of the

[3] Goyeneche, "Consultationes,"—*CpR,* IV (1923), 340; Schäfer *De Religiosis,* p. 1032; Fanfani, *De Religiosis,* p. 529.

[4] *De Religiosis,* n. 164, a)-c).

[5] "Annotationes,"—*CpR,* I (1920), 161; Larraona, "Commentarium Codicis,"—*CpR,* XVI (1935), 430; Schäfer, *De Religiosis,* p. 464.

[6] *AAS,* XI (1919), 477.

day, this day is not counted, and the fifteenth year is not completed until the end of the fifteenth birthday anniversary.[7]

C.) Those who are compelled to enter the society by grave fear, by deceit, or by force; or those who are received by a superior who admits them only because of such influences.

D). Married persons for the duration of the marriage. However, if the marriage has been dissolved, even by a dispensation, the impediment no longer exists.[8]

E). Those who have been professed members of another religious organization. However, if one was formerly enrolled in a quasi-religious society, he may, without a papal rescript, enter another quasi-religious society of a religious institute.[9]

F). Those who are subject to penalty for grave crimes of which they have been or can be accused. The person may be subject to such penalty either under the civil or under the ecclesiastical law, but the potential infliction of the penalty must exist as something imminent. Moreover, he must actually have committed the crime of which he is accused, or of which he is about to be accused.[10]

G). Either residential or titular bishops, even though they have not yet been consecrated.

H). Clerics who according to an ordinance of the Holy See are bound by oath to serve their diocese or mission, for such time as the obligation of the oath remains.[11]

The following are *illicitly* received into quasi-religious societies.

A). Clerics in sacred orders, without the knowledge of their local ordinary or against his will if his objection is based on the serious loss to souls that their withdrawal would impart, when that loss cannot by any means be otherwise avoided. The bishop has the sole right to make this judgment, though the cleric may seek redress against the decision by way of recourse to the Holy See. Pending the recourse, the Bishop's ruling would stand.[12]

---

[7] Schäfer, *De Religiosis,* p. 466.

[8] Vermeersch-Creusen, *Epitome,* I, n. 530.

[9] Goyeneche, "Consultationes,"—*CpR,* I (1920), 178; Schäfer, *De Religiosis,* pp. 471, 1037; Beste, *Introductio in Codicem,* p. 360; Berutti, *De Religiosis,* p. 500; Vermeersch-Creusen, *Epitome,* I, n. 682.

[10] Vermeersch-Creusen, *Epitome,* I, n. 532.

[11] Can. 542, n. 1.

[12] Vermeersch-Creusen, *Epitome,* I, n. 536.

B). Those who have debts to pay and cannot pay them.

C). Persons who are under an obligation of giving an account, e.g., those who have positions of trust, or those who are implicated in other secular affairs which might involve the society in lawsuits or other annoyances.

D). Children whose parents or grandparents are in great want and in need of help and who, unless they receive the help of their children or grandchildren, will suffer hardships. Likewise parents whose aid is needed for the education and the support of their children.

E). Candidates for the priesthood who suffer some irregularity or other canonical impediment. If the irregularity or the impediment will cease before the actual time of ordination, the candidate may be received.[13]

F). Catholics of an Oriental Rite who are received into a society of the Latin Rite without the written permission of the Sacred Congregation for the Oriental Church. The Pontifical Commission for the Authentic Interpretation of the Canons of the Code declared on November 10, 1925, that an Oriental may be received into a novitiate of a religious institute of the Latin Rite, provided that he retain his own Rite, and provided that the purpose of his entrance be to establish later on a house or a province of that institute in the Oriental Rite.[14]

Although the response of the Commission was explicitly intended for religious institutes, it may likewise be applied to quasi-religious societies. It was an authentic interpretation of canon 542, n. 2. Therefore its import should extend to all those who are subject to the prescriptions of the canon itself. Quasi-religious societies, in virtue of canon 677, are bound by the prescriptions of canon 542 and consequently must, like religious institutes, abide by the interpretation furnished in the Commission's response.

If in the approved constitutions of any society there are enacted additional requirements for a valid or licit admission, these conditions retain their force, provided that they set down requirements

[13] Blat, *De Religiosis*, pp. 290-291; Vermeersch-Creusen, *Epitome*, I, n. 540; Schäfer, *De Religiosis*, p. 482; Larraona, "Commentarium Codicis,"—*CpR*, XVIII (1937), 150.

[14] *AAS*, XVII (1925), 583; can. 542, n. 2.

over and above (praeter) the prescriptions of canon 542. If, however, they are contrary to these prescriptions they are invalid.[15]

The Pontifical Commission for the Authentic Interpretation of the Canons of the Code on June 3, 1918, declared that the prescriptions of canon 2411, whereby superiors who accept candidates contrary to the regulations of canon 542 are to be gravely punished, even with the deprivation of office, are to be applied to the superiors of quasi-religious societies.[16]

However, canon 2352, which states that all who force anyone to enter a religious institute are automatically excommunicated, does not apply in the case of one forced to enter a quasi-religious society. This conclusion is in accordance with the prescription of canon 2219, § 3, namely that a penalty is not to be extended from person to person nor from one case to another, though there is the same or even a greater reason for holding a person guilty.[17]

Section 1. Military Service

The Sacred Congregation of Religious on January 1, 1911, issued the decree *"Inter reliquas."* This decree contained legislation for those in religious institutes who are subject to military service.[18]

Number IX of this decree applied its legislation to the quasi-religious societies in which simple promises were pronounced as binding the members to the respective societies.[19]

Although the only quasi-religious societies explicitly mentioned in the decree were those societies in which simple promises were taken, there seems to be no reason why only one type of these societies should be included within the scope of the decree. Consequently, it seems justifiable to apply the principles of canon 18 and extend the prescriptions of the decree to all quasi-religious societies. For otherwise there would exist no regulations to provide for similar cases in these other classes of quasi-religious societies.

---

[15] Schäfer, *De Religiosis*, p. 107; can. 6, n. 1.

[16] *AAS*, X (1918), 347.

[17] Ayrinhac, *Penal Legislation in the New Code of Canon Law* (revised ed., New York: Benziger Bros., 1936), p. 246; Blat, *De Religiosis*, p. 290.

[18] *AAS*, III (1911), 37.

[19] *AAS*, III (1911), 39.

The Sacred Congregation of Religious on July 15, 1919, stated that the prescriptions of the decree "*Inter reliquas*" were still to be observed after the promulgation of the Code. However, certain norms were laid down, explaining in greater detail the legislation governing the cases of profession as provided for in the decree of 1911.[20]

The legislation comprised in the original decree of 1911 together with the clarification of 1919 in so far as quasi-religious societies are affected is as follows. If novices of a quasi-religious society in which perpetual bonds are pronounced are subject to military service, then after the completion of their novitiate they are to pronounce temporary bonds effective until the day they enter military service and thus become subject to military discipline, or until the day they are absolutely declared unfit for military service.

During the time of military service the member of the society, although not bound by his promise, or by any other form of bond, still continues to be a member of the society, under the authority of his superiors, who should take care of him by frequently writing to him, and by arranging for him to visit frequently some house of the society or, if this is impossible, at least by insisting he regularly visit some priest from whom the superior may receive testimonials of the virtue and life of the member during his military service.[21]

When the member is definitely dismissed from the army, he must immediately return to his proper house. If his conduct has been satisfactory, he may pronounce temporary promises, or any other form of temporary bond, for at least one year. The time of temporary profession is to be counted from his first profession, excluding the time spent in military service.

The original decree of 1911 declared that, if during the time of service or at any time before final profession the member showed any signs of faltering, the Superior General with the consent of his council could dismiss him. However, as is stated by Sweeney,

---

[20] *AAS*, XI (1919), 322.

[21] However, according to canon 637, a member may freely leave the society whenever he so wishes.

this procedure is supplanted by canon 637, so that the response of 1919, after referring to canon 637, accordingly declares that the society may, for just and reasonable causes, declare the subject dismissed.[22] The word *"dismissal,"* as used in the response of 1919, is, in the opinion of Coronata, a reference to the exclusion from profession and is used in the broad sense. He draws this conclusion from the fact that the response of 1919 refers to canon 637 which concerns exclusion from profession.[23]

The procedure to be observed in the case of voluntary departure from the society, as expressed in the original decree of 1911, has been changed by reason of the prescriptions of canon 637 and the response of 1919. For the response declares that the subject is not bound by his vows when he enters the service, consequently there would be no need of a dispensation from vows, in case of a voluntary withdrawal from the society, and canon 637 states that a person can freely withdraw from a religious institute on the completion of the period of temporary profession.[24]

Section 2. Incorporation and the Proper Diocese

According to the prescriptions of canon 585, a perpetually professed religious by the very action of the law itself in view of the act of profession loses the proper diocese which he had in the world. However, this canon applies only to religious properly so called. Consequently it does not apply to members of quasi-religious societies, even though some of these societies do have a form of perpetual profession.

Goyeneche claims that one cannot appeal to canon 20 in order to make the prescription of canon 585 applicable to those quasi-religious societies which have a form of perpetual profession. He argues that canon 115 specifically states that a person is excardinated from his proper diocese through the kind of religious

[22] *The Reduction of Clerics to the Lay State,* the Catholic University of America Canon Law Studies, n. 223 (Washington, D. C.: The Catholic University of America Press, 1945), p. 84.

[23] *Institutiones,* I, 773.

[24] Sweeney, *The Reduction of Clerics to the Lay State,* pp. 84-85; Bouscaren, *The Canon Law Digest* (2 vols., Milwaukee: Bruce, 1934, 1943), I, 106-108.

profession that is specified in canon 585. To employ analogy with a view to increasing the cases of excardination would be contrary to the Code. Therefore, he continues, it is not permissible to make use of canon 20 in an attempt to apply its prescriptions to quasi-religious societies.

Accordingly, the members of quasi-religious societies, even though they make a perpetual profession, never lose the proper diocese they had in the world. Goyeneche further states that while the Code was in preparation there were many requests that canon 585 be extended to include the members of quasi-religious societies, but that these requests were always refused.[25]

Section 3. The Profession of Members of Quasi-Religious Societies in Danger of Death

The Sacred Congregation of Religious on December 30, 1922, declared that the novices of religious institutes, as well as the aspirants to membership in quasi-religious societies, who are gravely ill and considered to be in extreme danger of death, may make their profession or incorporation, according to the constitutions of the institute or society, even though they have not completed the time of their novitiate or probation.[26]

Before the privilege of profession in danger of death may be used, the following conditions must be satisfied. The candidate must have at least begun his canonical year of the novitiate, or the actual period of probation in a society which does not have a novitiate. The profession must be received either by the major superiors who under the prescriptions of the constitutions are competent to accept the profession or the act of incorporation or by any one who is actually ruling the house where the novitiate is located as a delegate of the aforesaid superiors. The formula of profession as used by the society must be employed in this profession or incorporation without any mention of time or per-

[25] "Consultationes,"—*CpR,* I (1920), 177; Cocchi, *De Religiosis,* n. 165 b; Schäfer, *De Religiosis,* p. 1032; Piontek, *De Indulto Exclaustrationis necnon Saecularizationis,* The Catholic University of America Canon Law Studies, n. 29 (Washington, D. C.: The Catholic University of America, 1925), p. 224.

[26] *AAS,* XV (1923), 157.

petuity. The only effect of this profession or incorporation is to entitle the novice to all the indulgences, suffrages and graces which ordinarily are granted by reason of a profession or incorporation.

Consequently, if the member thus professed or incorporated should die, the society cannot claim any of his goods or rights. Moreover, if the person thus incorporated should recover, he must return to the same position in which he was before the profession or incorporation was made. Therefore he is perfectly free to leave the society whenever he so desires, and he may be dismissed just as any other novice or aspirant. He must, likewise, complete the entire period of the novitiate and, following the completion of the novitiate, he must make a new profession or incorporation.[27]

Section 4. The Effects of the Incorporation of Members into Quasi-Religious Societies

As a result of incorporation into a quasi-religious society, a member is expected to live his life in common with the rest and in conformity with the constitutions of his society. In this regard the Pontifical Commission for the Authentic Interpretation of the Canons of the Code on June 3, 1918, declared that the prescriptions of canon 2389 should be applied to clerical quasi-religious societies if their members live a common life. Canon 2389 states that if a member of a religious institute—and by application of the response, also a member of a society—should seriously fail in the observance of the common life as prescribed in the constitutions of his institute or society, he should be admonished, and that, if he should fail to amend his ways, he should be punished even by privation of vote and eligibility for office and, in the case of a superior of office itself.[28]

Finally, it should be noted that one does not automatically lose any previously held ecclesiastical office by reason of an incorporation into a quasi-religious society. Canon 188, n. 1, states that any ecclesiastical office is tacitly and automatically renounced if a cleric should make a religious profession. However, the incorpora-

---

[27] Schäfer, *De Religiosis,* pp. 561-562.

[28] *AAS,* X (1918), 347.

tion into a quasi-religious society is not a religious profession properly so called because such a profession demands the pronouncing of public vows. Public vows are never pronounced in a quasi-religious society.

ARTICLE II. THE ARRANGEMENT OF STUDIES AND THE ORDINATION OF MEMBERS OF QUASI-RELIGIOUS SOCIETIES

Canon 678 states: In those things which pertain to the arrangement of studies and the ordination of members of quasi-religious societies, the norms established by the common law for secular aspirants are to be applied, in addition to the particular prescripts given each society by the Holy See.

Quasi-religious societies are not obliged to observe the prescripts of canon 587 and 588, which determine the arrangement of studies for the clerical members of religious institutes. However, if the particular constitutions of a quasi-religious society should incorporate the prescriptions of these canons in providing for the studies of its own members, these prescriptions would then have to be observed.[29]

Consequently, no clerical quasi-religious society, nor any province of such a society, is obliged to have its own proper house of studies. When a proper house of studies is lacking, these societies may send their members to a house of studies of another society or of a religious institute, to a diocesan seminary, or to a Catholic university.[30] However, the course in theology cannot be taken privately. It must be pursued in a school destined for that purpose in accordance with the prescriptions of canon 1365.[31]

The course of philosophy, together with other allied subjects, must be pursued by the members of quasi-religious societies for two complete years. The course in theology must last at least four full years. Besides dogmatic and moral theology, the course must include sacred scripture, canon law, liturgy, sacred eloquence, ecclesiastical chant and lectures on pastoral theology, with particular stress placed on the methods of teaching catechism to the children,

---

[29] Schäfer, *De Religiosis*, pp. 632, 1032; Cocchi, *De Religiosis*, n. 165 (a).
[30] Berutti, *De Religiosis*, p. 370.
[31] Can. 976, § 3.

the hearing of confessions, the visiting of the sick, and the care of the dying.[32]

Throughout the course of their studies the members of quasi-religious societies are to receive the various minor and major orders in accordance with the prescriptions of the common law.

No member is to be admitted to first tonsure before he has begun his course in theology. Subdeaconship may not be conferred until the latter part of the third year of theology; deaconship may be received only at the commencement of the fourth year of theology, while priesthood must be deferred until the first semester of the fourth year is completed.[33]

In addition to the prescriptions just mentioned, the following norms concerning the age of the candidate must be observed. Subdeaconship cannot be conferred until the completion of the twenty-first year of age; deaconship, until the completion of the twenty-second year, and priesthood until the completion of the twenty-fourth year.[34]

The various orders must be received in proper succession so that the omission of any is absolutely forbidden.[35]

Furthermore, certain intervals of time must be observed between the reception of the various orders. The intervals between the first tonsure and the first of the minor orders, and between the individual minor orders, are left to the prudent judgment of the bishop. Unless in the opinion of the bishop necessity demands otherwise, there must be at least one year's interval between the last minor order and subdeaconship, and at least three months between subdeaconship and deaconship as also between deaconship and priesthood. Without special permission of the Roman Pontiff, minor orders and subdeaconship, or two major orders, cannot be conferred on the same day. Nor is it lawful to confer tonsure together with one minor order, or also all of the minor orders, on one and the same day.[36]

After the completion of their studies, the priest members of quasi-religious societies must undergo each year for three years an

---

[32] Can. 1365.

[33] Can. 976, §§ 1, 2.

[34] Can. 975.

[35] Can. 977.

[36] Can. 978, §§ 1-3.

examination in the various branches of the sacred sciences, designated and announced a sufficient length of time before the date of the examination.[37]

In accordance with the prescriptions of canon 590, priest members of religious institutes must undergo this examination for five years.

The constitutions of a clerical quasi-religious society may demand a longer period for these examinations, and they may also determine what members of a society are excused from the necessity of taking these examinations.

The Sacred Consistorial Congregation on April 30, 1918, issued the decree *"Nemo de clero."* This decree laid down certain regulations concerning clerics who pursued various studies in secular universities. It stressed the fact that clerics generally should not attend these institutions, and if it was deemed necessary that they attend them, proper permission had to be secured from the local ordinary or proper superiors. Moreover, priests attending these institutions were not only obliged to take the prescribed junior clergy examinations for the first three years of their priesthood, but in addition they were to be subjected to a stricter examination, lest their interest in theological studies should become weakened because of their interest in their secular studies.[38]

The articles of this decree were made binding on both secular and religious priests. Consequently, whether priest members of quasi-religious societies be strictly considered as secular priests, or broadly considered as religious, in either case they are subject to the prescriptions of this decree.[39]

Quasi-religious clerical societies are not obliged, as are clerical religious institutes, to hold monthly discussions on moral and liturgical subjects. However, if their own constitutions do not contain prescriptions concerning regular discussions on these subjects, the members of the society must then attend the diocesan conferences provided for by the prescriptions of canon 131, § 1.[40]

Priests who in violation of the prescriptions of canon 131, § 1,

---

[37] Vermeersch-Creusen, *Epitome,* I, n. 679; Cocchi, *De Religiosis,* n. 165.

[38] *AAS,* X (1918), 237; Blat, *De Religiosis,* p. 431.

[39] Blat, *loc. cit.*

[40] Schäfer, *De Religiosis,* p. 1032; Vermeersch-Creusen, *Epitome,* I, n. 679.

stubbornly refuse to attend the diocesan conferences should be punished at the discretion of the ordinary.[41] If members of quasi-religious societies which do not have their own conferences fail to attend the diocesan conferences in accordance with the prescriptions of canon 131, § 1, they become subject to the penalties enacted in canon 2377.[42]

Canon 678 states that quasi-religious societies are subject to any particular prescriptions of the Holy See concerning the matter of studies and ordination. The Sacred Congregation of Religious on December 1, 1931, issued the instruction *"Quantum religiones omnes ac societates."* It is specifically mentioned in various numbers of the instruction that quasi-religious societies are included within the scope of the instruction.[43]

This instruction is concerned with the training of members for the priesthood and the testing of their vocation before the reception of orders. The provisions of the instruction place on superiors the obligation of securing from novices before their first profession or incorporation a written petition expressing their conviction that they have a vocation to the clerical state. The petition should also state their firm resolve to give themselves forever to the clerical state in the common life. Superiors are likewise warned that no member should be allowed to receive any major order before perpetual religious profession or incorporation. In a quasi-religious society the members are forbidden to be promoted to major orders before they have made their perpetual promise to remain in the society, provided, of course, that the society is one whose constitutions provide for this perpetual choice. If, on the other hand, the constitutions do not prescribe a perpetual choice, the superiors may not allow any member to receive major orders before the expiration of three full years from the time of their first reception into the society following the period of novitate or probation.

Before their promotion to the subdiaconate, an inquiry into their intention to remain forever in the ranks of the clergy must again be made. Moreover, before the reception of the subdiaconate the candidates must sign a declaration in their own handwriting and

---

[41] Can. 2377.

[42] Berutti, *De Religiosis,* p. 370.

[43] *AAS,* XXIV (1932), 74-81; Schäfer, *De Religiosis,* pp. 842-848.

in the presence of the superior, attesting the fact that they are receiving the order freely and with the desire of promotion to the subdiaconate, with full knowledge of the obligations involved, especially concerning the obligations of chastity and celibacy, and finally, that they embrace unqualified subjection to the authority of their superiors.[44]

Section 1. Prerequisites for the Reception of Orders

In accordance with the prescriptions of canon 992, all members of quasi-religious societies who are candidates for ordination must in good time, either in person or through another, manifest either to the bishop or to his representative a desire to be ordained.[45]

They must likewise procure the following testimonials:

1) Testimony of the last ordination conferred on them or, if they are to receive first tonsure, certificates of baptism and confirmation.

2) Testimony of the completion of the required courses of study as demanded for the various orders by canon 976.[46]

3) Testimony of the rector of the seminary as to their good conduct. If, in an exceptional case, a candidate has been permitted to live outside a seminary, the priest to whose care the seminarian was entrusted must, in accordance with the prescriptions of canon 972, § 2, submit this testimony of good conduct. Furthermore, in accordance with the prescriptions of canon 1000, § 1, the pastor who publishes the name of the candidate who is to receive major orders must likewise be questioned as to the morals of the candidate.[47]

4) Testimonials from the ordinaries of the dioceses in which the candidate has lived for six months after the age of puberty, or for three months while in military service.[48]

5) Testimonial letters of the major superior of the society.[49]

---

[44] Schäfer, *loc. cit.*

[45] Can. 992.

[46] Cf. *supra*, p. 194; can. 993, n. 1.

[47] Cans. 972, §§ 2, 3; 993, n. 2; 1,000 § 1.

[48] Cans. 993, n. 4; 994, § 1.

[49] Can. 993, n. 5.

If the local superior spoken of in n. 4 cannot testify as to whether or not the candidate has incurred an impediment during his stay in that particular diocese, the ordinary must require the candidate to state under oath whether or not he has incurred an impediment while in the diocese.[50]

Candidates for ordination must undergo an examination with reference to the orders which they are to receive. Moreover, candidates for major orders must be examined in the other tracts of theology which are required before the reception of the various major orders. A bishop who ordains candidates who are sent to him with dimissorial letters may accept the testimony of the proper superior that these examinations were successfully passed or he may himself examine the candidates.[51]

The name of the candidate to receive major orders must be announced publicly in the parish church of the candidate.[52]

However, if the society has been given the privilege of issuing dimissorial letters for major orders, then, in the opinion of the authors, the ordinations of its candidates are to be governed by the prescriptions regulating the ordination of religious. Consequently, the names of the candidates for major orders belonging to societies possessing this privilege need not be announced.[53]

Stanton (✠ 1941) states that if dimissorial letters for major orders are given by the superiors of quasi-religious societies, then in accordance with canon 995, § 2, the ordaining bishop needs no other testimonial letters. This provision, he asserts, excludes the necessity of the pastor's announcing the names of the members of these societies who are to receive major orders, since by the prescription of canon 1000, § 1, the purpose of these announcements is the testimonial which the pastor making them is to communicate to the ordinary.[54]

---

[50] Can. 994, § 2.

[51] Cans. 996-997.

[52] Can. 998; Vermeersch-Creusen, *Epitome,* I, n. 679.

[53] Schäfer, *De Religiosis,* p. 1033; McBride, *Incardination and Excardination of Seculars,* The Catholic University of America Canon Law Studies, n. 145 (Washington, D. C.: The Catholic University of America Press, 1941), p. 343; Berutti, *De Religiosis,* p. 370.

[54] *De Societatibus,* p. 137.

Candidates for first tonsure must make a spiritual retreat for at least three full days prior to the reception of tonsure; candidates for major orders, for at least six full days. If the candidates are to receive several major orders within six months, the ordinary may reduce the number of the days of the retreat before deaconship to not less than three full days. If after the retreat the ordination is delayed for more than six months, it is left to the judgment of the ordinary whether or not the retreat is to be repeated.[55]

If a society has not the right of issuing dimissorial letters, then the proper local ordinary of each candidate is to be consulted concerning the retreat. Moreover, the local ordinary who should conduct the requisite examination should also be the proper ordinary of each candidate. If the society does have the privilege of issuing dimissorial letters, it seems that the local ordinary of the place where the house of the candidates is located may reduce the period required for retreat in accordance with canon 1001. Finally, in an exempt society the ordinary would be the major superior.[56]

The conclusions just stated concerning the determination of the proper ordinary were deduced from the principle already stated, namely, that if a society has the privilege of issuing dimissorial letters for major orders, its candidates are to be governed by the prescriptions regulating the ordinations of religious.[57]

It will be noted that the various prescriptions applied in this article with regard to the ordination and studies of quasi-religious are the prescriptions of the common law determining the ordinations and studies of secular clerics. This conclusion is justified by the prescription of canon 678, which states that in those things which pertain to the arrangement of study and ordinations, members of clerical quasi-religious societies are held to the same norms as secular aspirants to the priesthood.

Section 2. The Proper Bishop for Ordination

In accordance with the prescriptions of canon 955, everyone is to be ordained by his proper bishop, or with the dimissorial letters of the latter. The proper bishop for ordination, in accordance with

[55] Can. 1001, §§ 1, 2.

[56] Schäfer, *De Religiosis*, p. 837.

[57] Cf. *supra*, pp. 198, 205.

the prescription of canon 956, is the bishop of the diocese in which the candidate has his domicile and place of origin, or simply his domicile. In the latter case, however, the candidate must declare under oath his intention of remaining permanently in the diocese, except in those cases mentioned in canon 956.[58]

According to the prescriptions of canon 585, perpetually professed religious lose their proper diocese which they had in the world. However, quasi-religious societies, even though they may have a form of perpetual profession, are not included within the scope of this canon. Consequently, their members never lose their diocese which they had in the world prior to their incorporation in the society.[59]

Moeder states that even if a member of a quasi-religious society has pronounced perpetual promises, he does not lose his proper diocese which he had in the world. Furthermore, it cannot be said that by virtue of canon 111, § 1, the members of these societies are incardinated in or became affiliated with their respective societies by the reception of first tonsure. The prescription of canon 111, § 1, applies only to religious properly so called. Consequently, after their reception of first tonsure the members of quasi-religious societies belong to the bishop of the proper diocese they possessed previous to its reception, and it is the right of this bishop to ordain them or to issue the dimissorial letters for their ordination. It could be said that in a certain sense the proper bishop loans them to the respective societies.[60]

Therefore, in determining the proper bishop for the ordination of the members of quasi-religious societies one must hold to the norm enacted in canon 956. Accordingly, members of these societies who are candidates for ordination must be ordained by the bishop of the diocese they had prior to their entrance into the society. If

---

[58] Can. 955.

[59] Cf. *supra,* pp. 190-191; Vermeersch-Creusen, *Epitome,* I, n. 679; McBride. *Incardination and Excardination of Seculars,* p. 344; Berutti, *De Religiosis,* p. 370; Cocchi, *De Religiosis,* n. 165, b); Schäfer, *De Religiosis,* p. 1033; Beste, *Introductio in Codicem,* p. 456.

[60] *The Proper Bishop for Ordination and Dimissorial Letters,* The Catholic University of America Canon Law Studies, n. 95 (Washington, D. C.: The Catholic University of America, 1935), pp. 113-114.

they are ordained by any other bishop, they must receive dimissorial letters from their proper bishop.[61]

As was previously affirmed, the proper bishop of ordination in accordance with canon 956 is the ordinary of the diocese in which the candidate has his domicile and place of origin, or simply his domicile. In the latter case an oath of remaining in the diocese must be taken. McBride, in discussing this obligation, mentions the prescription of canon 956, which states that the oath of remaining in the diocese need not be taken if, in accordance with canon 964, n. 4, the ordination involved is that of religious who are not exempt and who must follow the rules for the ordination of seculars. He concludes that quasi-religious societies are, for all practical purposes, religious following the rules for the ordination of seculars, and therefore fall under the exemption of canon 964, n. 4. Consequently, if the candidates of these societies have only a diocesan domicile which is not at the same time identified with their place of origin, they need not take an oath of remaining in the diocese.[62]

The writer favors the opinion of McBride. Under any contrary view there would occur the impractical situation whereby a member of a quasi-religious society would be required to take an oath of remaining in a diocese and at the same time be subject to superiors who are empowered by the constitutions to send him to any diocese in which the society might have an establishment.

In cases in which dimissorial letters are issued by the superiors of quasi-religious societies, the bishop who has the right of conferring ordination is determined by canon 965.[63]

Canon 965 sets the norm relative to the ordination of religious. With the application of the prescriptions of this canon to the quasi-religious societies in which the proper superior has the privilege of issuing dimissorial letters, the following conclusions are warranted. The letters are to be sent by the superior to the bishop of the diocese wherein is located the house to which the candidate belongs. The superior may send these letters elsewhere only if the bishop of the diocese has given the requisite permission, or if he is of a different

---

[61] Schaaf, "Episcopus Proprius Ordinationis Religiosorum,"—*AER*, XC (1934), 504.

[62] *Incardination and Excardination of Seculars,* pp. 343, 345; Moeder, *op. cit.,* p. 75; cans. 956; 964, n. 4.

[63] Berutti, *De Religiosis,* p. 370; Moeder, *op. cit.,* p. 114.

rite than the candidate, or if he is absent, or if he does not intend to have ordinations on the next following regular ordination days, or finally if the diocese is vacant and the ordinary in charge does not possess the episcopal character. In each of the above mentioned cases it is necessary that the ordaining bishop know through an authentic statement from the curia of the bishop who has the original right of ordination that the superior is entitled to send his subjects to him.[64]

The superiors of societies possessing the right of granting dimissorial letters are forbidden to send their subjects to a house in another diocese with a view to circumventing the bishop of the diocese in which the house of the candidate is located, or to delay intentionally the issuing of dimissorial letters until a time when the bishop either will be absent or will not confer ordinations.[65]

On June 3, 1918, the Pontifical Commission for the Authentic Interpretation of the Canons of the Code declared that the penalties in canon 2410, whereby superiors who presumptuously violate the prescriptions of canon 966 are to be suspended from the celebration of Mass for a month, were to be applied to superiors of quasi-religious societies who abused their privilege of granting dimissorial letters.[66]

Another important question is the status of an ordained member of a quasi-religious society who leaves the society legitimately, either with the proper permission, or through his use of the right given him by the constitutions of the society. It seems quite certain from the norms of the common law that a subject thus returning to the world retains his proper diocese which he had before he entered the society, and that the bishop of that diocese has an obligation of receiving him.[67]

Vermeersch-Creusen mention the fact that it seems to be an unjust obligation placed on a local ordinary to require him to receive

[64] Cans. 965; 966.

[65] Can. 967.

[66] *AAS*, X (1918), 347.

[67] Veermeersch-Creusen, *Epitome*, I, n. 679; Pointek, *De Indulto Exclaustrationis necnon Secularizationis*, pp. 181, 224-225; Beste, *Introductio in Codicem*, p. 456; Stanton, *De Societatibus*, p. 141; Moeder, *The Proper Bishop for Ordination and Dimissorial Letters*, p. 113; Bastien, *Directoire Canonique*, p. 345.

into his diocese these ordained members of quasi-religious societies who have legitimately left their societies. This is especially true, they claim, of the case of those members who were ordained upon the issuance of dimissorial letters by their own superiors, since in that case the local ordinary had no connection whatsoever with the ordination.[68]

While it is true that at first glance this does seem to place an unjust obligation on the local ordinary, still when actual practice is considered, this objection does not hold. In the first place, as some of the authors point out, when the privilege of granting dimissorial letters is given to superiors of quasi-religious societies, it is rarely without the addition of a clause stating that, if the ordained members leave the society, they must find a benevolent bishop who will receive them.[69]

This proviso relieves the bishop, for all practical purposes, from the obligation of receiving into his diocese an ordained member of a quasi-religious society when his ordination had followed upon dimissorial letters issued by his own superior. Finally, even in cases in which a member has received major orders, the dimissorial letters having been issued either by his proper bishop or by his superior from a privilege, he will nevertheless most probably be held to find a benevolent bishop before being allowed to depart from the society. Even though the privilege of granting the dimissorial letters may set down no such condition it will most probably be demanded either by the constitutions of the society or by the direct intervention of the Holy See.

The Pontifical Commission for the Authentic Interpretation of the Canons of the Code on June 3, 1918, declared that canon 2387 is applicable to quasi-religious societies. Consequently, a member of a quasi-religious society who through his own fault has made an invalid profession and subsequently has received minor orders should be dismissed from the clerical state, and in the event that he has received major orders he is to remain suspended until the Holy See makes special provision to the contrary.[70]

---

[68] *Epitome,* I, n. 679.

[69] Vermeersch-Creusen, *Epitome,* I, n. 679; Stanton, *De Societatibus,* p. 139; Beste, *Introductio in Codicem,* p. 456.

[70] *AAS,* X (1918), 347.

Section 3. Title for Ordination

In accordance with the prescription of canon 979, § 1, the title of ordination for secular clerics is the title of *benefice.* If that title be lacking, then the title of *patrimony* or *pension* must be secured. Furthermore, the title must be secure for the whole life of the cleric and truly sufficient for his proper support, according to the standards laid down by respective local ordinaries and based on the needs and circumstances of the respective localities and times.[71]

If none of the mentioned titles of ordination be available, the secular cleric may be ordained under the title of *service of the diocese,* and in places subject to the Sacred Congregation for the Propagation of the Faith under the title of the *mission.* In these cases the candidate must take an oath to serve the diocese or the mission forever under the authority of the local ordinary. The local ordinary must provide a benefice, an office, or a salary sufficient for their support to all candidates ordained under either of these two titles.[72]

These various titles of ordination for secular clerics are available also to clerics who are members of quasi-religious societies. In accordance with the general prescription of canon 678, all that concerns the ordination of seculars is to be applied to the members of quasi-religious societies. Consequently, in determining the title of ordination for these members, which is a legal requirement for the reception of major orders, one must apply to them the norms which obtain for secular clerics. Canon 974, n. 7, affirms the need of a title of ordination for the reception of major orders.

The titles of *service of the diocese* and of the *mission* would rarely be used by quasi-religious societies. An exception to this rule would probably occur in the case of a society whose rule did not require a complete common life and whose works were essentially the parochial care of souls, especially in the mission fields; or possibly also in the case of a diocesan society which existed in only one diocese or mission and had no expectations of spreading into another diocese or mission.

---

[71] Can. 979, § 2.
[72] Can. 981.

In practically all cases quasi-religious societies are given an apostolic privilege of ordaining their members under the titles permitted for religious institutes.[73]

Schäfer, agreeing with the general principle already stated, namely that a privilege of granting dimissorial letters to its subjects makes a quasi-religious society, in the legal obligations concerning ordination, similar to a religious institute, claims that, as a result of this similarity, the members of quasi-religious societies ordained upon the issuance of dimissorial letters by their own superiors are to use the titles provided for religious institutes. These titles are listed in canon 982, § 2. These same titles are used by exempt clerical quasi-religious societies.[74]

Canon 982, § 2, states that for religious who are professed with simple perpetual vows the title of ordination for major orders may be the title of the *common life* (*mensae communis*), the title of the *congregation,* or some similar one as specified in the constitutions of the society.

Scholion I. Irregularities to Orders in Quasi-Religious Societies

In this chapter on ordination it should be noted that the irregularity for orders incurred in virtue of canon 985, n. 3, by one who contracts marriage with a religious, bound by either temporary or perpetual vows, is not incurred by reason of contracting marriage with a woman who is a member of a quasi-religious society. The canon specifically uses the terms *votis religiosis adstricta* as being the foundation of the irregularity, while the various bonds of union existing in quasi-religious societies are never the vows of religion properly so called. Similarly, should a member of a quasi-religious society of men attempt or contract marriage, while under obligation to the society, he would not on that account incur the irregularity *ex delicto* specified in canon 985, n. 3. This irregularity is incurred only when one bound by the vows of religion attempts or actually contracts marriage.

---

[73] Wernz-Vidal, *De Religiosis,* n. 458.

[74] *De Religiosis,* pp. 1033-1034; Vermeersch-Creusen, *Epitome,* I, n. 679; Berutti, *De Religiosis,* p. 379; Moeder, *The Proper Bishop for Ordination and Dimissorial Letters,* p. 114.

CHAPTER IX

The Obligations and the Privileges of Members of Quasi-Religious Societies

ARTICLE I. THE OBLIGATIONS OF MEMBERS OF QUASI-RELIGIOUS SOCIETIES

Canon 679 states that the members of quasi-religious societies, in addition to the special obligations imposed upon them by the constitutions of the society, are likewise bound by the common obligations of clerics, unless the nature of the law, or its context, shows that the law is not intended for them. They must observe the enclosure according to their constitutions, under the supervision of the local ordinary. They are also bound by the obligations of religious as specified in canons 595-612, unless their constitutions rule otherwise.

The obligations of clerics, to which the members of quasi-religious societies are bound by canon 679, § 1, are specified in canons 124-144. However, several of the prescriptions contained in these canons are also contained in the canons treating of the obligations of religious, to which the members of quasi-religious societies are also held. In these cases the members are not held to any of those common obligations of clerics which are more accurately determined, either for them in their own constitutions or for religious in the prescriptions of canons 595-612.[1]

Moreover, several of the prescriptions of canons 124-144 contain obligations binding only clerics. Consequently, the members of lay quasi-religious societies are not bound by them. Similarly, societies of women are not bound by the prescriptions which obviously are intended only for societies of men. It must also be stated that among the canons establishing the obligations of clerics there are some prescriptions which regulate duties arising from subjection to a diocese, duties which clearly are not consistent with

[1] Berutti, *De Religiosis,* p. 371.

the functions of these quasi-religious societies. Consequently, these prescriptions are not to be applied to the latter. Furthermore, rescripts which for groups of religious rather than for seculars urge a more rigorous application of canons 124-144 do not apply to quasi-religious societies since the latter are obliged to the observance of these canons in the measure in which they affect seculars, and not as they affect religious.[2]

Section 1. Obligations Which the Members of Quasi-Religious Societies Have in Common with Seculars

The interior life and the exterior conduct of all the members of quasi-religious societies should be superior to that of the laity, to whom they should furnish an example of virtue and good deeds.[3]

All the members of these societies are bound by a special duty to respect and obey their ordinary, whether he be their own proper ordinary, or the ordinary of the place where their house is located.[4]

After their ordination to the priesthood, clerics of these societies must not neglect study, especially that of the sacred sciences. In these studies they must always follow the sound doctrines handed down by the Fathers and commonly accepted by the Church, and they must avoid profane novelties of expression and what is erroneously called science.[5]

It must be left to the constitutions of each quasi-religious society to determine whether or not the members of the society are bound by any added obligations with regard to the observance of chastity. If special oaths, promises or private vows of chastity are demanded by the constitutions, then any violation of chastity would certainly be a sacrilege in the wide sense of the word. The authors dispute whether or not the violation of a private vow of chastity is a

---

[2] Blat, *De Religiosis*, p. 434.

[3] Can. 124.

[4] Can. 127.

[5] Can. 129. The obligations binding priests of these societies to yearly examinations for three years following ordination and to attendance at theological conferences, either at their own houses or at the diocesan meeting, have already been discussed in a previous chapter.—*Supra*, pp. 194-195.

sacrilege in the strict meaning of the term.[6] However, it is the opinion of the writer, that the authors who contend that the violation of a private vow of chastity is not a sacrilege in the strict sense, are considering the private vow as pronounced by a person living in the world and not the private vow of a member of a quasi-religious society. These same authors state that because a public vow juridically dedicates a person to the Church, a violation of a public vow of chastity would constitute a sacrilege in the strict sense. Therefore it would seem that the fact of public dedication to the Church effected by a public vow and the lack of this dedication in the private vow makes an offense against the former a sacrilege strictly so-called and an offense against the latter a sacrilege in the wide meaning of the word. However, it is the writer's opinion that the official recognition of quasi-religious societies by the Church in Her common law gives to the members of these societies a juridical dedication similar to that enjoyed by religious strictly so-called. Consequently, members of quasi-religious societies are juridically dedicated to the Church and therefore even violations of their private bonds would constitute sacrileges in the strict sense.

In accordance with canon 132, clerics of these societies who are in major orders, regardless of their constitutions, are so bound by the obligation of observing chastity that any sin against chastity is a sacrilege and any attempt at marriage is invalid. If a cleric in minor orders contracts marriage he becomes automatically reduced to the lay state.[7]

In accordance with the prescriptions of canon 214, if a member of a quasi-religious society received major orders as a result of force or grave fear, and did not ratify his ordination at least tacitly by the exercise of the orders received, which would imply a voluntary assumption of the obligations attached to these orders, he can bring his case before the bishop, and, if he can offer adequate proof, he must be pronounced free from the obligations attaching to the major orders, even though obligations arising from the incorporation in the society remain.[8]

---

[6] Noldin-Schmitt, *Summa Theologiae,* II, 170.

[7] Cans. 132, § 1; 646, § 1, n. 3.

[8] Can. 214, § 1. Canons 1933-1998, refer to the process to be observed in these cases.

It is the writer's opinion that the prescriptions of canon 133 do not apply to quasi-religious societies. Canon 133 prescribes certain precautions to be observed in the employment of women in clerical residences. From the context of the canon it could safely be concluded that the legislator had in mind the ordinary parish house of the secular clergy. This is especially evident from the legislation which, as there enacted, leaves the final decision in particular cases to the local ordinary. It would commonly be expected that the constitutions of a society would adequately provide for the necessary precautions in these cases. Furthermore, the obligation of vigilance placed on superiors of societies would likewise prevent any imprudence along these lines on the part of subjects. This conclusion is an application of the norm of canon 679, which states that the obligations of clerics apply to quasi-religious societies, unless the nature of the law, or its context, show that the law is not intended for these societies.[9]

Clerics in major orders are under the obligation of reciting daily all the Canonical Hours according to the proper and approved liturgical books. If, in accordance with canon 214, a cleric has been reduced to the lay state, he is not obliged to recite them. The question of choir obligation which may exist in quasi-religious societies will be discussed in a later part of this chapter.[10]

Members of quasi-religious societies are forbidden to give bail or to be surety for any one, even with their own money, unless they have the permission of the local ordinary.[11]

They must abstain absolutely from all things unbecoming their state. They must not practice unbecoming arts, habitually play games of chance for money, carry weapons, indulge in hunting associated with great display and publicity. Nor may they visit saloons or other places of that nature except in cases of necessity or for other just reasons approved by the local ordinary.[12]

They must also avoid occupations which, although not unbecom-

---

[9] Cf. cans. 133; 679. Schäfer claims that religious institutes likewise are not bound by canon 133, since the precautions of the cloister parallel the prescriptions of this canon.—*De Religiosis*, p. 662.

[10] Cf. *infra*, pp. 222-223; can. 135.

[11] Can. 137.

[12] Can. 138.

ing in themselves, are foreign to the clerical state. Without an apostolic indult they cannot practice medicine or surgery; or act as a public notary, except in the ecclesiastical curia; nor may they accept public offices that entail secular jurisdiction or administrative duties.[13]

Without the permission of their ordinaries, the members of quasi-religious societies may not act as agents for the property of lay people, or assume secular offices that impose the obligation of rendering an account, or exercise the office of solicitor or attorney, except in the ecclesiastical court, or in the civil court when there is question of a case affecting them or their houses. They cannot take any part at all, not even as witnesses, unless they are put under constraint, in a criminal case in the secular courts, if the case be one in which the criminal may be punished with a grave penalty.[14]

Without the permission of the Holy See they are not allowed to compete for, or accept, the office of senator or representative in those countries where this is forbidden by the Holy See; in other countries they cannot seek or accept these offices without the permission of their own ordinary as well as the ordinary of the place where the election is to take place. The permission of the superior would also have to be secured, but in all probability the constitutions would entirely exclude the possibility of a member ever holding public office.[15]

The proper ordinary, in the application of canon 139, §§ 3, 4, in virtue of canon 679 to exempt clerical quasi-religious societies, would be the major superior.[16]

The members of quasi-religious societies must avoid those theatrical performances, dances and shows, especially in public theatres, which are unbecoming to their state and the attendance at which might cause scandal.[17]

They should not volunteer for military service, unless they have the permission of their proper ordinary and do so for the purpose of sooner liberating themselves from the service in countries in

[13] Can. 139, §§ 1, 2.

[14] Can. 139, § 3.

[15] Can. 139, § 4.

[16] Can. 198, § 1.

[17] Can. 140.

which there is compulsory military training for all men including priests and religious. They may not take part in, or help in any way, internal revolts or disturbances of public order. If members of a clerical society in minor orders, in violation of this law, volunteer for military service, they are automatically reduced to the lay state. Permission of the proper superiors would also have to be secured, in accordance with the constitutions, by those who wished to take advantage of the prescriptions of this canon. The proper major superiors in clerical exempt societies would be included under the office of proper ordinary in the application of canon 141 to quasi-religious societies.

The members of quasi-religious societies are forbidden to engage either personally or through others in any business or trading, whether for their own benefit or for that of others.[18]

It is a common opinion that these members may make investments in stocks and bonds, provided the investments are really economic and not speculative. They must also be prepared to obey any mandate of the Holy See in this matter and they must not have any part in the direction of the business.[19]

It will be noted that the various obligations of quasi-religious as mentioned in this section are obligations of the common law placed on clerics. The application of these obligations to quasi-religious societies is justified in virtue of the norm of canon 679. This canon states that the members of quasi-religious societies are bound by the common obligations of clerics, unless the nature of the law, or its context, show that the law is not intended for them.

ARTICLE II. OBLIGATIONS WHICH THE MEMBERS OF QUASI-RELIGIOUS SOCIETIES HAVE IN COMMON WITH RELIGIOUS

It is to be noted that in speaking of the obligations which the members of quasi-religious societies have in common with religious, canon 679 uses the phrase *"nisi constitutiones aliud ferant."* Accordingly, in the case of quasi-religious, the constitutions are to be followed in these matters which are legislated for religious by canons 595-612, even though they be contrary to the law of the

[18] Can. 142.

[19] Schäfer, *De Religiosis,* p. 667.

Code as contained in these canons. Canons 595-612 list the obligations which the law has placed on religious. These obligations, by virtue of canon 679, are likewise applicable to quasi-religious societies in the qualified sense as just explained. However, if the constitutions contain no prescriptions governing any of these matters, then the prescriptions of the Code which specify this matter as obligatory for religious must also be observed by the members of quasi-religious societies.[20]

Furthermore, canon 679, § 2, states that with reference to the cloister the norms of the constitutions are to be observed, under the vigilance of the local ordinary.

Consequently, canons 597-604, which treat of the cloister for religious Orders and congregations, are not applicable to quasi-religious societies. This is true even though canon 679, § 1, applies to the latter all the canons which contain enacted obligations for religious, including the canons on the cloister. If the obligations of canons 579-604, which affect the cloisters of religious likewise applied to quasi-religious societies, then canon 679, § 2, would be useless, for the matter contained in it would have already been treated in the first paragraph of the same canon.[21]

In accordance with canon 595, the superiors of quasi-religious societies are charged with the obligation of seeing to it that all their subjects make a retreat each year, that all are present at daily Mass, make the meditations and perform the spiritual exercises prescribed by the constitutions, and finally, that all make their confession at least once a week. The superiors must likewise promote among their subjects the practice of frequent Communion; and even daily Communion must be allowed to subjects who are properly disposed. If, however, a subject since his last confession has given scandal to the community, or has committed an external mortal sin, the superior can forbid that person to go to Holy Communion until he has again gone to confession. If a society has certain days for Holy Communion prescribed in the rules or constitutions, such regulations shall be considered as merely directive norms.[22]

---

[20] Blat, *De Religiosis*, p. 434.

[21] Vermeersch-Creusen, *Epitome*, I, n. 680; Berutti, *De Religiosis*, p. 371; Blat, *De Religiosis*, pp. 476-477.

[22] Can. 595.

All members should, in the house as well as outside, wear the habit proper to their society, unless in the judgment of the major superior there is grave reason to make an exception.[23]

Some authors claim that this particular ruling should be applied to quasi-religious societies with great latitude because of the special nature of the work in which they frequently engage, work which at times necessitates their going about in the garb of laymen. This is especially true of several quasi-religious societies of women, the principal work of which is the nursing of the poor sick at home or in hospitals. Of their very nature other works would, in the case of quasi-religious societies, also require a broad interpretation of this canon, such as census work and the work of conversion among unfriendly peoples.[24]

A. The Cloister in Quasi-Religious Societies

As has already been mentioned, the prescriptions of the constitutions are to be followed in the determination of the exact nature of the cloister of each quasi-religious society.[25] However, as stated in canon 679, § 2, the vigilance over the observance of this cloister is reserved to the local ordinary, even though the society may have pontifical approval.[26]

In an exempt society the local ordinary, outside the time of visitation, has no direction over the cloister of the society. Nevertheless, according to canon 617, § 1, if any abuse creeps into the house of an exempt religious institute and the superior, after a warning, fails to correct it, the local ordinary is bound to refer the matter to the Holy See. The prescription of canon 617, § 1, as affecting exempt religious institutes, is also applicable to exempt quasi-religious societies. This is true in virtue of the general principle, already stated, that in regard to exemption all the prescriptions of the common law concerned with the exemption of religious institutes apply equally to exempt quasi-religious societies.[27] Consequently, if any abuse has crept into the observance of the cloister

---

[23] Can. 596.

[24] Blat, *De Religiosis*, p. 477; Stanton, *De Societatibus*, pp. 143-144.

[25] Cf. *supra*, p. 212.

[26] Blat, *De Religiosis*, p. 434.

[27] Cf. *supra*, pp. 109-110.

of an exempt society, and the superior, after a warning, has failed to correct it, the local ordinary must refer the matter to the Holy See.[28]

All those who, according to the constitutions of each society, have the custody of the enclosure shall see to it that during the visits of outsiders the discipline is not relaxed or the spirit of the society weakened by useless conversation.[29]

The superiors of quasi-religious societies must ensure the faithful observance of the laws of their constitutions regarding the departure of their subjects from the cloister and their receiving visits from and paying visits to outsiders.[30]

The authors likewise maintain that the prescription of canon 606, § 1, is to be applied only in a wide sense to quasi-religious societies in view of the nature of their work which frequently demands their going out of their houses for reasons of physical and spiritual necessity.[31]

It is not lawful for the superiors of these societies to allow their subjects to remain outside of their houses, except for a just and grave cause, and for as brief a period as possible in accordance with the prescriptions of the constitutions. For an absence of six months, except for the purpose of study, the permission of the Holy See is required.[32]

According to the general legislation of canon 679, § 1, if the constitutions are at variance with the obligations imposed on religious by the common law, the constitutions are to be followed. Consequently, if the constitutions allow a longer period than six months for the absence of a member from a house of the society without recourse to the Holy See, the constitutions are to be observed. On the contrary, if the constitutions do not legislate on this particular matter, the common law as binding religious applies.[33]

It is the common opinion of authors that a brief departure from the house of a religious institute, and consequently also from the

---

[28] Schäfer, *De Religiosis,* p. 1036; Vermeersch-Creusen, *Epitome,* I, n. 680.
[29] Can. 605.
[30] Can. 606, § 1.
[31] Blat, *De Religiosis,* pp. 476-477; Stanton, *De Societatibus,* p. 144.
[32] Can. 606, § 2.
[33] Cf. can. 679, § 1.

house of a quasi-religious society, e.g., an absence of a few hours for the purpose of a walk or a visit, without the proper permission as required by the constitutions is not to be considered as flight or apostasy from the institute or the society. Particular constitutions may fix certain penalties for departure without permission. However, they cannot make something a grave matter which is not such by its nature, unless in the case of particular aggravating circumstances, as would be involved, v.g., in an habitual mode of conduct.[84]

B. Correspondence of Members of Quasi-Religious Societies

All members of quasi-religious societies are allowed to send letters, free from inspection, to the Holy See and to its legates in the respective country; to their cardinal protector, if they have one; to their own major superiors; to their own local superior when he is absent, and to the local ordinary to whom they are subject. Likewise they may receive letters from all these persons free from all inspection.[85]

The principle of canon 611, applied to quasi-religious societies through canon 679, indirectly states that the subjects of quasi-religious societies are under the obligation of renouncing the ordinary rights of privacy in the matter of writing and receiving letters. Consequently, this canon implies that the local superiors have the right of examining all the outgoing and the incoming correspondence of the subjects, except in the cases specifically mentioned in canon 611. It is to be noted that canon 611 does not mention the correspondence carried on with confessors and spiritual directors. The law does not seem to contemplate that such communications may be made in writing, since ordinarily they should be carried on personally.

However, if a member wishes to correspond with his confessor or spiritual director he should seek this permission from his supe-

---

[84] Schäfer, *De Religiosis,* pp. 736, 976-977; Vermeersch-Creusen, *Epitome,* I, n. 648, 2; Wernz-Vidal, *De Religiosis,* n. 432; Woywod, *A Practical Commentary on the Code of Canon Law,* I, 257-258. (As will be explained later, apostasy, in regard to quasi-religious societies, is used in a wide sense.)

[85] Can. 611.

rior, and the superior should allow it without creating any difficulty. Once the superior has authorized the sending or receiving of these letters of "conscience," he is not allowed to read them. Nevertheless, if in any particular case there is a well founded suspicion that the inscription *"case of conscience"* is used for deception, then the superior may read just enough of the letter to ascertain the fact and if he discovers it really is a matter of conscience then he is bound by the natural law to read no further. This would also be true in the case of letters of this sort sent or received without any special permission. For even in these cases, once the superior has discovered that the contents of a letter pertain to matters of conscience he would be obliged by the natural law not to read the letter.[36]

C. The Care of Souls Entrusted to Quasi-Religious Societies

It will be noted that this entire section treats of various obligations which the common law places on religious institutes. These obligations are applicable to quasi-religious societies in virtue of the general prescriptions of canon 679, § 1, which state in part that all the obligations which are placed on religious institutes by the common law in canons 595-612, are to be applied to quasi-religious societies, unless the constitutions prescribe otherwise. It is the application of this canon which has justified the various applications of the obligations of the members of religious institutes to quasi-religious. By virtue of this same principle, canon 608 is applicable to quasi-religious societies with the following conclusions.

With regard to the care of souls, the superiors of quasi-religious societies should see to it that, without any prejudice to the discipline of the society, its subjects shall cheerfully discharge the sacred ministry in their own churches, or in public oratories, especially in the dioceses in which they are stationed whenever their services are required by the local ordinary or by the pastors to meet the spiritual needs of the faithful. Reciprocally, local ordinaries and pastors should willingly use the services of these members, especially when the latter reside in their dioceses, for the exercise of

[36] Schäfer, *De Religiosis*, pp. 739-740.

the sacred ministry and especially for the administration of the sacrament of penance.[37]

Similarly, canon 609 is applicable to quasi-religious societies with the following conclusions. If the church attached (*pleno iure*) to the residence of the society is also a parochial church, then all the pertinent regulations of canon 415 are to be observed.[38] Since by reason of canon 679, § 1, the prescriptions of canon 609 are applicable to quasi-religious societies, it may safely be concluded that canon 415, specifically mentioned in canon 609, § 1, is likewise applicable to quasi-religious societies. Canon 415 considers the relations existing between the pastor and the chapter in a collegiate church which is at the same time a parish church. These same relations should exist, then, whenever they are pertinent, between the pastor and the society, when the church of the society is also the parish church.[39]

Now, canon 415, which has already been shown to be applicable to quasi-religious societies, demands a parochial vicar who will be able to perform the various functions listed in the canon, which ordinarily are performed by the pastor of a parish church. Nowhere in the Code is there any specific legislation regulating the appointment of a parochial vicar in quasi-religious societies. Consequently, by an application of canon 20, laws laid down in similar cases must be applied. Therefore it seems justified to apply canon 456, which provides for the appointment of pastors in churches belonging to religious institutes, to quasi-religious societies. Canon 456 states that in parishes given to religious institutes the superior presents the pastor, and the bishop has the right to examine him as to his fitness for the position, but, if he finds him qualified, he must give him the canonical institution. In virtue of canon 20, superiors of quasi-religious societies may similarly present parochial vicars to the bishop, and the bishop has the same right of examination and the same obligation of appointment if the subject is found qualified.

Canon 415, in enumerating the various functions which must be performed by pastors, and, in virtue of the application just made, also the functions to be performed by the parochial vicars of quasi-

[37] Can. 608.

[38] Can. 609, § 1.

[39] Schäfer, *De Religiosis*, p. 918.

religious societies, includes mention of the parochial functions listed in canon 462. Consequently, since canon 415 incorporates the prescriptions of canon 462, the latter canon likewise becomes applicable to quasi-religious societies. Therefore by an application of the prescriptions of canons 415 and 462 to quasi-religious societies, the following conclusions may be stated.

A member of a quasi-religious society who has been nominated and installed as a parochial vicar must apply the *Missa pro populo,* preach, give catechetical instructions, keep the parochial books, attest copies of the records, and perform the parochial functions proper to the pastor as specified in canon 462. He may also discharge other functions which are not strictly parochial but which are usually observed in parishes. He may likewise collect alms for the poor of the parish, accept them when directly or indirectly offered and administer and dispense them according to the will of the donors.[40]

The society itself is charged with the custody of the Blessed Sacrament, but one key to the tabernacle must be in the hands of the vicar. The society itself must see to it that the vicar observes the liturgical laws in his functions in the church. The society must likewise take care of the church building, and administer its goods and its pious legacies. The local ordinary is to decide any controversy which may arise between the vicar and the society. The society is bound in charity to assist the vicar in his work, especially if he has no assistants. However, the superiors generally determine the method in which this assistance shall be given.

It is the opinion of the writer that the prescriptions of canons 630-631 are also applicable to quasi-religious societies. Title XVII, Book II, of the Code does not contain any norms corresponding to the regulations of these two canons which prescribe essential regulations governing the administering of parishes by religious. Therefore, in virtue of canon 20, when there is no law governing a particular matter, laws enacted in similar cases are to be supplied. Consequently, the following conclusions are warranted.

A member of a quasi-religious society who rules a parish under the title of parish priest or vicar remains bound to the observance

---

[40] Canon 462 treats of the parochial administration of the sacraments.

of the prescriptions of the constitutions of the society, inasmuch as their observance is compatible with the discharge of his office.[41]

Accordingly, in matters pertaining to religious discipline, he remains subject to his proper superior who alone has the right to make inquiries regarding his observance of the rules and constitutions and to correct him if necessary.[42]

The member of the society must acquire all property which comes to him for the parish in the name of the parish. He must receive all other property in accordance with the prescriptions of the constitutions of the society.[43]

He may gather and receive alms, when they are offered in any manner whatever, for the good of the parishioners or for Catholic schools or pious institutions connected with the parish, and this would in no way violate any bond of poverty that might be prescribed by the constitutions. He has the right to administer any alms thus received or collected and according to his prudent judgment he may spend those alms, always keeping in mind any special wish of the donors. However, in all these transactions he remains subject to the vigilance of his proper superior.

If the church is owned by the quasi-religious society the superior of the house to which the parish is joined has the right to collect, keep, and administer those alms and donations which are given for the building, upkeep, restoration, and adornment of the parish church; otherwise these rights are vested in the local ordinary.[44]

Every member of a quasi-religious society who is a pastor or vicar is immediately subject to the entire jurisdiction, visitation, and correction of the local ordinary, just as are secular pastors, even though the member of the society should exercise his ministry in a house which is the ordinary residence of his major superior. Matters pertaining to the personal religious observance of the pastor are excluded from this supervision.[45]

---

[41] Can. 630, § 1.

[42] Can. 630, § 2.

[43] Can. 630, § 3.

[44] Can. 630, § 4. If the parish church is not owned by the society, the local ordinary has the administrative rights given to the superior by this canon; Wernz-Vidal, *De Religiosis*, n. 416.

[45] Can. 631, § 1.

Therefore, the local ordinary may issue opportune decrees and impose penalties whenever he finds that the pastor has been neglectful in his parochial duties. The superior of the quasi-religious member may likewise punish the pastor in these circumstances. However, should the ordinary and the superior issue contrary orders, the decree of the ordinary must prevail.[46]

Canon 631, § 3, states that the removal of a religious pastor or vicar should be governed by the law of canon 454, § 5, and that the administration of the temporal goods of the parish is to be governed by canons 533, § 1, n. 4, and 535, § 3, n. 2.

The application of the prescriptions of this paragraph of canon 631 to quasi-religious societies results in the following conclusions.

Either the local ordinary or the superior of the society may remove from office the member of the society who has been acting as pastor or vicar of the parish without any obligation of giving the reason for their action to the other.[47]

The society member acting as pastor or vicar must obtain the previous consent of the ordinary before investing any parish money, whether this money was given directly to the parish or to the pastor for the sake of the parish.[48] On the occasion of the canonical visitation of the parish, the pastor of the parish must give a financial account of these investments to the ordinary.[49]

In virtue of canon 679, § 1, canon 609 applies to quasi-religious societies in the following ways.

A church attached to the house belonging to a quasi-religious society of women cannot be made into a parochial church.[50]

In non-parochial churches belonging to quasi-religious societies it is the obligation of the superior to see to it that the celebration of divine services in them does not interfere with the catechetical instructions or the preaching of the Gospel given in the neighboring parochial churches. It pertains to the local ordinary to judge whether or not this hindrance exists.[51]

---

[46] Can. 631, § 2.
[47] Can. 454, § 5.
[48] Can. 533, § 1, n. 4.
[49] Can. 535, § 3, n. 2.
[50] Can. 609, § 2.
[51] Can. 609, § 3.

If the local ordinary thinks that a conflict does exist between the religious services in the non-parochial churches of quasi-religious societies and the services in the parochial churches, he has a right to demand that the society arrange its services at an hour which would forestall all conflict. If the society refuses to accede to the demands of the local ordinary, the entire case must be put before the Sacred Congregation of Religious. Meanwhile, the society must comply with the directions of the local ordinary.[52]

In accordance with the prescriptions of canon 1345, it is desirable that a short sermon on the Holy Gospel or on other points of Christian Doctrine be given on Sundays and holy days in all churches and public oratories whenever the laity assist at Mass in them. If preaching be prescribed by the local ordinary, then the ruling applies to quasi-religious societies inasmuch as the canon expressly adverts to *all churches and public oratories* without making any exception. It can further be stated that the end of the law is concerned with the laity attending the religious services, and not with the question of who is conducting the services. Consequently, even in view of the purpose of the law, quasi-religious societies are included within the prescriptions of canon 1345. This canon also states that, if the local ordinary has enacted any special regulations concerning the provisions of this canon, they must be obeyed, even by exempt religious. This last prescription likewise is applicable to quasi-religious societies because of the very wording of the canon. The canon expressly mentions as subjects of this latter prescription, not only the secular clergy but also religious, even if exempt. Consequently, whether the members of quasi-religious societies be strictly considered as secular clerics or regarded rather as religious in the broad meaning of the term, in either case they are held to the entire legislation of canon 1345.

According to canon 1334, if in the judgment of the local ordinary the help of religious is deemed necessary for the catechetical instruction of adults, the proper superiors, even of exempt institutes, are obliged upon the request of the ordinary to give such catechetical instruction, either in person or through their subjects, especially in their own churches. However, such instruction need not be given to the detriment of their own discipline.

---

[52] Schäfer, *De Religiosis*, p. 741.

While it is true that the prescriptions of canon 1334 does not specifically mention quasi-religious societies as subject to its legislation, nevertheless it is the opinion of the writer that quasi-religious societies are so bound. This conclusion is based on the following reason. Canon 608, § 1, which by virtue of canon 679, § 1, obliges quasi-religious societies, states that the superiors of religious institutes, and consequently also the superiors of quasi-religious societies, should see to it that their subjects shall cheerfully discharge the sacred ministry, especially in the diocese in which they are stationed, whenever their services are required by the local ordinary or by the pastors to meet the spiritual needs of the faithful. Now, in the opinion of the writer, canon 1334 is to all practical purposes an application of canon 608, § 1. Consequently, quasi-religious societies are included within its scope.

If the local ordinary for a public reason prescribes the ringing of bells, the recitation of certain prayers, or the celebration of sacred solemnities, all quasi-religious societies, even though they be exempt, must obey, without prejudice, however, to the constitutions and privileges of each society.[53] The application of canon 612 to quasi-religious societies is justified in virtue of the prescription of canon 679, § 1. This latter canon states that the obligations of religious as listed in canons 595-612 are applicable to quasi-religious societies. This same norm has warranted all the applications which have been made in this entire section regarding the various obligations incumbent on quasi-religious societies.[54]

D. The Divine Office and Quasi-Religious Societies

Canon 610, as applied to quasi-religious societies by canon 679, § 1, imposes the following obligations. In all quasi-religious societies in which there exists the obligation of choir, the Divine Office must be recited daily in common, conformable to the constitutions, in every house with at least four members who are bound to choir, and who are not at the time lawfully impeded. If the constitutions so prescribe, even fewer than four may be obliged to recite the Divine Office in common. The Mass corresponding to the Office

[53] Can. 612.

[54] Schäfer, *De Religiosis*, p. 1036; Blat, *De Religiosis*, pp. 437-438.

of the day, according to the rubrics, must also be celebrated daily in the local communities of men, and, whenever possible, even in the local communities of women.[55]

If the constitutions of a quasi-religious society prescribe that the Office is to be said, either privately or in common, by those members who are not bound by reason of ordination to recite the Office, such prescriptions have no juridical force or obligation other than that expressly stated in the constitutions.[56]

If the constitutions prescribe that the Office of the Blessed Virgin is to be recited, either in choir or privately, the only obligation of saying this Office is that which is expressed in the constitutions. Moreover, if the constitutions do not prescribe the contrary, the Office of the Blessed Virgin may be said in the vernacular, as long as the text is approved by the proper ecclesiastical authority.[57]

The constitutions may even impose on the novices the obligation of reciting the Office, either in common or privately. However, as in all cases concerning the recitation of the Office by the members or aspirants of quasi-religious societies, except with reference to the obligation imposed by the common law on those who are in major orders, the force of the obligation depends entirely upon the constitutions.[58]

Causes legitimately excusing one from choir duty can be either physical or moral impossibilities, such as sickness or injury, the exercise of the ministry, and other similar reasons. In the absence of an adequately excusing cause a dispensation can free one from the obligation.

E. The Celebration of Mass

Members of quasi-religious societies who are priests are obliged, as are all priests, to say Mass several times a year.[59]

According to the authors this obligation of saying Mass several times a year is substantially satisfied if Mass is said three or four times a year. Circumstances may make a more frequent celebration

[55] Can. 610.
[56] Schäfer, *De Religiosis*, p. 742.
[57] Schäfer, *De Religiosis*, p. 744.
[58] Schäfer, *loc. cit.*
[59] Can. 805.

of Mass obligatory, as, for instance, the necessity of satisfying a certain number of Mass stipend obligations every month as prescribed by the constitutions.[60]

Canon 831, § 3, states that all, even exempt religious, are obliged to observe the law of the diocese, or the custom of the diocese, in the matter of Mass stipends.

This canon is applicable to quasi-religious societies by reason of the general extension of its prescription. Its enacted obligation extends to all priests, secular and religious. Consequently, whether the quasi-religious be considered as seculars in a strict sense or as religious in a wide meaning of the term, they are under either aspect obliged to follow the regulations of canon 831, § 3, that is, they must observe the diocesan law or custom in the matter of Mass stipends.

In accordance with the prescriptions of canon 1546, the written consent of the local ordinary is required for the acceptance of any pious foundations by moral persons, inclusive of quasi-religious societies. Moreover, it is the right of the local ordinary to establish the limits below which a pious foundation may not be accepted. He may not give his consent for the acceptance of a foundation until he has ascertained that the society can satisfy the obligations attached.[61]

The money and movable goods given for the endowment of a foundation must be deposited in a safe place to be designated by the local ordinary, and kept there until they can be safely and profitably invested. The investments must be made according to the good judgment of the local ordinary, after he has consulted the interested parties and the diocesan board of administrators.[62]

A record of the pious foundations must be kept in the archives of each society as well as in the diocesan archives. Likewise, apart from the record book of manual stipends there must also be kept by the rectors of all churches belonging to quasi-religious societies a book containing a statement of all the obligations arising from foundations, with reference to their fulfillment and the stipend paid,

---

[60] Schäfer, *De Religiosis,* p. 754.

[61] Cans. 1545; 1546.

[62] Can. 1547.

so that an exact account of these items may be given to the local ordinary.[63]

In all churches belonging to exempt quasi-religious societies the rights and duties of the local ordinary, as defined in canons 1545-1549, pertain to the major superiors.[64] Canons 1550 can thus be applied to exempt quasi-religious societies in virtue of the general principle already stated, that the exemption of quasi-religious societies has the same extension as the exemption of religious institutes.[65]

The prescriptions of canons 1545-1549 were applied to quasi-religious societies in the foregoing paragraphs in virtue of the general extension of the prescriptions of these canons whereby they are intended to include all churches and institutions regardless of the authority charged with their direction.

Canon 843 places the obligation on the rectors of all churches, whether the churches belong to the secular or the religious clergy, of keeping a special book for the recording of the number of manual Mass stipends, the specific intentions, the amount of the stipends, and the fulfillment of the intentions. Ordinaries are obliged to inspect these books at least once a year, either in person or through others.[66]

Since the obligations enacted in this canon are placed on the rectors of all churches, regardless of the secular or religious administration of them, the rectors of churches of quasi-religious societies are necessarily included within the scope of these obligations. Furthermore, in exempt clerical societies the obligation of inspecting these books at least once a year, either in person or through another, rests on the major superiors of the society. This follows in virtue of the principle that, in regard to the privilege of exemption, the exempt quasi-religious societies parallels the exempt religious institutes.[67]

Canons 842 and 844, § 1, place certain obligations on local ordinaries with regard to the satisfaction of Mass stipends by the

---

[63] Can. 1548; 1549.

[64] Can. 1550.

[65] Cf. *supra*, pp. 109-110.

[66] Can. 843.

[67] Cf. Can. 198, § 1; *supra*, pp. 109-110.

secular clergy, and similar obligations on religious superiors in relation to their own subjects. Although these two canons do not mention quasi-religious societies, still it seems quite evident both from the end of the law and from the mind of the legislator that superiors of quasi-religious societies are held to their prescriptions. For undoubtedly, the superior of a quasi-religious society is best suited to see to it that these obligations are fulfilled.[68]

Accordingly, the following applications may be stated as flowing from this conclusion. The right and duty to see that the obligations of Mass stipends are satisfied pertains to the proper superiors of churches belonging to quasi-religious societies. Furthermore, in accordance with canon 844, § 1, the superiors of quasi-religious societies who entrust Mass obligations to their subjects or to others, should mark down at once the proper order of the Masses they have accepted together with the offering made, and should see to it that these Masses are said as soon as possible.

All priests of these societies must make an accurate record of the Mass intentions they have received and of those whose fulfillment they have satisfied. This obligation is mentioned in canon 844, § 2. It obliges all priests whether secular or religious. Consequently, priest members of quasi-religious societies are certainly included under this obligation whether they be considered as religious or as seculars.

F. Fast and Abstinence in Quasi-Religious Societies

In accordance with the prescription of canon 1253, if the constitutions of quasi-religious societies prescribe days of fast and abstinence in addition to those prescribed by the common law, the constitutions must be observed.

In keeping with the principle already established, namely, that the privilege of exemption affords a quasi-religious society all the rights granted to exempt religious institutes by the common law, canon 1245, § 3, may be applied to exempt clerical quasi-religious societies. Consequently, the superiors of exempt clerical quasi-religious societies may exercise for their professed subjects, for the novices, for those who live night and day in the house of the society

---

[68] Cf. can. 18.

for the purpose of education, health or hospitality, the same faculties concerning fast and abstinence as the pastor exercises for his parishioners. Accordingly, these superiors may in individual cases and for a just cause dispense individual members of the above mentioned groups from the common law of fast or abstinence as also from the observance of the holy days of obligation. However, only the superiors specifically mentioned in the constitutions may dispense from the obligations of fast and abstinence which are imposed by the constitutions.[69]

ARTICLE II. PRIVILEGES OF QUASI-RELIGIOUS SOCIETIES

Canon 680 states that all quasi-religious, even laics, enjoy all the privileges of clerics as enumerated in canons 119-123. They also enjoy any privileges directly conceded to them. However, without a special indult, they do not enjoy the privileges of religious. It is the opinion of some authors that the novices and aspirants in quasi-religious societies likewise enjoy the privileges specified in canon 680.[70]

It likewise seems to be the opinion of authors that the words, "*directe concessis,*" as used in canon 680, are to be understood in the sense of canon 613, § 1; that is to say, in the future no society may obtain any privileges by way of sharing in those directly conceded to other societies.[71]

On December 30, 1937, the Pontifical Commission for the Authentic Interpretation of the Canons of the Code was asked whether the words of canon 613, § 1, which preclude for the future the enjoyment of privileges acquired by way of inter-participation, were to be so understood that they revoked also the privileges which had been obtained by religious institutes by way of mutual inter-participation before the Code. The Commission replied in the negative.[72]

---

[69] Cf. *supra,* pp. 109-110, can. 1245, § 3; Creusen, *Religious Men and Women in the Code* (5. ed., Milwaukee, U. S. A.: Bruce Co., 1940), p. 240.

[70] Berutti, *De Religiosis,* p. 371; Schäfer, *De Religiosis,* p. 1036.

[71] Fanfani, *De Religiosis,* pp. 362, 530; Berutti, *De Religiosis,* p. 282; Vermeersch-Creusen, *Epitome,* I, n. 681; Cocchi, *De Religiosis,* n. 166.

[72] *AAS,* XXIX (1937), 73.

This response of the Code Commission was in keeping with the prescriptions of canon 4, which leaves acquired rights (*iura quaesita*) stand intact, if such rights were possessed and in use at the time of the enactment of the present Code.[73]

While this response was explicitly intended only for religious institutes, still, in virtue of the fact that many authors interpret canon 680 in the light of canon 613, § 1, it seems proper to extend the response to include quasi-religious societies.

In accordance with the prescription of canon 63, § 1, quasi-religious societies may also acquire privileges through legitimate prescription or custom. Moreover, the possession of a privilege for one hundred years or from time immemorial produces a presumption in favor of an original concession of the privilege.[74]

A society cannot renounce the privileges which were granted to it in the form of law, nor can it repudiate the privileges which are beneficial to the Church or other persons. No individual member of any society may renounce any privilege which has been granted to the society of which he is a member.[75]

However, members may lose their personal possession of the privileges granted to their society when they are reduced to the lay state or when they are perpetually deprived of the habit of the society. Yet, upon a remission of the penalties and consequent on a re-admission to the society such persons can regain the privileges they had lost in these ways.[76]

The members of all quasi-religious societies, including laic societies, and the novices of all quasi-religious societies possess the privileges of clerics enumerated in canons 119-123.[77]

Section 1. The Privilege of the Canon

All the faithful owe to the members of quasi-religious societies reverence in accordance with their rank and position. Moreover, the

---

[73] Fanfani, *De Religiosis*, p. 363; Vermeersch-Creusen, *Epitome*, I, n. 615.

[74] Can. 63, §§ 1, 2.

[75] Can. 72, §§ 3, 4.

[76] Fanfani, *De Religiosis*, p. 530; Berutti, *De Religiosis*, p. 371; Cocchi, *De Religiosis*, n. 166, b; can. 123.

[77] Can. 680.

faithful become guilty of sacrilege if they inflict a real injury on any member of a quasi-religious society.[78]

There is some discussion among the authors as to whether the penalty enacted in canon 2343, § 4, which inflicts an excommunication on anyone who maliciously strikes those who enjoy the privilege of the canon, is to be applied when the injury affects novices of religious institutes and members of quasi-religious societies. The doubt is due to the fact that they are not religious strictly so-called, in spite of their enjoyment of the privilege of the canon. It is the opinion of some authors that the penalty is applicable in both cases.[79]

Goyeneche states that the application of the penal sanction is necessitated by the completeness of the concept inherent in the canon. He claims that the privilege of the canon consists of two elements; first, the obligation to show reverence to those who possess this privilege, and secondly, the penalty for its violation. From this he argues that all members of religious institutes and quasi-religious societies possess the privilege integrally, i.e., they are immune from real injury, and any violation of that immunity is punishable with an excommunication to be automatically incurred. Secondly, he appeals to the pre-Code law, stating that no change has been introduced by the Code. Under pre-Code law, novices were protected by a penalty of excommunication to be incurred by any who maliciously assaulted them.[80]

The Code has reproduced the penal enactments for violations of the privilege of the canon as they were contained in the Constitution *"Apostolicae Sedis"* of October 12, 1869, except that in the Code the word *monachos* has been changed to *religiosorum*. It is evident from the old law that novices were included in the term *monachos*. Now, canon 2343 restates the pre-Code law, and in

---

[78] Can. 119.

[79] Several authors holding this opinion are mentioned by McGrath, *The Privilege of the Canon,* The Catholic University of America Canon Law Studies, n. 242 (Washington, D. C.: The Catholic University of America Press, 1946), p. 79. However, it should be noted that McGrath himself does not adhere to this opinion.

[80] "Consultationes,"—*CpR,* VII (1926), 187-190; c. 21, *de sententia excommunicationis, suspensionis et interdicti,* V, 11, in VI°.

accordance with the principles of canon 6, nn. 2, 3, it is to be interpreted in the light of the pre-Code legislation.[81]

Consequently, it seems safe to conclude that novices of religious institutes by virtue of the privilege of the canon are protected from real injury by means of the penalty which canon 2343, § 4, imposes on those who assault them. Since this sanction can be applied in the case of novices, it seems equally justifiable to apply it to quasi-religious. Both enjoy the privilege of the canon, without being religious properly so called.[82] Novices of quasi-religious societies likewise are protected by the penal sanction of canon 2343, § 4. However, since the postulants of these societies do not enjoy the privileges of the society, the penalty of canon 2343, § 4, is not incurred by those who are guilty of the malicious striking of one of them.[83]

Section 2. The Privilege of the Forum

All lawsuits against members of quasi-religious societies, both civil and criminal, must be brought before an ecclesiastical court, unless in some countries other provisions have been legitimately made.[84]

The supreme head of a quasi-religious society of pontifical law cannot be brought into a secular court without the permission of the Holy See, while other members may not be civilly cited without the permission of the ordinary of the place where the case is to be tried.[85]

However, if a member of a society is sued in the secular courts by one who has not obtained the proper permission, he may, compelled by necessity, put in an appearance to avoid greater evil, but he must inform the authority from whom permission should have been obtained.[86]

---

[81] Fontes, n. 552; can. 2343, § 4; McGrath, *The Privilege of the Canon,* pp. 80-81.

[82] McGrath, *The Privilege of the Canon,* p. 82; Cipollini, *De Censuris Latae Sententiae iuxta Codicem Iuris Canonici* (Taurini: Marietti, 1925), p. 172; Goyeneche, *loc. cit.*

[83] Schäfer, *De Religiosis,* p. 775.

[84] Can. 120, § 1.

[85] Can. 120, § 2.

[86] Can. 120, § 3.

The legislation on the privilege of the forum granted to clerics by the Code has up to this point been applied to quasi-religious societies in virtue of canon 680. However, the following applications of the common law to these societies are based on the oft-stated principle, that in regard to exemption quasi-religious societies enjoying this privilege are entitled to all the concessions granted by the Code to exempt religious institutes.[87]

In virtue of this principle the following applications of the common law are justified. If a controversy should arise between two members of the same exempt clerical society, the judge in the first instance, unless the constitutions prescribe otherwise, is the provincial superior.[88] The competent provincial superior is the provincial superior of the defendant, in accordance with the prescription of canon 1559, § 3. The provincial superior is also competent to judge cases between two or more houses of the same province of exempt clerical societies. If the houses are of different provinces, the judge in the first instance is the provincial superior of the defendant house.[89]

If the controversy is between two provinces of an exempt clerical society, the judge in the first instance is the Superior General or his delegate.[90]

Finally, if the controversy is between two physical or moral persons of different exempt clerical societies, or between persons of the same non-exempt clerical society or of any lay society, or between a member of a society and a secular cleric or a layman, the judge in the first instance is the ordinary of the place where the house of the society to which the defendant belongs, is established, or of the residence of the secular cleric or layman if either of these be the defendant.[91]

In cases in which the local ordinary is the judge in the first instance the appeal goes to the Metropolitan of the respective local ordinary.[92]

[87] Cf. can. 680; *supra*, pp. 109-110.

[88] Can. 1579, § 1.

[89] Can. 1559, § 3; Schäfer, *De Religiosis*, p. 778.

[90] Can. 1579, § 2.

[91] Can. 1579, § 3. Beste is of the opinion that in a lawsuit between two different clerical exempt societies the case must be tried before the Roman Rota, in accordance with canon 1557, § 2, n. 2, *Introductio in Codicem*, p. 768.

[92] Can. 1594, § 1.

In cases in which the provincial superior of an exempt clerical society is the judge in the first instance the appeal is to the Superior General.[93]

If the Superior General is the judge in the first instance, the appeal goes to the Roman Rota. However, the case is sent to the Roman Rota through the agency of the Sacred Congregation of Religious. The final instance for all cases affecting societies is the Sacred Roman Rota.[94]

Canon 1652 states that, apart from the three exceptions mentioned in the canon, religious have no personal standing in court without the consent of their superiors. However, it is the opinion of the writer that, quasi-religious are not comprehended by the restrictive prescription of this canon. The canon expressly uses the word *religiosi* as the subjects of this law. By applying the canonical principle, *Odia restringi et favores convenit ampliari,* quasi-religious may be excluded from those comprehended in the word *religiosi,* and, consequently, considered as not being obliged by the law of the canon.[95]

Canon 2341 states the penalty incurred by those who violate the precepts of canon 120. By virtue of canon 680, quasi-religious enjoy the privilege of the forum as established in canon 120. Consequently, anyone who violates this right with respect to a member of a quasi-religious society incurs the penalty of canon 2341.

Consequently, if anyone dares to cite the supreme superior of a quasi-religious society of pontifical law before a secular judge, he incurs automatically an excommunication simply reserved to the Holy See; if without the proper permission, a lay person cites before a secular court any member of a quasi-religious society enjoying the privilege of the forum, he should be punished with condign penalties in proportion to his guilt by the proper ordinary; if a cleric commits this offense he is automatically suspended from office, which suspension is reserved to the ordinary.[96]

---

[93] Can. 1594, § 1.

[94] Schäfer, *De Religiosis,* p. 779.

[95] Can. 1652; Krol, *The Defendant in Contentious Trials,* p. 71.

[96] Can. 2341; Schäfer, *De Religiosis,* p. 1036.

Section 3. The Privilege of Immunity

By virtue of canon 680, the prescription of canon 121 becomes applicable to quasi-religious societies. Therefore all members of quasi-religious societies are exempt from military service and from all civil duties and offices which are alien to the clerical state.

Section 4. The Privilege of Competency

The prescription of canon 122 is likewise applicable to quasi-religious societies in virtue of canon 680. Accordingly, members of these societies, when compelled to pay their creditors, may not be deprived of what is necessary for their decent maintenance, according to the prudent judgment of the ecclesiastical judge. But they remain under the obligation of satisfying their creditors as soon as possible.

SCHOLION I. THE CELEBRATION OF MIDNIGHT MASS

In accordance with the prescriptions of canon 821, § 3, in all religious houses or pious houses having an oratory with the faculty of habitually reserving the Blessed Sacrament, one priest may say the three ritual Masses at midnight on Christmas or one only. Attendance at this Mass will satisfy the obligation of hearing Mass for all who assist at it, and Holy Communion may be given to those who wish to receive.[97]

In the opinion of authors the privilege stated in canon 821, § 3, is applicable to quasi-religious societies, in view of the general extension of the term *pious houses.*[98]

SCHOLION II. THE CONFERRING OF BENEFICES ON QUASI-RELIGIOUS

Canon 1442 states that secular benefices are to be conferred on secular clerics exclusively; and that religious benefices are to be conferred on members of that religious organization to which the benefices belong. However, the exclusion of religious from secular

[97] Can. 821, § 3.

[98] Fanfani, *De Religiosis,* p. 406; Augustine, *A Commentary on Canon Law,* IV, 166; Schäfer, *De Religiosis,* p. 759.

benefices is not to be extended to members of clerical quasi-religious societies. This conclusion is based on the restrictive use of the words, *religiosa sodalibus illius religionis.* Members of quasi-religious societies are not *religious,* nor are quasi-religious societies *religious organizations.*[99]

By an application of the canonical principle, *Odia restringi et favores convenit ampliari,* it seems warranted to draw the following conclusion. Quasi-religious are given the protection afforded to religious by canons 1422 and 1430. Consequently, any transfer, division and dismemberment of benefices belonging to these societies is reserved to the Holy See. Likewise, the ordinary cannot convert a benefice belonging to a quasi-religious society into a secular benefice.[100]

---

[99] Beste, *Introductio in Codicem,* p. 710.

[100] Cf. cans. 1422; 1430. An explanation of the principle mentioned has already been given. Cf. *supra,* p. 74.

CHAPTER X

The Transfer, the Departure and the Dismissal of Subjects of Quasi-Religious Societies

ARTICLE I. THE TRANSFER OF SUBJECTS OF QUASI-RELIGIOUS SOCIETIES

Canon 681, which deals with the question of the transfer of members of quasi-religious societies, states the following: In addition to the prescriptions of the constitutions of each society, regulating the transfer of members to other societies without vows or to some religious institute properly so called, the prescriptions of canons 632-635 must likewise be observed in so far as it is possible, in accordance with the nature of each society.

The prescriptions of the constitutions must not be contrary to, though they may be more stringent than, the general prescriptions of the Code, However, even in the event that the prescriptions of the constitutions are contrary to the Code, they still retain their binding force if the constitutions received approval after the advent of the present Code.[1]

A transfer occurs when one, who is bound by obligations to a certain religious institute or quasi-religious society of which he is a member, commutes these into obligations which derive from another institute or society.[2]

Accordingly, there can be no question of a transfer properly so called on the part of a member of a society in which there are no bonds of perseverance, at least of a temporary nature. For in such a society a member is bound by the obligations deriving from the society only for the length of time during which he remains in the society. Just as soon as he leaves this society to join a new society or institute, all his obligations in the former cease. When a member does pass from such a society to another society or institute

[1] Blat, *De Religiosis*, p. 534.

[2] Wernz-Vidal, *De Religiosis*, n. 458; Schäfer, *De Religiosis*, p. 928.

there actually is a departure from one society with a subsequent admission into another society or institute. No special permissions are required for such a quasi-transfer, for then there is not had any transfer properly so called, nor did the incorporation in the former society constitute an impediment for admission into another society or institute. As has already been mentioned, a religious profession properly so called is contemplated in the restrictions enacted in canon 542, n. 1, and not a previous incorporation in a quasi-religious society.[3]

The writer disagrees in part with Goyeneche, who in discussing the question of the transfer of members of quasi-religious societies seems to confuse the notion of a transfer with that of a member's departure from his society and subsequent admission into a new society or institute. As a consequence of this confusion, Goyeneche permits an authority subordinate to that of the Holy See to permit a transfer from a society which requires of its members a bond of perseverance. He argues that the permission necessary for a transfer from such a society must be secured from the person to whom the act of freeing from this bond is reserved. He consequently concludes that in diocesan quasi-religious societies the local ordinary may give the necessary permission for the transfer, unless the act of freeing the member from the bond of perseverance is reserved to the Holy See, while in pontifically approved quasi-religious societies the necessary permission for the transfer must be secured from the Holy See, or from the persons to whom the act of freeing from the bond is reserved by the constitutions.[4]

On the contrary, the writer holds that whenever the permission to leave a society is secured from the person to whom the act of freeing from the bond of perseverance is reserved, the member is relieved from all obligations to the society. When later this person enters another society or institute, there is no question of a transfer of his obligations. Rather, there actually has been a legitimate departure from one society, and then a subsequent admission into another society or institute. Consequently, as long as

[3] Cf. *supra*, p. 186; Vermeersch-Creusen, *Epitome*, I, n. 682; Wernz-Vidal, *De Religiosis*, n. 458, VI; Schäfer, *De Religiosis*, p. 930; Goyeneche, "Studia Canonica,"—*CpR*, I (1920), 296.

[4] "Studia Canonica,"—*CpR*, I (1920), 295-296, 359.

there exists some bond of perseverance for the member of a quasi-religious society, whether that society be one of pontifical or one of diocesan approval, and whether the bond be temporary or permanent in nature, such a member may not transfer from that society to another society or religious institute until he has secured the necessary papal permission as demanded by canon 632 for the transfer of religious generally. In canon 681 the prescription of canon 632 is expressly mentioned as binding quasi-religious societies.[5]

Accordingly, in keeping with the prescription of canon 632, no one may transfer from a quasi-religious society to another such society or to a religious institute without the permission of the Holy See, even though the transfer be to a stricter institute.[6] Similarly, no one may transfer from a religious institute to a quasi-religious society without the permission of the Holy See.[7]

A member transferring from a quasi-religious society to a religious institute must undergo a novitiate in the latter. During this period of the novitiate his rights and obligations in the society are suspended, and he must obey the superiors and the novice master of the religious institute just as the other novices are obliged to do. It would seem that if the quasi-religious was bound to a special obligation of obedience, as demanded by the constitutions of the society, he would be obliged to obey the superiors and novice master of the religious institute in virtue of this special obligation, which would retain its force until his religious profession. If he does not make a profession in the religious institute, he must return to the society, unless in the meantime his obligations with reference to the society have expired. These conclusions are a result of the application of the prescription of canon 633 to quasi-religious societies, warranted in virtue of canon 681.[8]

If the transfer takes place from one society to another quasi-religious society, a new novitiate must be made in the latter if its

---

[5] Wernz-Vidal, *De Religiosis,* n. 458; Blat, *De Religiosis,* p. 534; Berutti, *De Religiosis,* p. 372; Cocchi, *De Religiosis,* n. 167 (2).

[6] Vermeersch-Creusen, *Epitome,* I, n. 682.

[7] Blat, *De Religiosis,* p. 536; Goyeneche, "Studia Canonica,"—*CpR,* I (1920), 359.

[8] Blat, *De Religiosis,* pp. 538-539.

constitutions require a period of novitiate or trial. If incorporation in the latter does not take place, the person transferring is obliged to return to the former society, unless his obligations with reference to it have meanwhile come to an end.[9]

The Sacred Congregation of Religious on May 11, 1923, declared, in answer to a doubt, that if a member of a religious institute has obtained a papal indult to transfer to another institute, he must wear the habit of the novices of the latter during the time of his novitiate in it.[10]

Although the reply mentioned only members of religious institutes, it is the opinion of the writer that it must be applied also to quasi-religious. The doubt concerned itself with a legal process, which, by virtue of the common law itself, is equally applicable to religious institutes and quasi-religious societies. Therefore, it seems that any legislation concerning this process should likewise be equally applicable to both.[11]

In the case of the transfer of a member of a religious institute to a quasi-religious society, it seems safe to conclude that the religious is still bound by the prescription of canon 633, which regulates the transfer both of religious and of quasi-religious. Therefore, the religious in question must submit to the probation of the society, if it be demanded by the constitutions. In the meantime his rights and obligations in the religious institute are suspended. He must likewise obey the superiors and the novice master of the society in virtue of his vow of obedience, which retains its force until he is incorporated in the society. He, too, is obliged to return to the institute if he is not subsequently incorporated in the society, unless, in the meanwhile, his temporary vows have expired.

Canon 634 states that, if a religious who has made a profession of perpetual vows joins another institute in which perpetual vows are taken by the members, he must at the end of the novitiate either be admitted to perpetual profession, the temporary profession spoken of in canon 574 being omitted, or return to the former religious institute. The superior has a right to prolong the period

---

[9] Berutti, *De Religiosis*, p. 188 (1).

[10] *AAS,* XV (1923), 156.

[11] Can. 20.

of probation for not more than one year after the completion of the novitiate.

In accordance with the prescription of canon 681, canon 634 is applicable to quasi-religious societies not only in the transfer from one society to another society, but also in a transfer from a quasi-religious society to a religious institute. However, the application of canon 634 to quasi-religious societies presents several difficulties not only because of the divergent nature of the various societies but also inasmuch as canon 574, which demands a temporary profession before the profession of final vows, does not apply to quasi-religious societies.

Vermeersch is of the opinion that canon 634 is to be applied absolutely to quasi-religious societies. Accordingly, he claims if a member perpetually incorporated in a quasi-religious society transfers to a religious institute he must, at the completion of the novitiate, be admitted to perpetual vows or return to the society, unless the superior prolongs the probation for a time not beyond one year. He bases this conclusion on the following reasoning. Canon 681 states that canon 634 is to be applied to quasi-religious societies, *congrua congruis referando*. He interprets this clause in the light of the response of the Pontifical Commission for the Authentic Interpretation of the Canons of the Code, issued on March 1, 1921, stating that in the dismissal of members from quasi-religious societies the canons regulating the dismissal of temporarily professed religious are applicable to the dismissal of members temporarily incorporated in the society; while the members perpetually incorporated in the society are to be dismissed in accordance with the legislation regulating the dismissal of perpetually professed religious. Therefore, so the author claims, the canons concerning the transfer of religious in perpetual vows are likewise applicable to quasi-religious perpetually incorporated in their society; while the canons pertaining to the transfer of religious in temporary vows should be applied to members temporarily incorporated in quasi-religious societies.

The author further claims that this application of canon 634 is justified by reason of the undesirable effect that would follow from a lesser application of the canon. Thus, if a member perpetually incorporated in a quasi-religious society were to transfer to a religious institute in which perpetual vows are taken, he could, since he would not be held to the norm of canon 634, leave the institute after temporary vows in spite of his former will to remain forever in the special service of God. This, Vermeersch claims, is entirely contrary both to the mind and the practice of the Church.[12]

On this point Schäfer is of the same opinion as Vermeersch.[13] Blat, however claims that, inasmuch as quasi-religious societies are not bound by canon 574, which demands a temporary profession of at least three years prior to a perpetual profession, they likewise are not bound by canon 634. Therefore, he claims, if a member of a quasi-religious society transfers to a religious institute in which perpetual vows are taken, he must always make a temporary profession after the novitiate, regardless of his having made a perpetual or a temporary promise to the society.[14]

The writer is of the same opinion as Vermeersch and Schäfer, for he feels that this opinion best satisfies the prescription of canon 681, which states that canon 634 is applicable to quasi-religious societies not only in the case of a transfer from one society to another, but also from a society to a religious institute. Consequently, if a member perpetually enrolled in a society transfers to another society which grants perpetual incorporation he must after the time of probation as demanded by the constitutions either be admitted to perpetual incorporation or return to the former society, granted the right of the superior to extend the period of probation, not however beyond a year after the regular time.

Likewise, if a member of a religious institute in perpetual vows transfers to a society which grants perpetual incorporation, he must, after completing the period of trial, either be admitted to perpetual incorporation or return to the religious institute from which he made his transfer. The superior of the society has the right of demanding an additional probation period of not more than one year after the regularly prescribed period of trial.[15]

---

[12] De Transeunte ad aliam religionem,"—*Periodica,* XIX (1930), 164;* *AAS,* XIII (1921), 177.

[13] *De Religiosis,* p. 938.

[14] *De Religiosis,* p. 541; Goyeneche, *Iuris Canonici Principia,* Libri, II, pars II, III, *De Religiosis-De Laicis* (Roma: Herder S.A.L.E.R., 1938), II, 190.

[15] Schäfer, *De Religiosis,* p. 938.

Blat, although not allowing the application of canon 634 in the transfer of a member of a quasi-religious society to a religious institute, does partially satisfy the demand of canon 634 by allowing an application of its prescription in the transfer from one society to another society. Accordingly, he claims that a member who has been perpetually incorporated in a quasi-religious society, may upon a period of trial, as long as the constitutions do not prescribe otherwise, be subsequently admitted into perpetual incorporation in the new society to which he has transferred.[16]

It would seem advisable in view of the difference of opinion in this matter, that whenever there is a case of a transfer of a permanently incorporated member of a quasi-religious society to another society in which there is had a perpetual incorporation or to a religious institute in which perpetual vows are taken, there should be sought from the Holy See along with permission for the transfer, a clarification of its mind with regard to the manner of incorporation in the new society or institute.

In consequence of the application of canon 635 to quasi-religious societies, in accordance with canon 681, the following conclusions may be drawn. A member transferring from a quasi-religious society to another society or to a religious institute loses, from the moment of his new incorporation, all the rights which he possessed in the society from which he transferred, but at the same time he is freed of all the obligations which it imposed. Moreover, from the same moment he assumes the rights and duties which derive from the society or institute to which he has transferred. The society from which the transfer was made retains the ownership of the goods which it acquired in accordance with the prescription of canon 676, § 3. The administration, the ownership and the use of the personal property of the member must be regulated in accordance with the prescriptions of the constitutions of the society or the institute to which the transfer has been made.[17]

If a member of a quasi-religious society transfers to a religious institute he must, before his first profession, cede the administration of his goods to a person of his own free choice and, accord-

---

[16] *De Religiosis,* p. 541.

[17] Blat, *De Religiosis,* p. 543.

ing to his pleasure, dispose of the use and the income of his personal property, unless the constitutions of the new institute rule otherwise with regard to such disposal.[18] He must likewise, before his first profession, freely dispose by last will of the goods which he actually possesses, and such as may perchance come to him in the future.[19] If he has transferred to a religious institute in which solemn vows are taken he must, in accordance with the prescription of canon 581, § 1, within sixty days prior to his solemn profession, renounce all his goods actually possessed in favor of a person or persons of his choice.[20]

Similarly, if a person transfers from a religious institute to a quasi-religious society, the institute retains the goods which the member had acquired by reason of his affiliation with the religious institute (*intuitu societatis*), while the constitutions of the new society will determine the administration, ownership, and the use of his personal goods. If, in accordance with the prescription of canon 569, § 3, the former religious has made a will, it seems that the will retains its validity, unless the constitutions of the society prescribe otherwise. The common law does not apply to the members of quasi-religious societies the obligation of making a will; rather, it states in canon 677 that in the admission of candidates the constitutions are to be observed. Consequently, the writer concludes that the will of the former religious would be valid, unless the constitutions prescribed otherwise.[21]

If a member of a quasi-religious society of women transfers to a religious institute, she must observe, with regard to the dowry, the prescriptions of canon 547. Therefore if she transfers to a monastery of nuns she must pay the dowry as determined by the constitutions. This payment must be made before the taking of the habit, or it should at least be guaranteed at that time by some document which is binding in civil law, and in this case, it must be handed over at least before profession. If she transfers to an institute of simple vows the constitutions must be observed with regard to the dowry and the manner in which it shall be made up

[18] Can. 569, § 1.

[19] Can. 569, § 3.

[20] Can. 581, § 1.

[21] Cf. cans. 569, § 3; 635; 677.

If a member of an institute of women religious in which a dowry has been paid should transfer to a quasi-religious society of women, the society has the right to the income from the dowry during the time of probation, provided the new society demands something for the board of the aspirants. After the member has become incorporated in the society, the entire dowry belongs to the society, in the event that the constitutions of the society demand a dowry. However, it seems altogether proper that, if the constitutions of the new society do not demand a dowry, it should be returned to the newly incorporated member by the former institute.[22]

In accordance with the prescription of canon 635, n. 1, applicable to quasi-religious societies by virtue of canon 681, the simple vows of a religious who transfers to a quasi-religious society are automatically dispensed at the moment of his incorporation in the society. However, it should be noted that canon 636, which according to the common law is not applicable to quasi-religious societies, provides for the automatic cessation of the solemn vows of a religious who, upon a transfer to an institute in which simple vows are taken, makes a final profession of simple vows. Inasmuch as canon 681 specifically mentions only canons 632-635 as applicable to quasi-religious societies, some authors conclude that, if one who was solemnly professed transfers to a quasi-religious society, the solemn vows are not automatically extinguished, unless this fact is expressly mentioned in the apostolic indult which permitted the transfer.[23]

In the transfer of members of quasi-religious societies it seems right to conclude that the testimonials required are the same as in the case of the transfer of religious. Consequently, in accordance with the prescription of canon 544, § 5, the only testimonial needed after the reception of an apostolic indult which permits the transfer, is the testimony of the major superior of the relinquished society. It is presumed that the relinquished society had already received all the necessary testimonials previous to its acceptance

[22] Cf. can. 551; Goyeneche, *Iuris Canonici Summa Principia*, II, 93-94; Creusen, *Religious Men and Women in the Code*, p. 146.

[23] Schäfer, *De Religiosis*, p. 941; Bastien, *Directoire Canonique*, p. 118, note 1.

of the member so that it would be without purpose to require the newly adopted society or institute to seek them through other sources. An exception to the just mentioned conclusion would occur in the case of a transfer from a society which did not demand the particular testimonials of its candidates which are demanded of the condidates for a religious institute. In that case, the testimonials demanded by the religious institute but not by the society, would have to be furnished by the transferring member, in addition to the testimony of the major superior. Moreover, in accordance with the prescription of canon 544, § 6, the superior of the newly entered society or institute may, if he wishes, demand further testimony.[24]

ARTICLE II. THE LEGITIMATE DEPARTURE OF SUBJECTS FROM QUASI-RELIGIOUS SOCIETIES

In those quasi-religious societies in which there are no bonds of perseverance the members are free to leave at any time, as long as the prescriptions of the constitutions which regulate the procedure to be followed in departure are duly observed. If temporary bonds of perseverance are promised, the members are free to leave at their expiration, provided that they observe the prescriptions of the constitutions governing this departure. This conclusion considers only the legal freedom to depart, the moral obligations in question are beyond the scope of this discussion.[25]

If a member of a quasi-religious society wishes to leave the society while he is still bound by obligations of perseverance to the society, a dispensation must be sought from the person to whom the act of freeing from the bond of perseverance is reserved. The constitutions of the various societies will determine the proper authority.

In several societies the act of freeing a member from the bond of perseverance is reserved to the Holy See, v.g., among the Eudists, the Paulists, and in the Society of Saint Columbian. In the case of the Congregation of the Mission, the Pallottine Fathers,

---

[24] Can. 544, §§ 5, 6; Goyeneche, "Studia Canonica,"—*CpR,* I (1920), 359.

[25] Piontek, *De Indulto Exclaustrationis necnon Saecularizationis,* p. 181; Vermeersch-Creusen, *Epitome,* I, n. 675, note 1.

and in the Society of the African Missions the act of freeing from the bond of perseverance is also entrusted to the Superior General.[26]

An unusual case is presented by the Society of the Oratory of France. In this particular society a member may not be definitively incorporated in the Society until he has completed three years in the priesthood. If after that period the superiors do not wish to affiliate him permanently with the Society, they must find a benevolent bishop for him.[27]

The canons of the Code treating of the question of exclaustration and secularization do not apply to quasi-religious. These matters are contained in canons 638-640. The following reasons are given by the authors why these canons are not applied to quasi-religious societies. The prescriptions of these canons are concerned entirely with the question of release from the obligations of public vows, whether the release be temporary or permanent. However, in quasi-religious societies no public vows are pronounced. There can be no question then, of a release from public vows where no public vows have been taken. Finally, no general rules for departure from quasi-religious societies could possibly be given by the common law in view of the widespread difference of their constitutions.[28]

However, as Stanton points out, although canons 638-640 do not apply to quasi-religious societies, nevertheless the Sacred Congregation of Religious, when dealing with societies in which the act of freeing members from the bond of perseverance is reserved to the Holy See, frequently uses the words *secularization* and *exclaustration* with reference to these societies.[29]

In the case of some exempt clerical quasi-religious societies, the Sacred Congregation of Religious has granted a special indult whereby the effect of canon 585 is applied to them. Consequently,

---

[26] Berutti, *De Religiosis*, p. 372; Wernz-Vidal, *De Religiosis*, n. 458; Stanton, *De Societatibus*, p. 151.

[27] Stanton, *De Societatibus*, pp. 151-152.

[28] Piontek, *De Indulto Exclaustrationis necnon Saecularizationis*, p. 180; Wernz-Vidal, *De Religiosis*, n. 458, VII; Cocchi, *De Religiosis*, n. 167; Fanfani, *De Religiosis*, p. 531.

[29] *De Societatibus*, p. 152.

perpetual affiliation with the society brings about loss of the proper diocese of the members thus incorporated.[80]

If a cleric in major orders who is a member of such a society were to leave it, he would not be governed by the prescription of canon 641, § 2. This canon permits a bishop to receive an ex-religious into his diocese for a trial period of three years, which period he may extend for an additional duration of three years, upon the completion of which the cleric becomes automatically incardinated in the diocese if he has not been previously dismissed. This canon applies only to clerics in major orders who had been members of a religious institute. There exists no reason for the extending of its application to quasi-religious societies.[81]

Consequently, if a cleric in major orders has left a quasi-religious society in which, by reason of special legislation or privilege, he has lost his proper ordinary, he can be put on an indefinite period of trial during which the ordinary may dismiss him regardless of the number of years of probation that may have elapsed.

In accordance with the prescription of canon 642, § 2, when a member of a quasi-religious society in sacred orders has been dispensed from his obligations of perseverance in the society, then, in the event that he had been bound by these obligations for at least six years, he becomes subject to the prohibitions enacted in canon 642, § 1.

Accordingly, such a dispensed member on his return to the world, though he may exercise his sacred orders, is forbidden without a new and special indult from the Holy See: 1) to hold any benefice in minor or major basilicas or cathedral churches; 2) to hold any professorship or office in a major or minor seminary, in a college in which clerics are educated, or in universities or institutions which enjoy the papal privilege of conferring academic degrees; and 3) to hold any office or position in the curia

---

[80] Vermeersch-Creusen, *Epitome*, I, n. 679. Quasi-religious do not lose their proper diocese by any prescription of the common law.

[81] Stanton, *De Societatibus*, p. 152; can. 641, § 2. However, Stanton cautions that it is always essential to consider well the indult of quasi-exclaustration granted to members of quasi-religious societies before denying them the benefits of canon 641.

of the bishop, or in religious houses of either men or women, even if these houses pertain to diocesan institutes.[32]

However it would appear that such a priest may hold a position or office in a quasi-religious society and be appointed confessor for such a society, for the houses of quasi-religious societies are not religious houses properly so called.

The prescriptions of canon 642, § 1, do not apply to members of quasi-religious societies who after six years of affiliation with a society through a temporary bond of perseverance have not thereafter renewed their bonds of perseverance but have legitimately left the society. To become subject to the prescriptions of this canon, a member must be dispensed from an actually existing incorporation in the society which has perdured beyond six years.

If contrary to the prescription of canon 642, § 2, a former member of a society or of a religious institute were given one of the positions forbidden by the prescriptions of this canon, the appointment would indeed be illicit but nevertheless valid.[33]

ARTICLE III. ILLEGITIMATE DEPARTURE OF SUBJECTS FROM QUASI-RELIGIOUS HOUSES

Since quasi-religious do not take public vows and consequently are not religious strictly so called, Lib. II, Tit. XVII, of the Code, does not refer to canon 644, § 1, wherein an *apostate* from religion is defined as one who while bound by perpetual vows, unlawfully leaves the religious house with the intention of not returning, or as one who, after legitimately leaving the house, does not return, having the mind of withdrawing himself from religious obedience. Hence it follows, that the penalty of canon 2385 incurred by apostates from religion is not to be applied to quasi-religious who depart their society with the same intention.[34]

However, the particular law of these societies may be invoked for the punishment of such members. Furthermore, superiors in exempt clerical societies may in virtue of their jurisdiction punish

[32] Can. 642, §§ 1, 2.

[33] Schäfer, *De Religiosis,* p. 968.

[34] Schäfer, *De Religiosis,* p. 975; Vermeersch-Creusen, *Epitome,* I, n. 682; Wernz-Vidal, *De Religiosis,* n. 458, VIII; Fanfani, *De Religiosis,* p. 531.

such members with a suitable penalty, and in all other societies, the superiors may do so in virtue of their dominative power.[85]

Canon 644, § 3, defines a *fugitive* from a religious institute as one who without permission of the superior has left the religious house but still intends to return to it. Authors also point out that this offense is likewise present when one leaves the house with permission of the superior but extends the absence beyond the time originally permitted by the superior. All commentators are agreed that two or three days of unlawful absence are required to constitute a fugitive in the canonical sense.[86]

The notion of profession through public vows is not essential to the concept of a fugitive from a religious institute. Consequently, members of quasi-religious societies and their novices may rightly be considered fugitives from their respective societies whenever they fulfill the conditions expressed in canon 644, § 3.[87]

However, to incur the penalties imposed on a fugitive from a religious institute one must be a religious properly so called, for canon 2386 mentions as subject to these penalties only religious who are fugitives. Therefore, fugitives from quasi-religious societies are not generally subject to these penalties. There is, however, an exception to this conclusion. On June 2-3, 1918, the Pontifical Commission for the Authentic Interpretation of the Canons of the Code declared that the penalties of canon 2386 were to be applied to fugitives from clerical quasi-religious societies in which the common life is observed.[88]

Consequently, fugitives from clerical quasi-religious societies in which the common life is observed are automatically deprived of any office they hold in the particular society, and, if they are in major orders, incur a suspension reserved to their major superiors. When they return to the society they are to be punished in accordance with the prescriptions of the constitutions. If the constitutions do not prescribe any penalty for this offense, the

---

[85] Voltas, "Consultationes," *CpR,* I (1920), 270-272; Schäfer, *De Religiosis,* p. 1039.

[86] Schäfer, *De Religiosis,* p. 976.

[87] Schäfer, *De Religiosis,* p. 976.

[88] *AAS,* IX (1918), 347.

major superiors shall inflict penalties in proportion to the offense committed.[39]

In exempt clerical quasi-religious societies the suspension mentioned in canon 2386 is certainly reserved in its remission to the major superiors of the society. However, the lifting of a suspension requires the power of jurisdiction, a power not possessed by the major superiors in non-exempt societies. Schäfer claims that in canon 2386 jurisdiction is given by the law even to superiors of non-exempt clerical societies and institutes for this one particular case. He states that until the Holy See declares otherwise, this opinion may be followed. The authors who hold a contrary opinion claim that a recourse must be had to the local ordinary by the members of non-exempt clerical institutes or societies for the lifting of this suspension.[40]

It has already been pointed out, that a subject who leaves a quasi-religious society with the intention of not returning cannot be called an apostate in the strict canonical sense, nor consequently, can he be subject to the penalty of canon 2385 incurred by apostates from religious institutes. Neither may he be considered a fugitive, for a fugitive is one who leaves a religious house with the intention of returning. Consequently, he is not liable to the penalties which are imposed on fugitives from a religious institute or from a clerical quasi-religious society. Schäfer offers a practical solution to the difficult problem of suitably punishing such members by calling them *"ad instar"* apostates and making them liable to the penalties which the constitutions may impose on such subjects.[41]

Moreover, an *"ad instar"* apostate from a quasi-religious society who is incorporated to the society by a temporary bond of perseverance can be dismissed in accordance with the prescriptions of canon 647 regardless of the fact whether he remains contumacious or whether he returns repentant to the society. For canon 647

---

[39] Can. 2386.

[40] Schäfer, *De Religiosis,* p. 981; Vermeersch-Creusen, *Epitome,* III, n. 590.

[41] *De Religiosis,* p. 1036; Riesner, *Apostates and Fugitives from Religious Institutes,* the Catholic University of America Canon Law Studies, n. 168 (Washington, D. C.: The Catholic University of America Press, 1942), pp. 54-55.

states that one who is temporarily affiliated with an institute may be dismissed for just causes and the commission of a crime is not required as a condition for dismissal. The desertion from a society by one of its members is, in the opinion of Vermeersch-Creusen, sufficient reason for dismissal.[42]

An *"ad instar"* apostate from a quasi-religious society who is perpetually incorporated to the society may be dismissed from the society, if the constitutions of the society consider such desertion from the society as a crime. In that case the desertion from the society may be considered as the crime which, in accordance with the prescription of canon 649, must be committed before a subject who is permanently affiliated with an institute or a society may be dismissed. Canon 656, n. 1, states that the crime which would be a sufficient cause to warrant the dismissal of a subject who is permanently incorporated to a religious institute need not be a crime in accordance with the prescriptions of the common law but it suffices if the action be a crime according to the prescriptions of the constitutions of the institute.[43] However, if the constitutions do not consider such desertion as a crime then the subject permanently incorporated in the society who commits such a desertion cannot be dismissed because the act is not a crime.[44]

The subjects of quasi-religious societies of women who are permanently affiliated to the society may be dismissed for an act of *"ad instar"* apostasy if they remain incorrigible, since not crimes but only grave external causes are sufficient reason for their dismissal.[45]

As has already been mentioned, the Pontifical Commission declared that fugitives from clerical quasi-religious societies are subject to the penalties of canon 2386. Authors dispute, however, whether this response refers only to clerical societies, or whether it is likewise applicable to lay quasi-religious societies. Riesner states that the answer to this question depends on whether the response of the Commission was intended as an extensive response

---

[42] *Epitome,* III, n. 589; Riesner, *Apostates and Fugitives from Religious Institutes,* p. 127.

[43] Riesner, *Fugitives and Apostates from Religious Institutes,* pp. 128-129.

[44] Riesner, *loc. cit.*

[45] Cf. cans. 681; 651, § 2.

or merely a declaratory response. If the response is extensive, then the members of lay societies are not held to the prescriptions enacted in canon 2386. However, if the response is a declaratory one, i.e., if it but points out what is already clearly stated in the law, then the penalties of canon 2386 are applicable to fugitives from lay quasi-religious societies. Riesner is of the opinion that the response is merely declaratory because the reason given by the Commission for applying the penalties of 2386 to the clerical societies is true of both clerical and lay quasi-religious societies, i.e., in so far as they lead a common life. The author concludes, however, that even if the opinion holding that the response is a declaratory one is more probable, yet, because of the extrinsic authority of those who hold it is extensive, it cannot be certainly held that the fugitive members of lay quasi-religious societies are liable to the penalties of canon 2386 because in penalties the more benign interpretation is to be used.[46]

Nevertheless, whenever a member of a quasi-religious society illicitly leaves a house of the society, whether he has the intention of returning or not, and whether he is or is not bound by a perpetual bond of perseverance, there rests upon him the natural obligation of returning to the house he illicitly left. Furthermore, canon 681 expressly declares that in so far as is possible the prescriptions of canon 645 are to be applied to quasi-religious societies. This canon states that any apostate or fugitive from a religious institute is bound to return to the institute as quickly as possible and, furthermore, that he is in no way relieved of his obligations to the institute by his illegal flight. With the application of this canon to a quasi-religious who illegally leaves his place of residence, it is seen that the fugitive or quasi-apostate from a society is not relieved of his obligations to the society and therefore is bound by the common law to return. Moreover, his superior is obliged to seek for him and to receive him, if he returns truly penitent.[47]

In accordance with the prescriptions of canon 643, any member who leaves a religious institute, either at the expiration of his

---

[46] *Apostates and Fugitives from Religious Institutes*, pp. 100-102.

[47] Vermeersch-Creusen, *Epitome*, I, n. 682; Fanfani, *De Religiosis*, p. 531; Schäfer, *De Religiosis*, pp. 1036-1037.

temporary vows or in consequence of a dispensation, as also a member who has been dismissed from the institute, cannot demand any compensation for services rendered to it by him.[48]

Nowhere in the Code is it explicitly mentioned that this canon is applicable to quasi-religious societies. However, it seems that in consideration of the very end of the law and of the nature of quasi-religious societies, so similar to that of religious institutes, legislation on this particular matter is essential for these societies. Since this legislation is not expressly contained in the Code, it must be supplied. Therefore, by an application of canon 20, the prescriptions of canon 643 must be referred to quasi-religious. Furthermore, the Code itself seems to favor this application. For canon 647, § 2, n. 5, applicable to quasi-religious societies of women, by virtue of canon 681, contains within its prescription the legislation of canon 643, § 2. However, it appears that the charitable subsidy called for in canon 643, § 2, is necessary principally because § 1, of this canon deprives a member of any right to compensation for services rendered. While it is true that this mode of reasoning makes canon 643, § 1, applicable only to quasi-religious societies of women and then only in the case of dismissal, still it would seem to indicate that the legislator intended to bind quasi-religious by the prescriptions of canon 643, § 1. For there seems to be no reason why the canon should apply in case of dismissal and not in the case of voluntary departure, nor why it should apply only to societies of women and not to societies of men.

In virtue of the application, then, of canon 643 to quasi-religious societies, the following conclusions may be drawn. Any member who leaves a society at the expiration of his bond of perseverance or after obtaining a dispensation, as also any member who has been dismissed from it, cannot demand any compensation for services rendered to the society by him. However, in the case of women who leave a society for any reason, if no dowry is to be returned to them and if they are not able to provide for themselves, the society must out of motives of charity and equity give them a sufficient subsidy to insure their safe return home and to provide equitably

---

[48] Can. 643, § 1.

for their support for a certain period, fixed by mutual agreement, or, in case of disagreement, by the local ordinary.[49]

ARTICLE IV. THE DISMISSAL OF SUBJECTS FROM QUASI-RELIGIOUS SOCIETIES

Canon 681 states that in the dismissal of subjects from quasi-religious societies the prescriptions of canons 646-672 are to be observed. These canons regulate the dismissal of members from religious institutes. Some of the canons mentioned regulate the dismissal of subjects in temporary vows, while others govern the dismissal of subjects who are perpetually professed. In view of this distinction the Commission for the Authentic Interpretation of the Canons of the Code was asked exactly how these canons were to be applied to quasi-religious societies in which no public vows at all, either temporary or perpetual, were pronounced. The Commission on March 1, 1921, replied that the canons which regulate the dismissal of those religious who are in temporary vows should be applied to the dismissal of subjects from quasi-religious societies who are affiliated with their societies by a temporary bond of perseverance, while the dismissal of subjects who are enrolled in their societies by a permanent bond of perseverance is to be regulated by the canons which legislate for the dismissal of religious who are in perpetual vows.[50]

Maroto (1875-1937) considers the case of a society in which the members take an oath for *"as long as I persevere."* He is of the opinion that the dismissal of members from such a society is to be regulated by the canons legislating for the dismissal of religious temporarily professed. He believes that in effect such an oath implies a temporary duration of the bond since, in order to be perpetual in its duration, an oath must be absolutely irrevocable on the part of the person taking the oath and on the part of the society accepting it. Consequently, since the oath under consideration is revocable on the part of the subject pronouncing it, the oath is not of perpetual but simply of temporary duration.[51]

[49] Can. 643, §§ 1, 2.

[50] *AAS,* XIII (1921), 117.

[51] "Annotationes,"—*CpR,* II (1921), 131-132.

This was the decision given by the Pontifical Commission for the Authentic Interpretation of the Canons of the Code with regard to the dismissal of a religious who took his vows under the same condition, namely, *"as long as I persevere."* The Commission replied that the vows were to be considered as implying merely temporary duration, and hence were to be regarded as temporary vows.[52]

Furthermore, there are certain quasi-religious societies in which no bond of perseverance whatsoever is effected, for example, the Society of the Oratorians of Saint Philip Neri. It seems that the dismissal of members from these societies is not considered at all in the law, and that consequently their dismissal would have to be carried out exclusively in accordance with the prescriptions of their constitutions.[53]

Wernz (1842-1914)-Vidal (1867-1938) compare the dismissal of members from a society in which there exists no bond of perseverance to the dismissal of a novice in a religious institute. They claim that if the constitutions are without any prescriptions regarding their dismissal, then the society is free to dismiss them for causes admitted by the constitutions without the formalities of law and the members are likewise juridically free to leave the society whenever they so desire.[54]

Section 1. Automatic Dismissal of Subjects from Quasi-Religious Societies

A. Delicts Effecting Automatic Dismissal

In accordance with the prescriptions of canon 646, applied to quasi-religious societies in virtue of canon 681, any member of a quasi-religious society, whether he be permanently or temporarily enrolled in it, or even if he has not assumed any obligations of perseverance whatsoever, is automatically dismissed if he commits

---

[52] *AAS,* XIII (1921), 177.

[53] Cocchi, *De Religiosis,* n. 167 (3); Vermeersch-Creusen, *Epitome,* I, n. 682.

[54] *De Religiosis,* n. 458, VII; Maroto, "Annotationes,"—*CpR,* II (1921), 129.

any of the following offenses: 1) public apostasy from the Catholic Faith; 2) flight with a person of the other sex; and 3) the contracting of marriage, or even the attempt to do so, even if there be question simply of a civil bond or union.

1) The act of apostasy does not necessarily postulate any affiliation with a non-Catholic sect. But the act of apostasy must have been a public act in the sense defined in canon 2197, n. 1.

2) The act of flight must likewise have been a public act; otherwise the dismissal is not automatically effective. The concerted action may be of a physical or of a moral character. If the parties conjoined their action in flight some short time after the member's departure from the society, the dismissal would still be effected if the united action of the parties had been agreed upon beforehand. If the accomplice had not yet reached the age of puberty, or if the two parties are related by consanguinity or affinity in the direct line or in the first degree of the collateral line, then it is the common opinion of the authors that the dismissal does not automatically follow.

3) There is question both of the contracted and of an attempted marriage. A valid marriage could of course follow if the status of the persons implied only a prohibitive impediment to marriage. An attempted marriage could result in consequence of any impediment precluding its validity. There is question likewise of the merely civil bond or union, whether attempted only or contracted. The bond or union here contemplated is that to which the civil law accords the status of a marital union.

In all these cases it suffices that the major superior with his council or chapter makes a declaration of the fact, in the manner prescribed by the constitutions of the society. The major superior must likewise take care to preserve in the records of the house the collected evidence of the fact. However, these obligations as placed on the major superior do not affect the validity of the automatic dismissal. Immediately on the commission of the misdeed, the dismissal automatically occurs.[55]

[55] Can. 646; Schäfer, *De Religiosis*, p. 987; Blat, *De Religiosis*, pp. 566-567; Palombo, *De Dimissione Religiosorum* (Taurini-Romae: Marietti, 1931), pp. 234-237.

However, it must be noted that the penalty of canon 2388, § 2, whereby all religious who, while professed with simple perpetual vows contract or attempt marriage, are excommunicated, does not apply to the members of quasi-religious societies. This is in accordance with the prescriptions of canon 2219, § 3, which states that a penalty is not to be extended from person to person, nor from one case to another, even though there be present an equal or even a stronger reason for holding a person guilty.[56]

Nevertheless, the prescription of canon 2388, § 1, whereby all clerics, who attempt marriage while in major orders, are excommunicated, obviously applies to the members of a clerical quasi-religious society who are in major orders. Likewise canon 2314, which states the penalties for all apostates from the Christian Faith, applies to any member of a quasi-religious society who commits the crime of apostasy.

B. The Effects of Automatic Dismissal

If a member of a quasi-religious society, whose affiliation with that society is by a temporary bond of perseverance only, should be automatically dismissed for one of the crimes mentioned in canon 646, he is at the same time automatically absolved from all his obligations to the society. Although this conclusion is not expressly stated in the law, it can nevertheless be deduced from the fact that canon 646 speaks of those who commit these crimes as being considered lawfully dismissed from the society, and that canon 648 provides that those in temporary vows who actually are lawfully dismissed from their institute, in accordance with canon 647, are automatically absolved from all their obligations to the institute. Therefore, it can be said that one of the effects of lawful dismissal from temporary vows is an automatic absolution from all the obligations consequent upon membership in an institute. Now, this same effect should follow any other form of dismissal which, although not actually the lawful dismissal of canon 647, is nevertheless considered as lawful, namely, the automatic dismissal which canon 646 itself designates as lawful dis-

[56] Blat, *De Religiosis,* p. 568.

missal. While this conclusion has been made with regard to religious properly so called, it can nevertheless be equally applied to quasi-religious societies in virtue of canon 681, which applies to quasi-religious societies all the canons considered in this paragraph.[57]

If a member, bound by a temporary bond of perseverance and automatically dismissed from a society for one of the crimes mentioned in canon 646, is a cleric in major orders he is obliged to return to his proper ordinary. This would be the case where a secular cleric in major orders had entered such a society. If he is a cleric in minor orders, he is automatically reduced to the lay state in accordance with the prescriptions of canon 648. These conclusions likewise are not specifically stated in the Code, but they seem to be natural conclusions of the principle just stated, namely, that when those under a temporary bond of perseverance are dismissed in accordance with the prescriptions of canon 646, then the same effects follow as though they had been dismissed in accordance with canon 647.[58] It could be objected that in the case of one in major orders who, during his temporary incorporation in the society, is automatically dismissed according to canon 646, the prescription of canon 670 should be applied, which states that any one in major orders who has committed one of the three crimes mentioned in canon 646 is forbidden ever to wear the clerical garb. However, while it is true that canon 670 states in general terms that any cleric in major orders committing these offenses is subject to the penalty specified, nevertheless, the general rubric of Chapter IV, of which canon 670 is a part, considers only the dismissal of those who are in perpetual vows. Consequently, the prescriptions of canon 670 can be applied only to those who are perpetually enrolled in a society.

It is the opinion of the writer that probably, in view of the infrequency of the cases in which a cleric in temporary vows would at the same time be in major orders, the legislator did not have them in mind when he drafted the canons involved here. If the question were proposed to the Pontifical Commission for the

---

[57] Cf. Cans. 646; 647; 648; Fanfani, *De Religiosis*, p. 519.

[58] Can. 648.

Authentic Interpretation of the Canons of the Code, it might respond that even a cleric under temporary profession, if at the same time he be in major orders, is subject to the penalty of canon 670, if he is automatically dismissed in consequence of his commission of one of the three crimes mentioned in canon 646. However, until a response is received from the Holy See, it seems that in accordance with the prescriptions of canon 2219, § 3, the penalties for those who are perpetually professed cannot be applied to those who are only temporarily professed. Consequently, the dismissed cleric would have to return to his proper ordinary, and it would rest with the good judgment of the ordinary to apply proper penalties for his offense.[59]

It seems correct to maintain that one, bound by only a temporary bond of perseverance and automatically dismissed for the commission of one of the crimes mentioned in canon 646, is under no obligation to return to the society. This would appear to follow from the fact that by his dismissal he is freed from all his obligations to the society. Similarly, if he should attempt to return to the society, the latter has no obligation to accept him notwithstanding his sorrow and reformation. Furthermore, if the society should be willing to accept him again, he would have to repeat his period of probation and become incorporated anew in the society in accordance with the constitutions, unless the constitutions provided a different arrangement for this particular case.

If a member of a society is dismissed from it, in consequence of the ruling of canon 646, while he is perpetually affiliated with the society, he remains bound by the obligations of the society, unless the constitutions or an apostolic indult declares otherwise. If at the time of his dismissal the perpetually incorporated member is a cleric in minor orders, he is by the very act of dismissal reduced to the lay state. If he is a cleric in major orders, he is perpetually deprived of the right of wearing the clerical garb, and he loses the rights and privileges of the clerical state. These conclusions follow in virtue of the application of canons 669 and 670 to

[59] Cf. cans. 646; 670; 2219, § 3; Blat, *De Religiosis*, pp. 610-611; Schäfer, *De Religiosis*, p. 1023.

quasi-religious societies as justified by the prescriptions of canon 681.[60]

Furthermore, by a declaration of the Pontifical Commission for the Authentic Interpretation of the Canons of the Code, issued on July 30, 1934, the prescriptions of canon 672, § 1, are *not* to be applied to those whose dismissal was effected by canon 646. According to the norms of canon 672, § 1, a dismissed religious, and consequently a dismissed quasi-religious, whose vows, or bonds of perseverance, have not been dissolved, is obliged to return to the cloister and, if signs of complete amendment are given for three years, the institute or society, is bound to receive him or submit the case to the judgment of the Holy See.[61]

By an application of the response of the Commission to quasi-religious societies, valid by virtue of canon 681, the following conclusion may be drawn. A member of a society who, while perpetually affiliated with the society, is dismissed from it in accordance with canon 646 has no right to be received again into the society, even after signs of complete amendment. He must consequently petition for a dispensation from his obligations or rely upon the charity of the society to reconsider his case. He likewise remains perpetually deprived of the right of wearing the clerical garb, unless he receives a special indult of pardon from the Holy See. Palombo is of the opinion that an institute should never, without first corresponding with the Holy See, receive back into the institute a member who has been dismissed in accordance with the norm of canon 646. He claims that, since the common law deprives such persons of the right of ever wearing the ecclesiastical garb, a dispensation from this penalty should be sought from the Holy See before the institute again accepts the member into its fold.[62]

---

[60] Cans. 669; 670; 681; 2304, § 2; Fanfani, *De Religiosis,* p. 517.

[61] *AAS,* XXVI (1934), 494.

[62] Cf. cans. 646; 672, § 1; 670; Palombo, *De Dimissione Religiosorum,* p. 255, note (1); Larraona, "Commentarium Codicis,"—*CpR,* III (1922), 318; Choupin, *Nature et Obligations de l'Etat Religieux* (Paris: Beauchesne, 1923), 528-529.

Section 2. The Dismissal of Subjects Temporarily Enrolled in Quasi-Religious Societies

In accordance with the prescription of canon 647, § 1, applicable, in virtue of canon 681, to pontifically approved quasi-religious societies in which there exists a temporary bond of perseverance, the temporarily affiliated members may be dismissed by the supreme head of the society with the consent of his council, given by a secret ballot. This consent of the council is required for the validity of the dismissal, while the securing of the consent by means of a secret ballot is a requirement that touches the lawfulness of the act. In a quasi-religious society of diocesan law, the ordinary of the place where the house of the member is located has the right of effecting the dismissal. However, the ordinary should not use this right without the knowledge of the Superior General of the society, or against the latter's reasonable objections. Nevertheless, if a local ordinary should issue a decree of dismissal for a temporarily enrolled member of a society of diocesan law, even without the knowledge of the Superior General or in opposition to the latter's reasonable objections, the decree is valid and must be observed. However, the society has a right of interposing a recourse with the Holy See.[63]

In order that the superiors who have the right of effecting the dismissal, as just described in the previous paragraph, may use this right validly and licitly, they must be certain of the conditions which are listed in canon 647. The prescriptions of canon 647 are applicable to quasi-religious societies in virtue of canon 681.

1) The reason for the dismissal must be grave, certain and external; however, the reason does not postulate an act which in its malice is the equivalent of a mortal sin.

2) The reason may exist either on the part of the subject, such as the loss of vocation, or on the part of the society, such as the inability of the subject to serve the purposes of the society. A lack of religious spirit in regard to the observance of the constitutions, if it proves a source of scandal to others, is a sufficient reason for dismissal, provided that repeated admonitions, at least two in

---

[63] Cans. 647, § 1; 681; Schäfer, *De Religiosis,* pp. 989-992; Blat, *De Religiosis,* pp. 570-572; Fanfani, *De Religiosis,* pp. 500-501.

number and accompanied with a salutary penance have produced no good effect. However, the poor health of a temporarily affiliated member is not a sufficient reason for dismissal unless it can be showed with certainty that the state of poor health was fraudulently concealed or disguised before incorporation.

3) Though the reason for dismissal must be known with certainty by the superior who issues the decree of dismissal, a formal judicial process is not necessary; an administrative process suffices. The member must be informed of the reason for his dismissal and must be given ample opportunity to answer the charges; this answer must be faithfully submitted to the superior who has the right of effecting the dismissal.[64]

The Sacred Congregation of Religious on February 5, 1925, declared that any member of a religious institute who became insane during the time of temporary profession cannot be dismissed for this reason, and that the institute is bound to care for him.[65]

Although this reply was directed explicitly to religious institutes, it is the opinion of the writer that it also obliges quasi-religious societies. It seems to be a further explanation of canon 647, § 2, n. 2, which prescription is binding on quasi-religious societies in virtue of canon 681.

The members of quasi-religious societies who are dismissed while they are affiliated with a temporary bond of perseverance have a right of recourse to the Holy See against the decree of dismissal, and, pending a reply, the dismissal has no juridical effect. Consequently, these members are bound to obey the superiors just as thought no decree of dismissal had been issued. Juridically, these members are still affiliated with the society, and hence enjoy all the concomitant rights and are held to all the obligations.[66]

The Sacred Congregation of Religious on July 20, 1923, declared that a religious wishing to have recourse against the decree of dismissal must forward the appeal within ten days from the time of the reception of the decree; this period of ten days is, furthermore, to be computed as *tempus utile,* that is, as a period

---

[64] Can. 647, § 2, nn. 1-3; Schäfer, *De Religiosis,* pp. 993-997; Palombo, *De Dimissione Religiosorum,* pp. 175-180.

[65] *AAS,* XVII (1925), 107.

[66] Can. 647, § 2, n. 4; Schäfer, *De Religiosis,* pp. 997-999.

during which the dismissed member not only knows of the right to invoke a recourse, but also is able to use that right.[67]

Although the decree of the Sacred Congregation mentioned only religious, it may logically be deduced that the decree relates also to quasi-religious. For the reply was a further explanation of canon 647, § 2, n. 4, which prescription, by virtue of canon 681, is likewise applicable to quasi-religious societies of women.

The prescription of canon 647, § 2, n. 4, states that, if a temporarily professed member of a religious institute of women is dismissed, canon 643, § 2, must be observed. Therefore with the application of this prescription to quasi-religious societies of women, in virtue namely of canon 681, it follows that when a member of a quasi-religious society of women, temporarily affiliated to it, is dismissed without a dowry and has no means of her own, the society must furnish her the necessary means to reach her home in safety and enable her to live awhile until she may be able to provide for herself.

It is to be noted that in accordance with the prescription of canon 647, § 2, n. 2, the superiors of quasi-religious societies may not, in view of the member's poor health, dismiss such a member while bound by a temporary bond of perseverance to the society. However, the prescription of canon 637, which forbids superiors, in consideration of the poor health of the religious, to exclude them at the time of the expiration of their temporary vows and prior to the renewal of the temporary vows or the making of their perpetual profession, does not apply to quasi-religious societies. Consequently, unless the constitutions provide otherwise, as is generally the case, subjects could be excluded for the reason of poor health at the completion of their temporary affiliation with the society.[68]

A member of a quasi-religious society, if dismissed while temporarily enrolled in the society is, in accordance with canon 648, automatically absolved from all obligations to it. However, if the dismissed member is a cleric in major orders, he must return to his proper bishop, and his proper bishop is obliged to

---

[67] Cf. can. 35; *AAS,* XV (1923), 457.

[68] Stanton, *De Societatibus,* p. 154, note (123) ; cans. 637; 647, § 2, n. 2.

receive him. As has already been stated, the proper bishop for members of clerical quasi-religious societies is the bishop of the diocese where the member had a domicile before his entrance into the society.[69]

If, however, by special indult a member of a quasi-religious society has lost his proper diocese, he cannot, subsequent to the decree of his dismissal from the society, exercise his major orders on his return to the world. He must first find a bishop who is willing to receive him, or wait until the Holy See has made other provisions for him.[70]

Canon 648, applicable in virtue of canon 681 to quasi-religious societies, further states that canon 642 is to be applied to those who are dismissed while temporarily affiliated with a society. Consequently, if a member who has been at least six years temporarily affiliated with a society is dismissed in accordance with canon 647, he cannot hold any of the various offices mentioned in canon 642, § 1.[71]

If a member of a quasi-religious society is refused permission to renew the bond of perseverance at the expiration of the temporary bond he is absolutely free from all obligations to the society and he may not demand any remuneration for his services to the society during the time of his incorporation in the society. Such a member is not held by the prescription of canon 642, § 2, even though he may have been affiliated with the society through the bond of perseverance for more than six years. This is true because the case does not involve a dispensation from his obligations, a prerequisite demanded by canon 642 if one is to become subject to its legislation.

If such a member who, either is unwilling to renew his obligations to a society at the expiration of the temporary bond of per-

---

[69] Cf. *supra*, pp. 199-201; can. 648.

[70] Can. 641, § 1, does not explicitly comprise quasi-religious under its prescriptions, nevertheless canon 648, which is applicable to quasi-religious societies, safeguards the law of canon 641, § 1, in its own legislation. Consequently, by virtue of canon 648, quasi-religious societies are likewise made subject to the law of canon 641, § 1.

[71] Cf. *supra*, pp. 246-247; Palombo, *De Dimissione Religiosorum*, p. 258; cans. 642; 648; 681.

severance, or is refused permission to do so, and consequently returns to the world, should be at the same time a cleric in major orders, he is bound to return to his proper bishop, just as a cleric in major orders who has been dismissed from a society, while he was still bound by his temporary obligations. If he is in minor orders, it seems that then, too, he is obliged to return to his proper bishop. However, the latter may reduce him to the lay state immediately, or the subject himself may of his own free will revert to the lay state, after first notifying the local ordinary of his intention, as prescribed in canon 211.[72]

Section 3. The Dismissal of Subjects Permanently Enrolled in Non-Exempt Quasi-Religious Societies of Men

In non-exempt quasi-religious societies of men the permanently affiliated members are dismissed by means of a decree which is administrative in nature, whereas in an exempt quasi-religious society of men the decree of dismissal is a judicial sentence. In the former case there is no judicial process properly so called; there is rather an extrajudicial process, carried on to determine whether or not the member is deserving of dismissal.[73]

In accordance with the prescription of canon 649, applicable to quasi-religious societies in virtue of canon 681, a member of a non-exempt quasi-religious society of men who is permanently enrolled in it cannot be dismissed unless he has previously committed three offenses and has been twice admonished without any fruitful results. The offenses must be grave, external and notorious, committed against the common law or against the particular laws of the society. These offenses may be three of the same species, or, if they belong to different species, they must be such that, taken together, they manifest perversity of will and obstinacy in sin. Furthermore, one continued offense which is virtually made threefold because of the two distinct admonitions during the con-

---

[72] Palombo, *De Dimissione Religiosorum,* pp. 259-261; Fanfani, *De Religiosis,* p. 515.

[73] Schäfer, *De Religiosis,* p. 1002.

tinuance of the offense is sufficient to warrant the offender's dismissal from the society.[74]

An offense is notorious in fact when it is publicly known and was committed under such circumstances that it cannot be concealed by means of any subterfuge, or excused by means of any claim admitted in law. It is notorious in law after judgment by a competent judge which has become *res iudicata,* or after a confession by the culprit in open court according to canon 1750.[75]

The investigations which might be required may be carried out by the major superiors themselves; however, as a rule, they should be made by a member delegated for this purpose by the major superior. A member should not be generally delegated to the office of investigator. On the contrary, as they arise, a member should be delegated for the individual case. It is left entirely to the discretion of the immediate major superior whether or not an investigation of the actions of a subject should be made.

The major superior should not pay any attention to denunciations which are made by manifest enemies of the subject denounced, by vile and unworthy persons, or by means of anonymous letters destitute of the qualities and elements which could lend any probability of truth to the accusations made. If the superior deems an investigation necessary, it is to be carried out in secrecy and with caution, lest the rumor of the offense be spread about and the good reputation of the subject be endangered.

The member acting as investigator may question persons whom he believes to have a knowledge of the matter. He may constrain them under an oath to tell the truth and to maintain secrecy.

Finally, when the investigation is completed, the investigator should refer all the acts of the process along with an expression of his own opinion to the immediate major superior. It is then left to the judgment of the superior to decide the value of the investigation.[76]

---

[74] Cans. 656; 657; 658.

[75] Cf. cans. 658; 2197, nn. 2-3; 1902; 1750.

[76] Cans. 658; 1939-1946; Schäfer, *De Religiosis,* pp. 785-787; Canon 658, applicable to quasi-religious societies through the norm of canon 681, justifies the application of canons 1939-1946 to these societies.

In accordance with the prescription of canon 649, there must be two admonitions during the course of the commission of the offenses before a perpetually affiliated member of a non-exempt quasi-religious society of men may be dismissed.[77]

The admonition must be given after each of the first two offenses, while in the case of a continued offense an interval of at least three whole days must elapse between the first and the second admonition.[78]

Moreover, inasmuch as the proceedings of dismissal, though not strictly judicial in nature, are nevertheless quasi-judicial in character, the admonitions should be given by the major superior or his delegate, unless the constitutions prescribe otherwise, and hence not generally by a local superior. Furthermore, the admonitions should always contain a threat of dismissal.[79]

The major superior should add to these admonitions appropriate exhortations and corrections, and impose penances and other penal remedies calculated to effect the amendment of the subject and the reparation of scandal. The superior is likewise bound to remove the offending subject from the occasions which could readily bring about a relapse into the same faults, and if necessary the subject should even be transferred to another house where these dangers do not exist.[80]

These admonitions are to be considered fruitless if the subject after the second admonition commits a new offense, or perseveres in the old one; a period of six days must elapse after the last admonition before any further steps may be taken.[81]

When the threefold offenses have been committed and the prescribed admonitions have been made without any consequent amendment in the subject, the supreme head of the society with his council, all the circumstances being duly considered, must deliberate whether there is sufficient cause for the dismissal.[82]

---

[77] Can. 649 becomes applicable to quasi-religious societies in virtue of the norm of canon 681.

[78] Can. 660. This canon is applicable to quasi-religious societies in virtue of canon 681.

[79] Palombo, *De Dimissione Religiosorum*, p. 213; can. 659.

[80] Can. 661.

[81] Can. 662.

[82] Can. 650, § 1.

However, it is proper to keep in mind the observation of Palombo that the process is not strictly a judicial one, and consequently the required proofs can be established without the formalities that a judicial process demands.[83]

The vote of the council in deliberating as to whether or not the offending subject is deserving of dismissal is of the nature of a decisive vote. If the majority of the votes favor the dismissal of the subject, the following prescriptions must be observed. In a society of diocesan approval the entire matter is to be referred to the ordinary of the place where the house of the permanently incorporated member is located, and that ordinary has the right to decide the matter according to his prudent judgment.

In a society of pontifical approval the supreme head of the society has the right of issuing the decree of dismissal, but in order to produce its effect the decree must be confirmed by the Holy See. In all cases the subject has a right to defend himself freely, and his defense must be faithfully entered in the acts of the proceedings.[84]

Although the Code does not mention any right of recourse to the Holy See on the part of the dismissed subject, who has been permanently affiliated with his organization, it would seem, nevertheless, that in virtue of canon 647, § 2, n. 4, whereby a right of recourse is given those who are dismissed as religious professed with temporary vows, that a similar right of recourse to the Holy See should be given to a subject when dismissed from a religious institute or from a quasi-religious society of men, to which he had been joined either by perpetual vow or by a perpetual bond of perseverance. However, this recourse when made by a member of a society or of an institute of pontifical approval would not have a suspensive effect after the confirmation of the decree of dismissal by the Holy See. But, with reference to a society or an institute of diocesan approval it seems correct to say that the

---

[83] *De Dimissione Religiosorum*, pp. 213-214.

[84] Can. 650, §§ 2, 3. Canons 650 and 660-662 are all applicable to quasi-religious societies in virtue of the ruling contained in canon 681.

full prescription of canon 647, § 2, n. 4, is to be applied, whereby the appeal to the Holy See suspends the effect of the decree.[85]
Berutti, *De Religiosis,* p. 346; Beste, *Introductio in Codicem,* p. 444.

Schäfer and Fanfani even go further and hold that the appeal with a suspensive effect against a decree of dismissal is to be admitted in the case of male institutes of pontifical as well as of diocesan law, when the subjects involved are those perpetually professed.[86]

Section 4. The Dismissal of Subjects Permanently Enrolled in Quasi-Religious Societies of Women

For the dismissal of members permanently enrolled in quasi-religious societies of women, there are required serious external causes together with incorrigibility. Incorrigibility is to be considered as present when attempts to correct the subject have proved unsuccessful, and the superioress judges that there is no hope of amendment. The offenses warranting dismissal need not be grave sins in the theological sense; it suffices that they be grave faults more serious in character than the faults warranting the dismissal of a woman who is only temporarily enrolled in a society. No specific number of faults is required. But the faults must be sufficiently public to yield potentially to the proof that they have been committed.

In the presently considered case the Code demands no double admonition coupled with the threat of dismissal; however, Schäfer states that the Holy See will not confirm a decree of dismissal if the double admonition together with the threat of dismissal has not been given beforehand.[87]

In accordance with the prescription of canon 651, § 2, the cause for dismissal must be made known to the subject, and she must be

---

[85] Palombo, *De Dimissione Religiosorum,* pp. 215-216; Blat, *De Religiosis,* pp. 578-579; Vermeersch, "Tempus Utile Recursui Religiosorum Dimissorum,"—*Periodica,* XII (1924), 101-104; Wernz-Vidal, *De Religiosis,* n. 441;

[86] *De Religiosis,* p. 1003; *De Religiosis,* p. 504.

[87] Can. 651, § 1; *De Religiosis,* pp. 1004-1005; Wernz-Vidal, *De Religiosis,* n. 442, I.

given an opportunity to defend herself. The defense thus given must be included in the acts of the case.[88]

A. Societies of Diocesan Approval

Canon 681 makes applicable, in the case of the dismissal of quasi-religious women permanently enrolled in diocesan societies, the prescription of canon 652, § 1. Consequently, if the major superioress considers that there are present sufficient reasons for the dismissal of a subject in accordance with the prescription of canon 651, § 1, she must transmit all the documents to the ordinary of the place in which the house of the particular subject is located. The ordinary will then consider the case, and if he sees fit, issue the decree of dismissal.[89]

Though the Code does not prescribe that the major superioress consult either her council or the local superioress before sending the case to the local ordinary, yet this should always be done. Frequently the constitutions of a society will demand these consultations as well as a deliberative or at least a consultative vote of the council. Accordingly, if the constitutions do not make such a demand, the consultations in question cannot be imposed as an obligation on the major superioress. However, it would appear very imprudent for a superior general to act in so important a matter without at least the consultive vote of her council. Schäfer and Larraona are of the opinion that by an analogy with canon 647, § 1, the superioress should seek the decisive vote of her council before submitting the case to the local ordinary.[90]

Palombo and others claim that the prescription of canon 647, § 2, n. 4, which allows an appeal with a suspensive effect against a decree of dismissal issued to a religious in temporary vows, should

---

[88] Can. 651, § 2. Canon 651 has been applied to quasi-religious societies in virtue of the general prescription of canon 681.

[89] Can. 652, § 1.

[90] Schäfer, *De Religiosis,* p. 1007; Larraona, "Commentarium Codicis,"—*CpR,* II (1921), 364-365. The opinion of these authors, although strictly intended for religious institutes, seems applicable to quasi-religious societies in this instance.

a fortiori be applied to a subject who is permanently incorporated in a diocesan society.[91]

B. Societies of Pontifical Approval

In accordance with the prescription of canon 652, § 3, applicable in virtue of canon 681 to quasi-religious societies, the following norms govern the dismissal of members permanently enrolled in pontifically approved societies of women.

In all pontifically approved quasi-religious societies of women the highest superioress of the society must refer all the acts and documents pertaining to the dismissal of a perpetually affiliated member to the Sacred Congregation of Religious. It is then left to the Sacred Congregation to decide what action is to be taken. However, if the Sacred Congregation issues a decree of dismissal, the prescription of canon 643, § 2, must be observed.[92]

In the dismissal of a member perpetually affiliated with a pontifically approved quasi-religious society of women, it seems that the following should be the proper method of procedure. The local superioress who has judged one of her subjects to be deserving of dismissal should make known the facts and the reasons for her judgment to the provincial superioress. The latter then should consider the matter together with her council, and if it still seems proper that dismissal should take place, the case should be directed to the supreme superioress. She should then consider the matter with her council. If the decision still favors dismissal, the entire proceedings should be submitted to the Sacred Congregation of Religious.[93]

The subjects dismissed in consequence of a decree issued by the

---

[91] *De Dimissione Religiosorum*, pp. 217-218; Fanfani, *De Religiosis*, p. 513; Beste, *Introductio in Codicem*, p. 445; Berutti, *De Religiosis*, p. 347.

[92] Can. 652, § 3. Canon 643, § 2, provides for the temporary support which is to be furnished to the member who, when dismissed without a dowry, has no means of her own.

[93] Palombo, *De Dimissione Religiosorum*, pp. 219-220. The procedure as outlined in these pages refers to cases of dismissal in religious institutes of women. However, since the same canons determine the procedure both for religious institutes and quasi-religious societies, it seems justifiable to apply this doctrine to quasi-religious societies.

Sacred Congregation of Religious have a right of a recourse against the sentence contained in the decree. However, such recourse has no suspensive effect, and the decree of dismissal must be observed until the Holy See declares otherwise.[94]

As has already been mentioned, the necessity of consulting the council is not placed on the superioresses by the Code. However, the seriousness of the matter and the rights in question in these cases of dismissal certainly place a moral obligation on the major superioresses of consulting their councils before they submit such cases to a higher authority for review or confirmation.[95]

Section 5. The Dismissal in Urgent Cases of Subjects Permanently Enrolled in Quasi-Religious Societies

By an application of canon 653 to quasi-religious societies, justified in virtue of the prescription of canon 681, a male or female member perpetually affiliated with a society may, in case of grave external scandal or of very serious imminent injury to the society, be dismissed immediately and deprived of his or her habit by the proper major superior or superioress with the consent of the respective council. If there be any danger in delay, and time does not permit recourse to the major superiors, the subject may be dismissed even by a local superior or superioress with the consent of the respective council and of the local ordinary. In these cases however, the major superior, or the local ordinary, as the case may be, must immediately submit the case to the Holy See. If for some reason or other even the local ordinary cannot be reached, it seems that the local superior could in that case act with only the consent of his council.[96]

Canon 653 may also be invoked during that period of time when the experiment of incorrigibility is being made according to canon 660, or while waiting for the decision of the Holy See if the decree

---

[94] Palombo, *De Dimissione Religiosorum,* p. 220; Berutti, *De Religiosis,* p. 348; Beste, *Introductio in Codicem,* p. 445.

[95] Cf. *supra,* p. 269.

[96] Can. 653; Schäfer, *De Religiosis,* p. 1007; Tabera, "Studia Canonica,"—*CpR,* XIV (1933), 58.

of dismissal has already been sent to the Holy See for confirmation according to the prescriptions of canons 652 and 665.[97]

The dismissal of a subject in accordance with the prescription of canon 653 is not effected through a decree of dismissal properly so called. The juridical decree of dismissal is present only if the Holy See issues such a decree on the receipt of the evidence submitted by either the local ordinary or the major superior. The evidence submitted to the Holy See should contain notice of the cause of dismissal, mention of the name of the authority who issued the note of dismissal, and a notice of the consent of the council.[98]

It is the opinion of some authors that by reason of the prescriptions of canon 650, § 2, n. 1, and 652, § 1, whereby the local ordinary is given the right to issue decrees of dismissal for both men and women members of diocesan institutes who are perpetually professed, the local ordinary may also issue the decree of dismissal for the members of diocesan institutes who are dismissed in accordance with the prescription of canon 653. This opinion removes the necessity of a recourse to the Holy See to secure the decree of dismissal in the cases considered.[99]

It seems correct to apply to quasi-religious societies these opinions expressed with regard to religious institutes. This application seems warranted for the following reason. The common law, which is the basis for the authors' opinions in this particular matter, is equally applicable to both religious institutes and quasi-religious societies. Consequently, whatever interpretations are given to these canons should extend equally to all included within their scope.

Section 6. The Dismissal of Subjects Perpetually Enrolled in Exempt Clerical Quasi-Religious Societies

In accordance with the prescription of canon 654, applicable to quasi-religious societies in virtue of canon 681, a member perpetually enrolled in an exempt clerical quasi-religious society cannot

[97] Can. 668. Canon 668 is applicable to quasi-religious societies in virtue of the general prescription of canon 681.

[98] Schäfer, *De Religiosis,* pp. 1008-1009; Wernz-Vidal, *De Religiosis,* n. 449, IV.

[99] Wernz-Vidal, *De Religiosis,* n. 449, iv, note (13) ; Schäfer, *De Religiosis,* p. 1022; Vermeersch-Creusen, *Epitome,* I, n. 625, c.

be dismissed without a canonical trial. Canon 654 revokes every contrary privilege. The only exceptions to the prescription of canon 654 are listed in canon 646, which treats of automatic dismissal in certain cases, and in canon 668, which provides for the dismissal of the members of exempt clerical institutes in urgent cases.

In accordance with the prescriptions of canon 655, also applicable to quasi-religious societies by the norm of canon 681, the power to issue the sentence of dismissal in these cases is vested in the supreme head of the society together with his chapter or council. The chapter or council must consist of at least four members of the society. If because of illness or travel, or for any other reason, four members of the council or of the chapter are not at hand, the president of the tribunal with the others who together with him constitute the collegiate tribunal must, under pain of the invalidity of the procedure, elect other members to complete the necessary number. This decision is to be determined by the majority vote of those who constitute the tribunal. The president with the consent of the other judges must likewise nominate a prosecutor, who in accordance with the prescriptions of canon 1589, §§ 1, 2, must be a member of the same society, a priest in good repute, an expert in canon law, and a person commended for his tried prudence and his zeal for justice.[100]

In order that the canonical trial be validly prosecuted there must be appointed, in addition to the prosecutor, a notary who, in accordance with the prescription of canon 503, must be deputed by a major superior of the society. Any acts of the process which are not signed by the notary are invalid in view of the ruling of canon 1585, § 1.

The president of the tribunal must likewise appoint one of the associate judges as referee, whose duty it is to report on the case in the meeting of the judges and to commit the sentence in writing; the president can for a just reason appoint another in his place.[101]

The member who is on trial must have an advocate, either selected by himself or given to him by the tribunal. This advocate,

---

[100] Berutti, *De Religiosis,* p. 352.

[101] Can. 1584.

too, must belong to the same society. If he is selected by the member on trial, he must be approved by the president of the tribunal.[102]

The prescriptions of the common law, which demand that the notary, the referee and the advocate be present at these trials are not specifically referred to in Book II, Title XVI, Chapter III, of the Code, which deals with the dismissal of members permanently professed in exempt clerical religious institutes. However, canon 654 demands that the dismissal be effected through a canonical trial, and consequently all the canons pertaining to canonical processes in the fourth book of the Code are applicable.[103]

Before a trial may be initiated the following conditions must be verified. The accused subject of the exempt clerical society must be guilty either of three grave external offenses committed against the common law or the particular laws of the society, or of one continued offense which is virtually threefold in view of the fruitless admonitions given during the course of the continuous crime.[104]

Two admonitions must also have been given by the immediate major superior of the accused subject, and appropriate exhortations and corrections must have been added to these admonitions.[105]

Finally, there must be evidence of a failure to amend, which evidence becomes manifest when a new offense is committed after the second admonition.[106]

These three conditions, which must exist before a canonical trial may be initiated for the dismissal of a member perpetually affiliated with an exempt clerical quasi-religious society, have already been discussed in the section dealing with the dismissal of perpetually affiliated members of non-exempt societies.[107]

After the admonitions and corrections have proved unavailing, the immediate major superior must carefully collect all the acts and documents and send them to the supreme head of the society.

---

[102] Cans. 1655, § 1; 1658, §§ 2, 4.

[103] Schäfer, *De Religiosis,* pp. 1011-1020; can. 664, § 1.

[104] Cans. 656, n. 1; 657.

[105] Cans. 656, n. 2; 658, § 1; 659-661.

[106] Cans. 656, n. 3; 662.

[107] Cf. *supra,* pp. 264-266.

The latter must give all these documents to the prosecutor, appointed with the consent of the other judges. The prosecutor must examine them and submit his conclusions.[108]

If the prosecutor should oppose the dismissal of the member, the provincial superior has a right of recourse to the Sacred Congregation of Religious.[109]

If the prosecutor is not completely satisfied with the evidence which is submitted for proof that the subject is deserving of dismissal, he may institute such further investigations as he thinks proper. Finally, when the prosecutor concludes that there is sufficient evidence to warrant the dismissal of the subject, the canonical trial must be begun.

This trial must be conducted in accordance with the rules of the canons prescribing the proper procedure for canonical trials, as contained in the First Part of the Fourth Book of the Code.[110]

In the course of the trial it must be established by proof that the accused committed the offenses charged against him, that the two admonitions were properly given, and that the subject failed to show any amendment.[111]

After a careful consideration of the charges of the prosecutor and of the defense of the accused, the tribunal should proceed to the pronouncement of a sentence of dismissal if they judge that the commission of the offenses, the giving of the admonitions and the failure of amendment have been reliably established by proof.[112]

In accordance with the prescription of canon 1577, the tribunal must act as a body and pronounce sentence according to the majority vote.

However, the sentence of dismissal cannot be executed unless it is confirmed by the Sacred Congregation of Religious. The president of the tribunal must forward the sentence with all the acts of the case to this Congregation as soon as possible.[113]

There is no possibility of an appeal or of a recourse with a

---

[108] Can. 663.

[109] Schäfer, *De Religiosis*, p. 1019.

[110] Can. 664, § 1.

[111] Can. 664, § 2.

[112] Can. 665.

[113] Can. 666.

suspensive effect against a sentence of dismissal which has been confirmed by the Sacred Congregation of Religious.[114]

There can be no dismissal if the Sacred Congregation of Religious does not confirm the sentence of dismissal.[115]

A. Cases in Far-away Regions

Canon 667, applicable to quasi-religious societies by virtue of canon 681, provides special legislation for the cases of dismissal of permanently affiliated members of exempt clerical societies when there is a great distance between the habitation of the Superior General and the location of the house of the subject. This canon is applicable even though the case be unattended by any extraordinary circumstances. In these particular cases the Superior General with the consent of his council may delegate the power of dismissal to trustworthy and prudent members of the society. The tribunal receiving this delegated power must consist of at least three members. These judges must proceed in accordance with the prescriptions of canons 663-666, which prescribe the general norms of procedure in dismissal trials when the Superior General and his council of at least four constitute the tribunal.[116]

A region can be said to be distant in this regard not only by the actual measurement of space but also by reason of the difficulty in communicating with the Superior General.[117]

It seems quite evident from the wording of the canon that the power of actually issuing the sentence of dismissal may be delegated to another tribunal by the Superior General. However, it seems proper, though not obligatory, that a delegated tribunal should send a copy of the proceedings and of the sentence of dismissal to the Sacred Congregation of Religious, through the office of the Superior General. In this way the latter could examine all the acts of the case and give them his approval.[118]

---

[114] Schäfer, *De Religiosis*, p. 1021; Berutti, *De Religiosis*, p. 359; Cocchi, *De Religiosis*, n. 155, c); Fanfani, *De Religiosis*, pp. 511-512.

[115] Schäfer, *De Religiosis*, p. 1021.

[116] Cf. can. 667.

[117] Wernz-Vidal, *De Religiosis*, n. 447 (10); Schäfer, *De Religiosis*, p. 1021.

[118] Wernz-Vidal, *De Religiosis*, n. 447 (11).

It will be noted that the process which has just been described for the dismissal of members permanently affiliated with exempt clerical quasi-religious societies is the process outlined in canons 654-667, which regulates the dismissal of the perpetually professed members of exempt clerical religious institutes. The application of these canons to quasi-religious societies is justified not only by the norm of canon 681, but also by reason of the already mentioned response of the Commission for the Authentic Interpretation of the Canons of the Code pertaining to the dismissal of members of quasi-religious societies.[119]

B. Cases of Urgency

The prescriptions of canon 668 provide for the dismissal in urgent cases of members who are perpetually professed in exempt clerical religious institutes. This canon, by virtue of canon 681, is likewise applicable to quasi-religious societies. Consequently, the following conclusions may be drawn.

In the case of grave scandal or very great and imminent harm to an exempt clerical quasi-religious society, a member may be immediately dismissed by his major superior. If there is danger in delay, and likewise no time for recourse to the major superior, the member may be dismissed by the local superior with the consent of his council. The member thus dismissed must immediately cease wearing his habit. After the dismissal of the member in accordance with the prescription of canon 668, the canonical trial must be begun immediately, if it has not as yet been started, and must be conducted in accordance with the prescriptions of the canons which govern the dismissal of a subject who is perpetually incorporated in an exempt quasi-clerical society.[120]

If in a special case the local superior dismissed a member in accordance with the prescription of canon 668, the consent of his council must be secured in a majority vote. This requirement is essential to the validity of the superior's action. Moreover, a member dismissed in accordance with the prescription of this canon

---

[119] Cf. can. 681, *supra*, p. 253.

[120] Cans. 668; 681.

is not considered as juridically dismissed until the tribunal of the Superior General of the society by a judicial process has issued a sentence of dismissal.[121]

ARTICLE V. THE JURIDICAL STATUS OF SUBJECTS DISMISSED FROM QUASI-RELIGIOUS SOCIETIES WHILE PERPETUALLY ENROLLED IN THE SOCIETY

In accordance with the prescription of canon 669, § 1, applicable to quasi-religious societies in virtue of canon 681, a member who is perpetually enrolled in a quasi-religious society remains bound after his dismissal by the obligations formerly assumed in the society, unless the constitutions or an apostolic indult declare otherwise.[122]

Although a person who was dismissed while he was bound by perpetual ties to the society still continues juridically to be a member of the society, he is not held to those obligations which refer to the common life. Moreover, he cannot exercise any right in the society, nor may he demand from it any means of support. An exception exists in the case of women members who are to be given assistance if they were received without a dowry and are not able to provide for themselves upon their dismissal from the society.[123]

If, by a declaration of the constitutions or in consequence of an apostolic indult, a dismissed member of a society is absolved from his obligations to the society, though he had been perpetually incorporated therein, it seems that if he wishes to re-enter the society, he would be required to undergo a new period of probation or trial in order to become affiliated again with the society.

In view of the fact that a dismissed member who has been perpetually incorporated in a society remains bound by his former obligations in relation to the society, he is accordingly obliged to return to it. If he gives proof of complete amendment for a period of three years the society is bound to take him back. If there are serious objections against his return, the matter should be re-

[121] Schäfer, *De Religiosis*, pp. 1021-1022.

[122] Schäfer, *De Religiosis*, p. 1002.

[123] Schäfer, *De Religiosis*, pp. 1022-1023.

ferred to the Holy See. The society may receive him back before the completion of the three year period if it judges he has sufficiently proven himself, however it is not obliged to do so. It would seem that the dismissed member has an obligation of amending his ways and also an obligation of returning to the society whenever the society is willing to receive him.[124]

Wernz-Vidal are of the opinion that it is quite difficult to imagine a dismissed religious wishing to return to his institute even after three years of complete amendment. This difficulty would arise, they assert, for several reasons, both on the part of the member himself and on the part of the society. In accordance with the prescription of canon 672, § 1, when these difficulties which prevent the return of an amended subject actually arise, the matter is to be submitted to the Holy See. Generally, they state, the Holy See will grant the subject an indult of secularization.[125]

When a dismissed member sufficiently proves his amendment and is again received into the society, he need not repeat the time of probation or become affiliated anew with the society, for the bond of union with the society was never broken. However, the right of precedence of the member is to be determined, not from the time of his first incorporation in the society, but from the day of his return to it.[126]

If an indult of quasi-secularization is granted to a dismissed member who is in major orders, he must return to his proper ordinary. Finally, if a dismissed cleric in major orders who has been absolved from his obligations to the society must seek a benevolent bishop, by reason of an indult granted to the society, which is generally the case if the society has the right of issuing dimissorial letters for its members, then such a cleric is like to a religious who has been granted an indult of secularization while in major orders. If he cannot find a benevolent bishop, then, like the secularized

---

[124] Can. 672, § 1; Schäfer, *De Religiosis,* p. 1026.

[125] *De Religiosis,* n. 451, b). Strictly considered there is no secularization of a quasi-religious, although the Holy See uses this term in their regard. Actually a dispensation from the obligations to the society is granted.

[126] Schäfer, *De Religiosis,* pp. 1026-1027; Palombo, *De Dimissione Religiosorum,* p. 252; Fanfani, *De Religiosis,* p. 522.

religious in the same situation, he must refer the matter to the Holy See.[127]

Moreover, a member of a society who was perpetually affiliated with it, and then was dismissed after he had received major orders, provided that he was dismissed for a less serious crime than those mentioned in canon 670, is automatically suspended until he receives absolution from the Holy See.[128]

In order to be absolved from this suspension, a dismissed member must undergo a period of trial, under the vigilance of some ordinary, to prove his worthiness of being absolved. This process is outlined in canon 671, nn. 1-7.

In accordance with the prescription of canon 671, n. 2, if the Sacred Congregation deems it expedient, the dismissed member is ordered to report to some diocese, and to remain there, dressed as a cleric, under the direction of the ordinary of that diocese. However, it seems that, if the Sacred Congregation does not prescribe to the contrary, then the member dismissed from a quasi-religious society, after being perpetually incorporated in it and after having received major orders, will have to report to the diocese of his own proper ordinary. For, as Palombo remarks, the only reason why a particular diocese is selected by the Sacred Congregation for the religious who is in major orders at the time of his dismissal is that the religious has lost his proper diocese by reason of his perpetual profession in accordance with canon 585. In quasi-religious societies the subject in major orders retains his own proper ordinary. Hence it seems that the latter is best suited to assist him in his efforts to amend his faults. However, since this particular point is not considered in the law, it remains with the Sacred Congregation to decide whether he is to return to his own diocese or whether he is to report to a diocese designated by the Sacred Congregation.[129]

Similarly, if the dismissed member has been absolved from his obligations to the society, he must return to his proper ordinary, and it seems that in this case also the proper diocese of the dis-

---

[127] Can. 672, § 2.

[128] Can. 671, n. 1. This application is made to quasi-religious societies by reason of canon 681.

[129] Cf. *De Dimissione Religiosorum,* p. 248; can. 585.

missed member should be the diocese in which his probation is to be made. Finally, if a member who has been absolved from his obligations to a society must seek a benevolent bishop, which is generally the case if the society has the privilege of issuing dimissorial letters for its subjects, it appears that the diocese of the benevolent bishop whom he is to seek should be identified with the diocese which canon 671, n. 2, prescribes as the place for his probation and trial. If a benevolent bishop cannot be found, recourse must be had to the Holy See, which in accordance with canon 672, § 2, will provide for the particular case.[180]

If the dismissed member refuses to stay in the specified diocese, whether this be his own proper diocese or the one selected by the Sacred Congregation, the society has no further obligations towards him. Under the same circumstances he is also deprived of the right of wearing the clerical garb. Similarly, if a member has found a benevolent bishop and the Holy See has not opposed the arrangements whereby the member remains in that diocese for the time of his probation, the local ordinary would have no further obligations towards him if he refuses to remain in the diocese.[181]

Consequently, a dismissed member of a quasi-religious society who refuses to remain in a particular diocese for a period of trial is punished in the same manner as those who commit the more serious offenses mentioned in canon 670, with this difference, however, that those who are deprived of the right of wearing the clerical garb in consequence of the prescription of canon 670 are perpetually deprived of this right, while those similarly punished in consequence of the prescription of canon 671, n. 3, are deprived of it only as long as they refuse to obey the injunctions of the Holy See.[182]

If the dismissed subject reports to the indicated probationary diocese, the local ordinary should send him to a house of penance, or commit him to the care of a pious and prudent priest. If the subject refuses to obey the orders of the ordinary, the society

---

[180] Palombo, *De Dimissione Religiosorum*, pp. 252-253.

[181] Can. 671, n. 3; Palombo, *loc. cit.*

[182] Schäfer, *De Religiosis*, p. 1025, note 151.

has no further obligations or responsibilities towards him and he likewise incurs the penalty of deprivation of the right of wearing the clerical garb, with all the consequences which follow from such a penalty. Once again there is to be noted the difference in duration between the penalty prescribed in canon 670 and the same kind of penalty as prescribed in canon 671, n. 4.[183]

If the dismissed subject who obeys the orders of both the Sacred Congregation and the local ordinary has no means of providing for himself, the society to which he belongs should in the spirit of charity furnish him with the support he needs for his maintenance, to be given him through the ordinary of the diocese where the dismissed subject is staying. It seems correct to say that, if the subject has been absolved from his obligations to the society and consequently no longer belongs to it, the benevolent bishop who is trying him, or his own proper ordinary to whom he has returned, should supply the charitable support.[184]

If the dismissed subject leads a life unworthy of a cleric, the local ordinary may after one year, or even sooner, deprive him of the maintenance charitably furnished by the society or by himself, order him out of the house where he has been staying while on probation, and deprive him of the right to wear the ecclesiastical garb. If the local ordinary deems it necessary to take this action against a dismissed subject, he must immediately report his action to the Sacred Congregation of Religious as well as to the society.[185]

If, however, the dismissed subject conducts himself so well during the time of probation that it can justly be considered that he has truly repented, the local ordinary should endorse his petition to the Holy See for absolution from the censure of suspension. After the necessary absolution has been obtained, the local ordinary should, with due precautions, allow the subject to say Mass and, if he sees fit, to discharge other functions of the sacred

---

[183] Can. 671, n. 4.

[184] Can. 671, n. 5.

[185] Can. 671, n. 6. If the member has been completely absolved from all obligations to the society, there seems to be no need of reporting this action to the society.

ministry by which he may properly support himself. In this case the society, or the ordinary, may discontinue its charitable assistance.[136]

If the subject has not been absolved from his obligations to the society, then after three years of successful probation he will have the right, as given him in canon 672, § 1, to be readmitted into the society. If there are serious reasons against his return, the matter must be referred to the Holy See. In this latter instance the Holy See would most probably grant him a dispensation from his obligations to the society and the subject would then either return to his own proper ordinary or seek a benevolent bishop.[137]

The various prescriptions of canon 671, nn. 2-7, as just enumerated, contemplate exclusively the case of a dismissed member of an institute or of a quasi-religious society who is a priest perpetually incorporated in the institute or in the society. If the dismissed member be a subdeacon or a deacon, then the matter must be referred to the Holy See.[138]

The Holy See will then decide without delay whether it is expedient without further trial or proofs to forbid the subject to advance to higher orders, or whether the dismissed subject in major orders should undergo a trial or probation to prove his worthiness to advance to the priesthood.[139]

If the cleric who was dismissed while he was under a perpetual bond in relation to the society should be in minor orders, he would automatically be reduced to the lay state. If after three years of amendment he should be readmitted into the society and wish again to enter the clerical state, the permission of his proper bishop would have to be obtained.[140]

In all cases it must be remembered that the prescriptions of canon 641 do not apply to quasi-religious societies. Consequently, a bishop who receives a dismissed member who has been absolved

---

[136] Can. 671, n. 7.

[137] Can. 672, § 1.

[138] Can. 671, n. 7. Canon 671 is applicable to quasi-religious societies through the norm of canon 681.

[139] Wernz-Vidal, *De Religiosis*, n. 452, c).

[140] Cf. cans. 212; 669.

from his obligations to the society is not limited to a trial period of six years before deciding whether or not he wishes to incardinate the subject.[141]

In accordance with the prescription of canon 670, applicable to quasi-religious societies in virtue of canon 681, a cleric in major orders who has committed one of the three offenses mentioned in canon 646, whereby he is automatically dismissed from the society, or who has been dismissed in consequence of a crime which is punished with a juridical loss of good repute (*infamia iuris*), or with depositions or degradation, is forbidden ever to wear the clerical garb.[142]

Consequently, what has already been said about the canonical position of a perpetually affiliated member of a society, who while in major orders has been automatically dismissed in accordance with the prescription of canon 646, applies also to clerics in major orders who have been dismissed in consequence of the commission of crimes which in the common law are punished with *infamia iuris,* deposition, or degradation. Accordingly, by reason of the response of the Pontifical Commission for the Authentic Interpretation of the Canons of the Code, such dismissed members have no right of being received again into the society. Therefore, if the society refuses to receive them, they must seek an absolution from their obligations to the society. The indult which the Holy See grants for this purpose is in an accommodated sense frequently designated as an indult of secularization.[143]

Palombo discusses the question whether or not a suspension is incurred by those who, in accordance with the prescription of canon 670, are perpetually deprived of the right of wearing the clerical garb. He states that all the authors agree on the fact that a suspension is incurred, but that the authors are not in agreement regarding the source from which the suspension derives. The writer agrees with the opinion of Palombo that the suspension is contained in the penalty of the perpetual deprivation of the clerical garb, although the two penalties are distinct. This can be deduced

---

[141] *Supra,* p. 246.

[142] Cans. 670; 646.

[143] Cf. *supra,* pp. 258-259.

from a consideration of canon 2300, which states in part that the deprivation of the clerical garb entails for the time of its duration the prohibition to exercise any ecclesiastical ministry and the deprivation of all clerical privileges. This to all practical purposes seems to be tantamount to saying that such a cleric is likewise suspended.[144]

Coronata, on the other hand, is of the opinion that the suspension arises from the fact that, in accordance with canon 671, n. 1, this penalty is incurred by all those who commit crimes not as serious as those mentioned in canon 670, and that accordingly all those who are guilty of the more serious crime to which canon 670 adverts must likewise be regarded as contracting the same penalty of suspension.[145]

This mode of reasoning should perhaps be questioned in the light of canon 2219, § 3, which in relation to penal matters makes it unallowable to regard the law as applicable to cases in which similar or even stronger reasons seems to call for punishment. Hence, though the conclusions of these two authors remains the same, it seems warranted rather for the reason that the penalty which deprives the cleric of the right to wear the ecclesiastical garb comprises implicitly the penalty of suspension, for such a cleric is barred from the exercise of any and all ecclesiastical ministries as well as from the enjoyment of the privileges proper to the ecclesiastical state.

---

[144] *De Dimissione Religiosorum,* pp. 247-248; can. 2300.

[145] *Institutiones,* I, 868.

CONCLUSIONS

1) The voluntary application of a subject for admission into a quasi-religious society along with the valid acceptance of the subject by the society produces the juridical bond which effects the public incorporation of the subject in the society. As a result of this incorporation the subject is legally bound to the society and shares in its privileges and obligations.

2) In the question of precedence quasi-religious societies may use the canonical principle, *"Odia restringi et favores convenit ampliari."* Consequently, the members of these societies are to be considered as religious in cases in which religious enjoy precedence, and as seculars in cases in which seculars enjoy it. Therefore they precede laymen, since they are considered as religious, while on the other hand clerical members of quasi-religious societies are considered as secular clerics, and consequently precede all religous even Regulars.

3) All members of quasi-religious societies are subject to the authority of the Roman Pontiff and are obliged to consider him as their supreme superior and to obey him by reason of the bond which makes them subject to their own proper superiors.

4) Quasi-religious societies of men are not allowed to have under their jurisdiction any religious institute or quasi-religious society of women, nor are they allowed to claim any special right to their direction or care.

5) Quasi-religious societies of women may not subject themselves to the jurisdiction or direction of any religious institute or quasi-religious society of men.

6) The common law dealing with the entire institution of the novitiate does not apply to quasi-religious societies. The constitutions alone determine whether or not a period of probation must be observed in these societies, and likewise set all the regulations which must be observed during this period.

7) Confessors of quasi-religious societies of women must possess the special jurisdiction requisite for the valid hearing of

the confessions of women religious as prescribed by canon 876, § 1. Confessors of the Daughters of Charity of Saint Vincent de Paul are the only exception to this rule. By reason of a special privilege, their confessors need only the jurisdiction to hear women's confessions. However, for the *lawful* hearing of the confessions of the latter the confessors must be selected by either the Superior General of the Congregation of the Mission or the provincial director of these women, and they must also be approved by the local ordinary as confessors for these women.

8) The members of quasi-religious societies possess the right of choosing the church for their funeral as well as the right of choosing the place of their burial.

9) If a member of a quasi-religious society of men does not choose the church for his funeral he must be brought to the church or the oratory of his proper house, or at least to that of some other house of his society.

10) All goods received by members of a quasi-religious society in view of their own private and personal labor and industry, which bear no relation to their society belong to the members and not to the society, provided the constitutions do not prescribe to the contrary.

11) A member of a quasi-religious society never loses his proper diocese by reason of his perpetual enrollment in the society, saving any particular enactment of the Holy See.

12) A member of a clerical quasi-religious society, even though he may be perpetually enrolled in his society, has for his proper bishop of ordination the bishop of the proper diocese which he had previous to his entrance into the society.

13) In quasi-religious societies in which there exists no bond of perseverance there cannot be any transfer, properly so called, from the society to another organization. There may be a transfer, broadly speaking, which in reality is a departure from the society and a subsequent admission in another society or in a religious institute.

14) If a perpetually enrolled member of a quasi-religious society should transfer to another society or to a religious institute, then on the completion of the period of trial or novitiate he must be

perpetually enrolled or professed in the new society or institute, the right of the superior to prolong the period of probation for not more than one year being duly acknowledged and safeguarded.

15) If a member of a religious institute of women transfers to a quasi-religious society in which no dowry is demanded, the dowry which she had in the religious institute must be returned to her and then provided for in accordance with the constitutions of the society. The interest earned by the dowry during her period of probation in the society belongs to the religious institute, provided the society does not demand any payment during the time of probation.

16) In quasi-religious societies in which there exists some bond of perseverance no transfer may take place without the permission of the Holy See.

17) Because of the absence of public vows on the part of members in quasi-religious societies, a member may never be considered as an apostate, properly so-called, from the society; nor may he, in a proper sense, obtain an indult of secularization or exclaustration.

18) Provided that he was not dismissed for the reasons mentioned in canon 670, it seems that a member dismissed from a quasi-religious society, if he was perpetually enrolled in the society and had previously received major orders, would have to report to the diocese of his proper ordinary, which he never loses, for the probation prescribed in canon 671, saving always any particular enactment of the Holy See.

19) The prescriptions of canon 641 do not apply to quasi-religious societies. Consequently, a bishop receiving a dismissed member who has been absolved from his obligations to the society is not limited to a maximum period of six years for deciding whether or not he wishes to incardinate the subject.

BIBLIOGRAPHY

Sources

Acta Apostolica, Bullae, Brevia et Rescripta in Gratiam Congregationis Missionis, Parisiis, 1873.

Acta Apostolicae Sedis, Commentarium Officiale, Romae, 1909-1929; Civitate Vaticana, 1929-.

Acta Sanctae Sedis, 41 vols., Romae, 1865-1908.

Baronius, Caesare, *Annales Ecclesiastici,* ed. A. Theiner, 37 vols., Vols. I-XXVIII, Silvae Ducis, 1864-1875; Vols. XXIX-XXXVII, Parisiis, 1876-1883.

Bullarum Diplomatum et Privilegiorum Sanctorum Romanorum Pontificum Taurinensis Editio, 24 vols., et Appendix, Augustae Taurinorum-Neapoli, 1857-1872.

Bouscaren, Lincoln, *The Canon Law Digest,* 2 vols., Milwaukee: Bruce, 1934-1943.

Codex Iuris Canonici Pii X Pontificis Maximi iussi digestus Benedicti Papae XV auctoritate promulgatus, Romae, Typis Polyglottis Vaticanis, 1917.

Codicis Iuris Canonici Fontes cura Emi Card. Gasparri Editi, 9 vols., Romae (postea Civitate Vaticana): Typis Polyglottis Vaticanis, 1923-1939. (Vols. VII, VIII, et IX cura et studio Emi Card. Serédi.)

Collection of Privileges and Indulgences for the Use of the Daughters of Charity, new edition, Paris, 1909.

Constitutions of the Priests of the Mission of St. Paul the Apostle, New York, 1920.

Corpus Iuris Civilis, 3 vols., Berolini, 1928-1929. *Institutiones,* quas recognovit P. Krueger; *Digesta,* quae recognovit T. Mommsen et retractavit P. Krueger; *Codex Iustinianus,* quam recognovit et retractavit P. Krueger; *Novelle,* quas recognovit R. Schoell et absolvit G. Kroll.

Corpus Iuris Canonici, editio Lipsiensis secunda post Aemilii Ludovici Richteri curas ad librorum manu scriptorum et editionis Romanae fidem recognovit et adnotatione critica instruxit Aemilius Friedberg, Lipsiae: Tauchnitz, 1879-1881.

Decretales D. Gregorii Papae IX, una cum glossis restitutae, Romae, 1582.

Decretum Gratiani Emendatum et Notationibus Illustratum una cum glossis, Romae, 1582.

Institutionum ad Oblatos S. Ambrosii Pertinentium Epitome, Caroli S.R.E. Cardinalis Tit. Sanctae Praxedis Archiep. Mediol. iussu Edita, Mediolani apud Dominicum Bellagattam, 1716.

Mansi, Ioannes, *Sacrorum Conciliorum Nova et Amplissima Collectio,* 53 vols. in 60, Parisiis, 1901-1927.

Monita ad Confessarios Puellarum Charitatis, Parisiis, 1923.

Monumenta Germaniae Historica, Legum Sectio III, Concilia, 3 vols., ed. A. Boretius et V. Krause, Hannoverae, 1883-1924.

Potthast, Augustus, *Regesta Pontificum Romanorum inde ab A. post Christum natum 1198 ad A. 1304,* 2 vols., Berolini, 1874-1875.

Schroeder, H., *Canons and Decrees of the Council of Trent,* St. Louis: Herder, 1941.

Reference Works

Antrobus, Frederick, *The Excellencies of the Oratory of St. Philip Neri,* London, 1881.

Aquinas, Thomas, *Summa Theologica,* 6 vols., Rome, 1886-1887.

Augustine, Charles, *A Commentary on the New Code of Canon Law,* 8 vols., St. Louis: B. Herder, 1920-1938. Vol. I, 4. ed., 1921; Vol. II, 5. ed., 1928; Vol. III, 5. ed., 1938; Vol. IV, 3. ed., 1925; Vol. V, 2. ed., 1920; Vol. VI, 3. ed., 1931; Vol. VII, 3. ed., 1930; Vol. VIII, 3. ed., 1931.

Ayrinhac, H. A.-Lydon, P. J., *Penal Legislation in the New Code of Canon Law,* revised edition, New York: Benziger Bros., 1936.

Bastien, Pierre, *Directoire canonique a l'usage des congregations a voeux simples,* 3. ed., Bruges: Charles Beyaert, 1923.

Berutti, Christophorus, *Institutiones Iuris Canonici,* 6 vols., Vol. III, *De Religiosis,* Taurini-Romae: Marietti, 1936.

Beste, Udalricus, *Introductio in Codicem,* 2. ed., Collegeville, Minnesota: St. John's Abbey Press, 1944.

Blat, Albertus, *Commentarium Textus Codicis Iuris Canonici,* 5 vols. in 7, lib. II, pars II-III, *Ius de Religiosis et Laicis iuxta Codicis Ordinem,* 3. ed., Romae: apud "Angelicum," 1938.

Blessed Gaspar del Bufalo, by a member of the same congregation, Carthagena, Ohio, 1933.

Boulay, *Vie de Venerable Jean Eudes,* 4 vols., Paris, 1906.

Butler, Edward Cuthbert, *Benedictine Monachism,* 2. ed., London, New York: Longmans, Green and Co., 1924.

Cance, A., *Le Code de Droit Canonique,* Vol. II, *Des Religieux,* 5. ed., Paris: Librairie Lecoffre, J. Gabalda, 1939.

Cappello, Felix, *Summa Iuris Canonici in Usum Scholarum Concinnata,* 3 vols., Vol. II, Romae: Apud Aedes Universitatis Gregorianae, 1930.

Catholic Encyclopedia, The, 15 vols., 2 Supplements and Index, New York: Appleton Co., 1907-1922.

Cayré, Fulbert, *Manual of Patrology and History of Theology,* translated from the French by H. Howitt, 2 vols., Paris: Desclée and Co., 1936-1940.

Chelodi, Ioannes, *Ius de Personis Iuxta Codicem Iuris Canonici,* ed. altera a Sac. Ernesto Bertagnolli recognita et aucta, Tridenti: Libr. Edit. Tridentum, 1927.

Choupin, S. I., *Nature et Obligations de l'Etat Religieux,* Paris: Beauchesne, 1923.

Cipollini, Albertus, *De Censuris Latae Sententiae iuxta Codicem Iuris Canonici,* Taurini: Marietti, 1925.

Cocchi, Guidus, *Commentarium in Codicem Iuris Canonici ad Usum Scholarum,* 8 vols. in 5, Liber II, pars II, *De Religiosis,* 3. ed., Taurinorum Augustae: Marietti, 1932.

Considine, John, *March Into Tomorrow,* Maryknoll, New York: Field Afar Press, 1942.

Coronata, Mathaeus, Conte a, *Institutiones Iuris Canonici ad Usum Utriusque Cleri et Scholarum,* 5 vols., Vol. I, 2. ed., Taurini: Marietti, 1939.

Costaggini, Dionisio, *Vita del Beato Giovanni Eudes,* Roma: Typografia Pontificia del Instituto Pio IX, 1909.

Coste, P., *Life and Labors of St. Vincent de Paul,* translated from the French by Joseph Leonard, C.M., 3 vols., London: Burns, Oates and Washbourne, 1934-1935.

———, *Le grand Saint du grand Siecle, Monsieur Vincent,* 3 vols., Paris: Desclée de Brouwer & Co., 1931.

Creusen, Joseph, *Religious Men and Women in the Code,* 5. ed., Milwaukee, U. S. A.: Bruce Co., 1940.

Currier, Charles, *History of Religious Orders,* New York, 1894.

Elliott, Walter, *The Life of Father Hecker,* 2. ed., New York, 1894.

Faillon, M., *Vie de M. Olier,* 4. ed., 3 vols., Paris, 1853.

Fanfani, Ludovicus, *De Iure Religiosorum ad Normam Codicis Iuris Canonici,* 2. ed., Taurini-Romae: Marietti, 1925.

Ferreres, Ioannes, *Institutiones Canonicae,* 2 vols., Barcinone: Subirana, 1918.

Gallik, George, *The Rights and Duties of Bishops Regarding Diocesan Sisterhoods,* St. Paul, Minnesota: Wanderer Printing Co., 1939.

Genicot, Eduardus-Salsmans, Iosephus, *Institutiones Theologiae Moralis,* 14. ed., 2 vols., Buenos Aires: Typis Desclée de Brouwer, 1939.

Georges, Emile, *St. Jean Eudes,* 3. ed., Paris: Lethielleux, 1936.

Gillis, James, *The Paulists,* New York: Macmillan Co., 1932.

Goyeneche, Servus, *Iuris Canonici Summa Principia Libri II,* pars. II, III, *De Religiosis-De Laicis,* Roma: Herder S.A.L.E.R., 1938.

Hefele, Carolus, et Leclercq, Henricus, *Histoire des Conciles,* 10 vols. in 19, Paris: Letouzey et Ané, 1907-1938.

Heimbucher, Max, *Die Orden und Kongregationem der katholischen Kirche,* 2. ed., 3 vols., Paderborn: Ferdinand Schöningh, 1907-1908.

Herbermann, Charles, *The Sulpicians in the United States,* New York: Encyclopedia Press, 1916.

Herbert, Mary, *Venerable Vincent Pallotti, Apostle and Mystic,* revised and enlarged by Nicholas M. Wilwers, P.S.M., Milwaukee: The Pallottine Fathers, 1942.

Lexikon für Theologie und Kirche, 2. ed., 10 vols., Freiburg: Herder & Co., 1930-1938.

Kelly, James, *Jurisdiction of the Confessor According to the Code of Canon Law,* New York: Benziger Bros., 1928.

Krol, John, *The Defendant in Contentious Trials,* the Catholic University of America Canon Law Studies, n. 146, Washington, D. C.: The Catholic University of America Press, 1942.

Maroto, Philippus, *Institutiones Iuris Canonici,* 2 vols., Romae, 1919-1921. Vol. I, 3. ed., Romae: Apud Commentarium pro Religiosis, 1921.

Martinez, J. Fernández, *Privilegios e Indulgencias de las Hijas de la Caridad de S. Vincente de Paul,* Madrid, 1945.

McBride, James, *Incardination and Excardination of Seculars,* The Catholic University of America Canon Law Studies, n. 145, Washington, D. C.: The Catholic University of America Press, 1941.

McCormick, Robert, *Confessors of Religious,* The Catholic University of America Canon Law Studies, n. 33, Washington, D. C.: The Catholic University of America, 1926.

McGrath, James, *The Privilege of the Canon,* The Catholic University of America Canon Law Studies, n. 242, Washington, D. C.: The Catholic University of America Press, 1946.

Merkelbach, Benedictus Henricus, *Summa Theologiae Moralis ad Mentem D. Thomae et ad Normam Iuris Novi,* 3. ed., 3 vols., Parisiis: Desclée de Brouwer, 1939.

Migne, J. P., *Patrologiae Cursus Completus, Series Graeca,* 161 vols., Paris, 1856-1866.

———, *Patrologiae Cursus Completus, Series Latina,* 221 vols., Paris, 1844-1864.

———, *Encyclopédie Théologique,* 3 séries, 168 vols., Série I, Vols. XX-XXIII, *Dictionnaire des Orders Religieux,* Paris, 1847-1859.

Moeder, John, *The Proper Bishop for Ordination and Dimissorial Letters,* The Catholic University of America Canon Law Studies, n. 95, Washington, D. C.: The Catholic University of America, 1935.

Montalembert, Charles, *The Monks of the West,* 2 vols., Boston, 1872.

Montez, Charles, *Father Eudes and His Foundations,* Boston, 1874.

Noldin, H.-Schmitt, A., *Summa Theologiae Moralis,* 26. ed., 3 vols., Oeniponte: Typis et Sumptibus Fel. Rauch, 1940.

Oesterle, Gerardus, *Praelectiones Iuris Canonici,* Vol. I, Romae, in Collegio S. Anselmi, 1931.

Palombo, Josephus, *De Dimissione Religiosorum,* Taurini-Romae: Marietti, 1931.

Passardière, Jourdan, *L'oratoire de St. Philippe de Neri,* 2 parts, Draguignan, 1879.

Paulists and Their Works, The, New York: Paulist Press, 1932.

Perraud, J., *L'Oratoire de France,* Paris, 1866.

Piontek, Cyrillus, *De Indulto Exclaustrationis necnon Saecularizationis,* The Catholic University of America Canon Law Studies, n. 29, Washington, D. C.: The Catholic University of America, 1925.

Pisani, Paul, *The Congregations of Priests from the XVI-XVIII Century,* translated by Mother Mary Reginald, O.P., St. Louis: B. Herder Co., 1930.

Powers, George, *The Maryknoll Movement,* Maryknoll, New York: Field Afar Press, 1920.

Prümmer, Dominicus, *Manuale Iuris Canonici,* 3. ed., Friburgi: Herder and Co., 1922.

Raus, J. B., *De Sacrae Obedientiae Virtute et Voto secundum Doctrinam divi Thomae et S. Alphonsi, iuxta Normas ac Codicem Iuris Canonici,* Lugduni-Paris: Typis Emmanuelis Vitte, 1923.

Reiffenstuel, Anacletus, *Ius Canonicum Universum,* 5 vols. in 3, Maceratae, 1864-1870.

Reisner, Albert, *Apostates and Fugitives from Religious Institutes,* The Catholic University of America Canon Law Studies, n. 168, Washington, D. C.: The Catholic University of America Press, 1942.

Sardi, Vincenzo, *Vita del B. Gaspare de Bufalo,* Roma, 1904.

Schäfer, Timotheus, *Compendium de Religiosis ad Norman Codicis Iuris Canonici,* 3. ed., Roma: S.A.L.E.R., 1940.

Stackpoole-Kenny, Louise, *St. Charles Borromeo,* New York: Benziger Bros., 1911.

Stanton, William, *De Societatibus sive Virorum sive Mulierum in Communi Viventium sine Votis,* 2. ed., Halifaxiae: apud Custodiam Librariam Maioris Seminarii a. Sanctissimo Corde B.V.M., 1936.

Sweeney, Francis, *The Reduction of Clerics to the Lay State,* The Catholic University of America Canon Law Studies, n. 223, Washington, D. C.: The Catholic University of America Press, 1945.

Suarez, Franciscus, *Opera Omnia,* ed. nova, a Carolo Berton, 28 vols., Parisiis: L. Vivès, 1856-1861.

Vermeersch, Arthurus-Creusen, Josephus, *Epitome Iuris Canonici,* 3 vols., Romae, 1921-1923.

Wernz, Franciscus, *Ius Decretalium,* 2. ed., 6 vols., Romae et Prati, 1906-1913.

Wernz, Franciscus-Vidal, Petrus, *Ius Canonicum ad Codicis Normam Exactum,* 7 tomes in 8 vols., Tom. III, *De Religiosis,* Romae: Apud Aedes Universitatis Gregorianae, 1933.

Woywod, Stanislaus, *A Practical Commentary on the Code of Canon Law,* 7. ed., 2 vols., New York: Wagner, 1943.

Articles

Bihlmeyer, K., "Beginen"—*Lexikon für Theologie und Kirche,* II, 89-90.

Dunford, David, "Canonesses"—*The Catholic Encyclopedia,* III, 255.

Goyeneche, S., "Consultationes"—*CpR,* I (1920), 140-145; 177-183; IV (1923), 336-341; VII (1926), 103-106; 186-190.

———, "Quaestio Canonica"—*CpR,* II (1921), 13-24; XVIII (1937), 89-96.

———, "Studia Canonica"—*CpR,* I (1920), 295-300; 355-360.

Larraona, Arcadius, "Commentarium Codicis"—*CpR,* II (1921), 364-366; III (1922), 318-329; IV (1923), 134-139; 168-170; 210-218; 273-276; V (1924), 41-49; 81-85; 256-261; 143-153; 261-269; 324-330; 417-436; VI (1925), 77-81; 127-135; 180-186; 291-295; VII (1926), 376-389; VIII (1927), 275-283; X (1929), 33-38; 446-463; XI (1930), 20-30; 75-78; 153-164; XII (1931), 353-359; 435-442; XIII (1932), 24-35; XIV (1933), 416-419; XVI (1935), 421-432; XVIII (1937), 148-155.

———, "Consultationes"—*CpR,* I (1920), 112-114; IV (1923), 281-283.

———, "Studia Canonica"—*CpR,* VIII (1927), 177-183.

Maroto, Philippus, "Commentarium Codicis,"—*CpR,* V (1924), 342-352; IV (1923), 199; II (1921), 325.

Ott, Michael, "St. Joseph's Society for the Colored Missions"—*The Catholic Encyclopedia,* VIII, 521-522.

De Oliveria, "Para Ouvir de Confesão as Filhas de Caridade ou Vincentinas Requer se Peculiar Judisdicão"—*Revista Ecclesiastica Brasileira,* IV (1944), 397-400.

Schaaf, Valentine, "Episcopus Proprius Ordinationis Religiosorum"—*AER,* XC (1934), 491-509.

Tabera, A., "Studia Canonica"—*CpR,* XIV (1933), 53-59.

"Traite de Congregations Seculières"—*Analecta Juris Pontificii,* V (1861), 52-105.

Vermeersch, Arthurus, "Instituta Iuris Diocesani"—*Periodica,* XI (1923), 173-179.

———, "Tempus Utile Recursui Religiosorum Dimissorum"—*Periodica,* XII (1924), 100-104.

———, "De Transeunti ad aliam Religionem"—*Periodica,* XIX (1930), 164*-165*.

Voltas, Petrus, "Consultationes"—*CpR,* I (1920), 270-272.

Muller, Ulrich, "A Few Observations on the Rule"—*The Messenger of the Precious Blood,* XXI (1915), 281-282.

Periodicals

Analecta Juris Pontifici, Romae, 1855-1869; Parisiis, 1872-1891.

American Ecclesiastical Review, The (later (1905), *The Ecclesiastical Review*), Philadelphia, 1889-.

Commentarium pro Religiosis (later (1935), *Commentarium pro Religiosis et Missionariis*), Rome, 1921.

Periodica de Re Canonica et Morali utili praesertim Religiosis et Missionariis, Brugis, 1905-.

Revista Ecclesiastica Brasileira, Petrópolis, Estado do Rio, 1941-.

ABBREVIATIONS

AAS—*Acta Apostolica Sedis*
ASS—*Acta Sanctae Sedis*
AER—*The American Ecclesiastical Review* (later (July, 1905-December, 1943), *The Ecclesiastical Review*)
Bull. Rom. Taur.—*Bullarium Romanum ed. Taurinensis*
CpR—*Commentarium pro Religiosis* (later (1935), *Commentarium pro Religiosis et Missionariis*)
Fontes—*Codicis Iuris Canonici Fontes cura . . . Gasparri editi. . . .*
Mansi—*Sacrorum Conciliorum Nova et Amplissima Collectio*
MGH—*Monumenta Germaniae Historica*
MPG—Migne, *Patrologia Graeca*
MPL—Migne, *Patrologia Latina*
Periodica—*Periodica de Re Canonica et Morali utili praesertim Religiosis et Missionariis*

BIOGRAPHICAL NOTE

Bernard Joseph Ristuccia was born in New York City, New York, on June 16, 1916. He began his elementary education at Holy Cross School, in New York City, and completed it at Saint Patrick's Parochial School, Brooklyn. He received his high school education at Saint Michael's Diocesan High School in Brooklyn, and his college training at Saint John's University, Brooklyn. He began his preparation for the Priesthood under the tutelage of the Congregation of the Mission, spending two years of Novitiate at Saint Vincent's Seminary in Philadelphia. He received his Major Seminary training at Mary Immaculate Seminary, Northampton, Pennsylvania, where he was ordained May 30, 1943. In September, 1944, after serving for a year as instructor in Saint John's Preparatory School, Brooklyn, he entered the Graduate School of Canon Law of the Catholic University of America. He received the degree of the Baccalaureate in Canon Law in May, 1945, and the degree of the Licentiate in Canon Law in June, 1946.

ALPHABETICAL INDEX

CANON LAW STUDIES*

1. FRERIKS, REV. CELESTINE A., C.PP.S., J.C.D., Religious Congregations in Their External Relations, 121 pp., 1916.
2. GALLIHER, REV. DANIEL M., O.P., J.C.D., Canonical Elections, 117 pp., 1917.
3. BORKOWSKI, REV. AURELIUS L., O.F.M., J.C.D., De Confraternitatibus Ecclesiasticis, 136 pp., 1918.
4. CASTILLO, REV. CAYO, J.C.D., Disertacion Historico-Canonica sobre la Potestad del Cabildo en Sede Vacante o Impedida del Vicario Capitular, 99 pp., 1919 (1918).
5. KUBELBECK, REV. WILLIAM J., S.T.B., J.C.D., The Sacred Penitentiaria and Its Relation to Faculties of Ordinaries and Priests, 129 pp., 1918.
6. PETROVITS, REV. JOSEPH J. C., S.T.D., J.C.D., The New Church Law on Matrimony, X-461 pp., 1919.
7. HICKEY, REV. JOHN J., S.T.B., J.C.D., Irregularities and Simple Impediments in the New Code of Canon Law, 100 pp., 1920.
8. KLEKOTKA, REV. PETER J., S.T.B., J.C.D., Diocesan Consultors, 179 pp., 1920.
9. WANENMACHER, REV. FRANCIS, J.C.D., The Evidence in Ecclesiastical Procedure Affecting the Marriage Bond, 1920 (Printed 1935).
10. GOLDEN, REV. HENRY FRANCIS, J.C.D., Parochial Benefices in the New Code, IV-119 pp., 1921 (Printed 1925).
11. KOUDELKA, REV. CHARLES J., J.C.D., Pastors, Their Rights and Duties According to the New Code of Canon Law, 211 pp., 1921.
12. MELO, REV. ANTONIUS, O.F.M., J.C.D., De Exemptione Regularium, X-188 pp., 1921.
13. SCHAAF, REV. VALENTINE THEODORE, O.F.M., S.T.B., J.C.D.,' The Cloister, X-180 pp., 1921.
14. BURKE, REV. THOMAS JOSEPH, S.T.D., J.C.D., Competence in Ecclesiastical Tribunals, IV-117 pp., 1922.
15. LEECH, REV. GEORGE LEO, J.C.D., A Comparative Study of the Constitution "Apostolicae Sedis" and the "Codex Juris Canonici," 179 pp., 1922.
16. MOTRY, REV. HUBERT LOUIS, S.T.D., J.C.D., Diocesan Faculties According to the Code of Canon Law, II-167 pp., 1922.
17. MURPHY, REV. GEORGE LAWRENCE, J.C.D., Delinquencies and Penalties in the Administration and the Reception of the Sacraments, IV-121 pp., 1923.

* Below n. 100 only the following numbers are still available: Nn. 3, 4, 9, 25, 34, 57 and 75. Beginning with n. 100 only the following are unavailable: Nn. 100-111 inclusive, and n. 113.

18. O'Reilly, Rev. John Anthony, S.T.B., J.C.D., Ecclesiastical Sepulture in the New Code of Canon Law, 11-129 pp., 1923.
19. Michalicka, Rev. Wenceslas Cyril, O.S.B., J.C.D., Judicial Procedure in Dismissal of Clerical Exempt Religious, 107 pp., 1923.
20. Dargin, Rev. Edward Vincent, S.T.B., J.C.D., Reserved Cases According to the Code of Canon Law, IV-103 pp., 1924.
21. Godfrey, Rev. John A., S.T.B., J.C.D., The Right of Patronage According to the Code of Canon Law, 153 pp., 1924.
22. Hagedorn, Rev. Francis Edward, J.C.D., General Legislation on Indulgences, II-154 pp., 1924.
23. King, Rev. James Ignatius, J.C.D., The Administration of the Sacraments to Dying Non-Catholics, V-141 pp., 1924.
24. Winslow, Rev. Francis Joseph, O.F.M., J.C.D., Vicars and Prefects Apostolic, IV-149 pp., 1924.
25. Correa, Rev. Jose Servelion, S.T.L., J.C.D., La Potestad Legislativa de la Iglesia Catolica, IV-127 pp., 1925.
26. Dugan, Rev. Henry Francis, A.M., J.C.D., The Judiciary Department of the Diocesan Curia, 87 pp., 1925.
27. Keller, Rev. Charles Frederick, S.T.B., J.C.D., Mass Stipends, 167 pp., 1925.
28. Paschang, Rev. John Linus, J.C.D., The Sacramentals According to the Code of Canon Law, 129 pp., 1925.
29. Piontek, Rev. Cyrillus, O.F.M., S.T.B., J.C.D., De Indulto Exclaustrationis necnon Saecularizationis, XIII-289 pp., 1925.
30. Kearney, Rev. Richard Joseph, S.T.B., J.C.D., Sponsors at Baptism According to the Code of Canon Law, IV-127 pp., 1925.
31. Bartlett, Rev. Chester Joseph, A.M., LL.B., J.C.D., The Tenure of Parochial Property in the United States of America, V-108 pp., 1926.
32. Kilker, Rev. Adrian Jerome, J.C.D., Extreme Unction, V-425 pp., 1926.
33. McCormick, Rev. Robert Emmett, J.C.D., Confessors of Religious, VIII-266 pp., 1926.
34. Miller, Rev. Newton Thomas, J.C.D., Founded Masses According to the Code of Canon Law, VII-93 pp., 1926.
35. Roelker, Rev. Edward G., S.T.D., J.C.D., Principles of Privilege According to the Code of Canon Law, XI-166 pp., 1926.
36. Bakalarczyk, Rev. Richardus, M.I.C., J.U.D., De Novitiatu, VIII-208 pp., 1927.
37. Pizzuti, Rev. Lawrence, O.F.M., J.U.L., De Parochis Religiosis, 1927. (Not Printed.)
38. Bliley, Rev. Nicholas Martin, O.S.B., J.C.D., Altars According to the Code of Canon Law, XIX-132 pp., 1927.
39. Brown, Mr. Brendan Francis, A.B., LL.M., J.U.D., The Canonical Juristic Personality with Special Reference to its Status in the United States of America, V-212 pp., 1927.

40. CAVANAUGH, REV. WILLIAM THOMAS, C.P., J.U.D., The Reservation of the Blessed Sacrament, VIII-101 pp., 1927.
41. DOHENY, REV. WILLIAM J., C.S.C., A.B., J.U.D., Church Property: Modes of Acquisition, X-118 pp., 1927.
42. FELDHAUS, REV. ALOYSIUS H., C.PP.S., J.C.D., Oratories, IX-141 pp., 1927.
43. KELLY, REV. JAMES PATRICK, A.B., J.C.D., The Jurisdiction of the Simple Confessor, X-208 pp., 1927.
44. NEUBERGER, REV. NICHOLAS J., J.C.D., Canon 6 or the Relation of the Codex Juris Canonici to the Preceding Legislation, V-95 pp., 1927.
45. O'KEEFE, REV. GERALD MICHAEL, J.C.D., Matrimonial Dispensations, Powers of Bishops, Priests, and Confessors, VIII-232 pp., 1927.
46. QUIGLEY, REV. JOSEPH A. M., A.B., J.C.D., Condemned Societies, 139 pp., 1927.
47. ZAPLOTNIK, REV. JOHANNES LEO, J.C.D., De Vicariis Foraneis, X-142 pp., 1927.
48. DUSKIE, REV. JOHN ALOYSIUS, A.B., J.C.D., The Canonical Status of the Orientals in the United States, VIII-196 pp., 1928.
49. HYLAND, REV. FRANCIS EDWARD, J.C.D., Excommunication, Its Nature, Historical Development and Effects, VIII-181 pp., 1928.
50. REINMANN, REV. GERALD JOSEPH, O.M.C., J.C.D., The Third Order Secular of Saint Francis, 201 pp., 1928.
51. SCHENK, REV. FRANCIS J., J.C.D., The Matrimonial Impediments of Mixed Religion and Disparity of Cult, XVI-318 pp., 1929.
52. COADY, REV. JOHN JOSEPH, S.T.D., J.U.D., A.M., The Appointment of Pastors, VIII-150 pp., 1929.
53. KAY, REV. THOMAS HENRY, J.C.D., Competence in Matrimonial Procedure, VIII-164 pp., 1929.
54. TURNER, REV. SIDNEY JOSEPH, C.P., J.U.D., The Vow of Poverty, XLIX-217 pp., 1929.
55. KEARNEY, REV. RAYMOND A., A.B., S.T.D., J.C.D., The Principles of Delegation, VII-149 pp., 1929.
56. CONRAN, REV. EDWARD JAMES, A.B., J.C.D., The Interdict, V-163 pp., 1930.
57. O'NEILL, REV. WILLIAM H., J.C.D., Papal Rescripts of Favor, VII-218 pp., 1930.
58. BASTNAGEL, REV. CLEMENT VINCENT, J.U.D., The Appointment of Parochial Adjutants and Assistants, XV-257 pp., 1930.
59. FERRY, REV. WILLIAM A., A.B., J.C.D., Stole Fees, V-136 pp., 1930.
60. COSTELLO, REV. JOHN MICHAEL, A.B., J.C.D., Domicile and Quasi-Domicile, VII-201 pp., 1930.
61. KREMER, REV. MICHAEL NICHOLAS, A.B., S.T.B., J.C.D., Church Support in the United States, VI-136 pp., 1930.
62. ANGULO, REV. LUIS, C.M., J.C.D., Legislation de la Iglesia sobre la intencion en la application de la Santa Misa, VII-104 pp., 1931.

63. Frey, Rev. Wolfgang Norbert, O.S.B., A.B., J.C.D., The Act of Religious Profession, VIII-174 pp., 1931.
64. Roberts, Rev. James Brendan, A.B., J.C.D., The Banns of Marriage, XIV-140 pp., 1931.
65. Ryder, Rev. Raymond Aloysius, A.B., J.C.D., Simony, IX-151 pp., 1931.
66. Campagna, Rev. Angelo, Ph.D., J.U.D., Il Vicario Generale del Vescovo, VII-205 pp., 1931.
67. Cox, Rev. Joseph Godfrey, A.B., J.C.D., The Administration of Seminaries, VI-124 pp., 1931.
68. Gregory, Rev. Donald J., J.U.D., The Pauline Privilege, XV-165 pp., 1931.
69. Donohue, Rev. John F., J.C.D., The Impediment of Crime, VII-110 pp., 1931.
70. Dooley, Rev. Eugene A., O.M.I., J.C.D., Church Law on Sacred Relics, IX-143 pp., 1931.
71. Orth, Rev. Clement Raymond, O.M.C., J.C.D., The Approbation of Religious Institutes, 171 pp., 1931.
72. Pernicone, Rev. Joseph M., A.B., J.C.D., The Ecclesiastical Prohibition of Books, XII-267 pp., 1932.
73. Clinton, Rev. Connell, A.B., J.C.D., The Paschal Precept, IX-108 pp., 1932.
74. Donnelly, Rev. Francis B,. A.M., S.T.L., J.C.D., The Diocesan Synod, VIII-125 pp., 1932.
75. Torrente, Rev. Camilo, C.M.F., J.C.D., Las Procesiones Sagradas, V-145 pp., 1932.
76. Murphy, Rev. Edwin J., C.PP.S., J.C.D., Suspension Ex Informata Conscientia, XI-122 pp., 1932.
77. MacKenzie, Rev. Eric F., A.M., S.T.L., J.C.D., The Delict of Heresy in its Commission, Penalization, Absolution, VII-124 pp., 1932.
78. Lyons, Rev. Avitus E., S.T.B., J.C.D., The Collegiate Tribunal of First Instance, XI-147 pp., 1932.
79. Connolly, Rev. Thomas A., J.C.D., Appeals, XI-195 pp., 1932.
80. Sangmeister, Rev. Joseph V., A.B., J.C.D., Force and Fear as Precluding Matrimonial Consent, V-211 pp., 1932.
81. Jaeger, Rev. Leo A., A.B., J.C.D., The Administration of Vacant and Quasi-Vacant Episcopal Sees in the United States, IX-229 pp., 1932.
82. Rimlinger, Rev. Herbert T., J.C.D., Error Invalidating Matrimonial Consent, VII-79 pp., 1932.
83. Barrett, Rev. John D. M., S.S., J.C.D., A Comparative Study of the Third Plenary Council of Baltimore and the Code, IX-221 pp., 1932.
84. Carberry, Rev. John J., Ph.D., S.T.D., J.C.D., The Juridical Form of Marriage, X-177 pp., 1934.
85. Dolan, Rev. John L., A.B., J.C.D., The Defensor Vinculi, XII-157 pp., 1934.

86. HANNAN, REV. JEROME D., A.M., S.T.D., LL.B., J.C.D., The Canon Law of Wills, IX-517 pp., 1934.
87. LEMIEUX, REV. DELISE A., A.M., J.C.D., The Sentence in Ecclesiastical Procedure, IX-131 pp., 1934.
88. O'ROURKE, REV. JAMES J., A.B., J.C.D., Parish Registers, VII-109 pp., 1934.
89. TIMLIN, REV. BARTHOLOMEW, O.F.M., A.M., J.C.D., Conditional Matrimonial Consent, X-381 pp., 1934.
90. WAHL, REV. FRANCIS X., A.B., J.C.D., The Matrimonial Impediments of Consanguinity and Affinity, VI-125 pp., 1934.
91. WHITE, REV. ROBERT J., A.B., LL.B., S.T.B., J.C.D., Canonical Ante-Nuptial Promises and the Civil Law, VI-152 pp., 1934.
92. HERRERA, REV. ANTONIO PARRA, O.C.D., J.C.D., Legislacion Ecclesiastica sobra el Ayuno y la Abstinencia, XI-191 pp., 1935.
93. KENNEDY, REV. EDWIN J., J.C.D., The Special Matrimonial Process in Cases of Evident Nullity, X-165 pp., 1935.
94. MANNING, REV. JOHN J., A.B., J.C.D., Presumption of Law in Matrimonial Procedure, XI-111 pp., 1935.
95. MOEDER, REV. JOHN M., J.C.D., The Proper Bishop for Ordination and Dimissorial Letters, VII-135 pp., 1935.
96. O'MARA, REV. WILLIAM A., A.B., J.C.D., Canonical Causes for Matrimonial Dispensations, IX-155 pp., 1935.
97. REILLY, REV. PETER, J.C.D., Residence of Pastors, IX-81 pp., 1935.
98. SMITH, REV. MARINER T., O.P., S.T.Lr., J.C.D., The Penal Law for Religious, VII-169 pp., 1935.
99. WHALEN, REV. DONALD W., A.M., J.C.D., The Value of Testimonial Evidence in Matrimonial Procedure, XIII-297 pp., 1935.
100. CLEARY, REV. JOSEPH F., J.C.D., Canonical Limitations on the Alienation of Church Property, VIII-141 pp., 1936.
101. GLYNN, REV. JOHN C., J.C.D., The Promoter of Justice, XX-337 pp., 1936.
102. BRENNAN, REV. JAMES H., S.S., M.A., S.T.B., J.C.D., The Simple Convalidation of Marriage, VI-135 pp., 1937.
103. BBUNINI, REV. JOSEPH BERNARD, J.C.D., The Clerical Obligations of Canons 139 and 142, X-121 pp., 1937.
104. CONNOR, REV. MAURICE, A.B., J.C.D., The Administrative Removal of Pastors, VIII-159 pp., 1937.
105. GUILFOYLE, REV. MERLIN JOSEPH, J.C.D., Custom, XI-144 pp., 1937.
106. HUGHES, REV. JAMES AUSTIN, A.B., A.M., J.C.D., Witnesses in Criminal Trials of Clerics, IX-140 pp., 1937.
107. JANSEN, REV. RAYMOND J., A.B., S.T.L., J.C.D., Canonical Provisions for Catechetical Instruction, VII-153 pp., 1937.
108. KEALY, REV. JOHN JAMES, A.B., J.C.D., The Introductory Libellus in Church Court Procedure, XI-121 pp., 1937.
109. MCMANUS, REV. JAMES EDWARD, C.SS.R., J.C.D., The Administration of Temporal Goods in Religious Institutes, XVI-196 pp., 1937.

110. Moriarty, Rev. Eugene James, J.C.D., Oaths in Ecclesiastical Courts, X-115 pp., 1937.
111. Rainer, Rev. Eligius George, C.SS.R., J.C.D., Suspension of Clerics, XVII-249 pp., 1937.
112. Reilly, Rev. Thomas F., C.SS.R., J.C.D., Visitation of Religious, VI-195 pp., 1938.
113. Moriarity, Rev. Francis E., C.SS.R., J.C.D., The Extraordinary Absolution from Censures, XV-334 pp., 1938.
114. Connolly, Rev. Nicholas P., J.C.D., The Canonical Erection of Parishes, X-132 pp., 1938.
115. Donovan, Rev. James Joseph, J.C.D., The Pastor's Obligation in Prenuptial Investigation, XII-322 pp., 1938.
116. Harrigan, Rev. Robert J., M.A., S.T.B., J.C.D., The Radical Sanation of Invalid Marriages, VIII-208 pp., 1938.
117. Boffa, Rev. Conrad Humbert, J.C.D., Canonical Provisions for Catholic Schools, VII-211 pp., 1939.
118. Parsons, Rev. Anscar John, O.M.Cap., J.C.D., Canonical Elections, XII-236 pp., 1939.
119. Reilly, Rev. Edward Michael, A.B., J.C.D., The General Norms of Dispensation, XII-156 pp., 1939.
120. Ryan, Rev. Gerald Aloysius, A.B., J.C.D., Principles of Episcopal Jurisdiction, XII-172 pp., 1939.
121. Burton, Rev. Francis James, C.S.C., A.B., J.C.D., A Commentary on Canon 1125, X-222 pp., 1940.
122. Miaskiewicz, Rev. Francis Sigismund, J.C.D., Supplied Jurisdiction According to Canon 209, XII-340 pp., 1940.
123. Rice, Rev. Patrick William, A.B., J.C.D., Proof of Death in Prenuptial Investigation, VIII-156 pp., 1940.
124. Anglin, Rev. Thomas Francis, M.S., J.C.D., The Eucharistic Fast, VIII-183 pp., 1941.
125. Coleman, Rev. John Jerome, J.C.D., The Minister of Confirmation, VI-153 pp., 1941.
126. Downs, Rev. Joseph Emmanuel, A.B., J.C.D., The Concept of Clerical Immunity, XI-163 pp., 1941.
127. Esswein, Rev. Anthony Albert, J.C.D., Extrajudicial Penal Powers of Ecclesiastical Superiors, X-144 pp., 1941.
128. Farrell, Rev. Benjamin Francis, M.A., S.T.L., J.C.D., The Rights and Duties of the Local Ordinary Regarding Congregations of Women Religious of Pontifical Approval, V-195 pp., 1941.
129. Feeney, Rev. Thomas John, A.B., S.T.L., J.C.D., Restitutio in Integrum, VI-169 pp., 1941.
130. Findlay, Rev. Stephen William, O.S.B., A.B., J.C.D., Canonical Norms Governing the Deposition and Degradation of Clerics, XVII-279 pp., 1941.
131. Goodwine, Rev. John, A.B., S.T.L., J.C.D., The Right of the Church to Acquire Property, VIII-119 pp., 1941.

132. Heston, Rev. Edward Louis, C.S.C., Ph.D., S.T.D., J.C.D., The Alienation of Church Property in the United States, XII-222 pp., 1941.
133. Hogan, Rev. James John, A.B., S.T.L., J.C.D., Judicial Advocates and Procurators, XIII-200 pp., 1941.
134. Kealy, Rev. Thomas M., A.B., Litt.D., J.C.D., Dowry of Women Religious, IX-152 pp., 1941.
135. Keene, Rev. Michael James, O.S.B., J.C.D., Religious Ordinaries and Canon 198, V-164 pp., 1942.
136. Kerin, Rev. Charles A., S.S., M.A., S.T.B., J.C.D., The Privation of Christian Burial, XVI-279 pp., 1941.
137. Louis, Rev. William Francis, M.A., J.C.D., Diocesan Archives, X-101 pp., 1941.
138. McDevitt, Rev. Gilbert Joseph, A.B., J.C.D., Legitimacy and Legitimation, X-247 pp., 1941.
139. McDonough, Rev. Thomas Joseph, A.B., J.C.D., Apostolic Administrators, X-217 pp., 1941.
140. Meier, Rev. Carl Anthony, A.B., J.C.D., Penal Administration Procedure Against Negligent Pastors, XI-240 pp., 1941.
141. Schmidt, Rev. John Rogg, A.B., J.C.D., The Principles of Authentic Interpretation in Canon 17 of the Code of Canon Law, XII-331 pp., 1941.
142. Slafkosky, Rev. Andrew Leonard, A.B., J.C.D., The Canonical Episcopal Visitation of the Diocese, X-197 pp., 1941.
143. Swoboda, Rev. Innocent Robert, O.F.M., J.C.D., Ignorance in Relation to the Imputability of Delicts, IX-271 pp., 1941.
144. Dubé, Rev. Arthur Joseph, A.B., J.C.D., The General Principles for the Reckoning of Time in Canon Law, VIII-299 pp., 1941.
145. McBride, Rev. James T., A.B., J.C.D., Incardination and Excardination of Seculars, XX-585 pp., 1941.
146. Krol, Rev. John T., J.C.D., The Defendant in Ecclesiastical Trials, XII-207 pp., 1942.
147. Comyns, Rev. Joseph J., C.SS.R., A.B., J.C.D., Papal and Episcopal Administration of Church Property, XIV-155 pp., 1942.
148. Barry, Rev. Garrett Francis, O.M.I., J.C.D., Violation of the Cloister, XII-260 pp., 1942.
149. Bolduc, Rev. Gatien, C.S.V., A.B., S.T.L., J.C.D., Les Études dans les Religions Cléricales, VIII-155 pp., 1942.
150. Boyle, Rev. David John, M.A., J.C.D., The Juridic Effects of Moral Certitude on Pre-Nuptial Guarantees, XII-188 pp., 1942.
151. Canavan, Rev. Walter Joseph, M.A., Litt.D., J.C.D., The Profession of Faith, XII-143 pp., 1942.
152. Desrochers, Rev. Bruno, A.B., Ph.L., S.T.B., J.C.D., Le Premier Concile Plénier de Québec et le Code de Droit Canonique, XIV-186 pp., 1942.

153. Dillon, Rev. Robert Edward, A.B., J.C.D., Common Law Marriage, X-148 pp., 1942.
154. Dodwell, Rev. Edward John, Ph.D., S.T.B., J.C.D., The Time and Place for the Celebration of Marriage, X-156 pp., 1942.
155. Donnellan, Rev. Thomas Andrew, A.B., J.C.D., The Obligation of the Misa pro Populo, VII-131 pp., 1942.
156. Eltz, Rev. Louis Anthony, A.B., J.C.L., Cooperation in Crime.
157. Gass, Rev. Sylvester Francis, M.A., J.C.D., Ecclesiastical Pensions, XI-206 pp., 1942.
158. Guiniven, Rev. John Joseph, C.SS.R., J.C.D., The Precept of Hearing Mass, XIV-188 pp., 1942.
159. Gulczynski, Rev. John Theophilus, J.C.D., The Desecration and Violation of Churches, X-126 pp., 1942.
160. Hammill, Rev. John Leo, M.A., J.C.D., The Obligations of the Traveler According to Canon 14, VIII-204 pp., 1942.
161. Haydt, Rev. John Joseph, A.B., J.C.D., Reserved Benefices, XI-148 pp., 1942.
162. Huser, Rev. Roger John, O.F.M., A.B., J.C.D., The Crime of Abortion in Canon Law, XII-187 pp., 1942.
163. Kearney, Rev. Francis Patrick, A.B., S.T.L., J.C.L., The Principles of Canon 1127
164. Linahen, Rev. Leo James, S.T.L., J.C.D., De Absolutione Complicis In Peccato Turpi, 114 pp., 1942.
165. McCloskey, Rev. Joseph Aloysius, A.B., J.C.D., The Subject of Ecclesiastical Law According to Canon 12, XVII-246 pp., 1942.
166. O'Neill, Rev. Francis Joseph, C.SS.R., J.C.D., The Dismissal of Religious in Temporary Vows, XIII-220 pp., 1942.
167. Prince, Rev. John Edward, A.B., S.T.D., J.C.D., The Diocesan Chancellor, X-136 pp., 1942.
168. Riesner, Rev. Albert Joseph, C.SS.R., J.C.D., Apostates and Fugitives from Religious Institutes, IX-168 pp., 1942.
169. Stenger, Rev. Joseph Bernard, J.C.D., The Mortgaging of Church Property, 186 pp., 1942.
170. Waldron, Rev. Joseph Francis, A.B., J.C.D., The Minister of Baptism, XII-197 pp., 1942.
171. Willett, Rev. Robert Albert, J.C.D., The Probative Value of Documents in Ecclesiastical Trials, X-124 pp., 1942.
172. Woeber, Rev. Edward Martin, M.A., J.C.D., The Interpellations, XII-161 pp., 1942.
173. Benko, Rev. Matthew Aloysius, O.S.B., M.A., J.C.L., The Abbot *Nullius.*
174. Christ, Rev. Joseph James, M.A., S.T.L., J.C.L., Dispensation from Vindicative Penalties.
175. Clancy, Rev. Patrick M. J., O.P., A.B., S.T.Lr., J.C.D., The Local Religious Superior, X-299 pp., 1943.

176. Clarke, Rev. Thomas James, J.C.D., Parish Societies, XII-147 pp., 1943.
177. Connolly, Rev. John Patrick, S.T.L., J.C.D., Synodal Examiners and Parish Priest Consultors, X-223 pp., 1943.
178. Drumm, Rev. William Martin, A.B., J.C.L., Hospital Chaplains.
179. Flanagan, Rev. Bernard Joseph, A.B., S.T.L., J.C.D., The Canonical Erection of Religious Houses, X-147 pp., 1943.
180. Kelleher, Rev. Stephen Joseph, A.B., S.T.B., J.C.D., Discussions with non-Catholics: Canonical Legislation, X-93 pp., 1943.
181. Lewis, Rev. Gordian, C.P., J.C.D., Chapters in Religious Institutes, XII-169 pp., 1943.
182. Marx, Rev. Adolph, J.C.D., The Declaration of Nullity of Marriages Contracted Outside the Church, X-151 pp., 1943.
183. Matulenas, Rev. Raymond Anthony, O.S.B., A.B., J.C.L., Communication, a Source of Privileges.
184. O'Leary, Rev. Charles Gerard, C.SS.R., J.C.D., Religious Dismissed After Perpetual Profession, X-213 pp., 1943.
185. Power, Rev. Cornelius Michael, J.C.L., The Blessing of Cemeteries.
186. Shuhler, Rev. Ralph Vincent, O.S.A., J.C.D., Privileges of Regulars to Absolve and Dispense, XII-195 pp., 1943.
187. Ziolkowski, Rev. Thaddeus Stanislaus, A.B., J.C.D., The Consecration and Blessing of Churches, XII-151 pp., 1943.
188. Heneghan, Rev. John Joseph, S.T.D., J.C.L., The Marriages of Unworthy Catholics: Canons 1065 and 1066.
189. Carroll, Rev. Coleman Francis, M.A., S.T.L., J.C.L., Charitable Institutions.
190. Ciesluk, Rev. Joseph Edward, Ph.B., S.T.L., J.C.L., National Parishes in the United States.
191. Coburn, Rev. Vincent Paul, A.B., J.C.L., Marriages of Conscience.
192. Connors, Rev. Charles Paul, C.S.Sp., A.B., J.C.L., Extra-Judicial Procurators in the Code of Canon Law.
193. Coyle, Rev. Paul Raymond, A.B., J.C.L., Judicial Exceptions.
194. Fair, Rev. Bartholomew Francis, A.B., S.T.L., J.C.L., The Impediment of Abduction.
195. Gallagher, Rev. Thomas Raphael, O.P., A.B., S.T.Lr., J.C.L., The Examination of the Qualities of the Ordinand.
196. Gannon, Rev. John Mark, S.T.L., J.C.L., The Interstices Required for the Promotion to Orders.
197. Goldsmith, Rev. J. William, B.C.S., S.T.L., J.C.L., The Competence of Church and State over Marriage—Disputed Points.
198. Goodwine, Rev. Joseph Gerard, A.B., S.T.B., J.C.L., The Reception of Converts.
199. Kowalski, Rev. Romuald Eugene, O.F.M., A.B., J.C.L., Sustenance of Religious Houses of Regulars.
200. McCoy, Rev. Alan Edward, O.F.M., J.C.L., Force and Fear in Relation to Delictual Imputability and Penal Responsibility.

201. McDevitt, Rev. Vincent John, Ph.B., S.T.L., J.C.L., Perjury.
202. Martin, Rev. Thomas Owen, Ph.D., S.T.D., J.C.L., Adverse Possession, Prescription and Limitation of Actions: The Canonical "Praescriptio."
203. Miklosovic, Rev. Paul John, A.B., J.C.L., Attempted Marriages and Their Consequent Juridic Effects.
204. Mundy, Rev. Thomas Maurice, A.B., S.T.L., J.C.L., The Union of Parishes.
205. O'Dea, Rev. John Coyle, A.B., J.C.L., The Matrimonial Impediment of Nonage.
206. Olalia, Rev. Alexander Ayson, S.T.L., J.C.L., A Comparative Study of the Christian Constitution of States and the Constitution of the Philippine Commonwealth.
207. Poisson, Rev. Pierre-Marie, C.S.C., A.B., Ph.L., Th.L., J.C.L., Droits Patrimoniaux des Maisons et des Eglises Religieuses.
208. Stadalnikas, Rev. Casimir Joseph, M.I.C., J.C.L., Reservation of Censures.
209. Sullivan, Rev. Eugene Henry, S.T.L., J.C.L., Proof of the Reception of the Sacraments.
210. Vaughan, Rev. William Edward, J.C.L., Constitutions for Diocesan Courts.
211. Paro, Rev. Gino, S.T.D., J.C.L., The Right of Apostolic Legation.
212. Balzer, Rev. Ralph Francis, C.P., J.C.L., The Computation of Time in a Canonical Novitiate.
213. Dougherty, Rev. John Whelan, A.B., S.T.L., J.C.L., De Inquisitione Speciali.
214. Dziob, Rev. Michael Walter, J.C.L., The Sacred Congregation for the Oriental Church.
215. Eidenschink, Rev. John Albert, O.S.B., B.A., J.C.L., The Election of Bishops in the Letters of Pope Gregory the Great.
216. Gill, Rev. Nicholas, C.P., J.C.L., The Spiritual Prefect in Clerical Religious Houses of Study.
217. Hynes, Rev. Harry Gerard, S.T.L., J.C.D., The Privileges of Cardinals, XII-183 pp., 1945.
218. McDevitt, Rev. Gerald Vincent, S.T.L., J.C.D., The Renunciation of an Ecclesiastical Office, XIV—179 pp., 1946.
219. Manning, Rev. Joseph Leroy, J.C.L., The Free Conferral of Offices.
220. Meyer, Rev. Louis G., O.S.B., A.B., S.T.B., J.C.D., Alms-Gathering by Religious, XII—163 pp., 1946.
221. O'Donnell, Rev. Cletus Francis, M.A., J.C.L., The Marriage of Minors.
222. Prunskis, Rev. Joseph, J.C.D., Comparative Law, Ecclesiastical and Civil, in Lithuanian Concordat, X—161 pp., 1945.
223. Sweeney, Rev. Francis Patrick, C.SS.R., J.C.D., The Reduction of Clerics to the Lay State, X—199 pp., 1945.

224. VOGELPOHL, REV. HENRY JOHN, J.C.L., The Simple Impediments to Holy Orders, XVI—190 pp., 1945.
225. BROCKHAUS, REV. THOMAS AQUINAS, O.S.B., A.B., J.C.L., Religious who Are Known as *Conversi*, X—127 pp., 1945.
226. GRIESE, REV. ORVILLE NICHOLAS, S.T.D., J.C.L., Marriage and the Procreation of Offspring, XVI—224 pp., 1946.
227. BOUDREAUX, REV. WARREN LOUIS, J.C.L., The *"ab acatholicis nati"* of Canon 1099, § 2, XII—110 pp., 1946.
228. BOWE, REV. THOMAS JOSEPH, A.B., J.C.L., Religious Superioresses, VIII—206 pp., 1946.
229. DIEDERICHS, REV. MICHAEL FERDINAND, S.C.J., J.C.L., The Jurisdiction of the Latin Ordinaries over their Oriental Subjects, XIV—153 pp., 1946.
230. DINGMAN, REV. MAURICE JOHN, A.B., S.T.L., J.C.L., The Plaintiff in Contentious Trials.
231. FRISON, REV. BASIL, C.M.F., M.MUS., J.C.L., The Retroactivity of Law, X—221 pp., 1946.
232. GALVIN, REV. WILLIAM ANTHONY, M.A., J.C.L., The Administrative Transfer of Pastors, XII—288 pp., 1946.
233. GORACY, REV. JOSEPH C., J.C.L., The Diriment Impediment of Major Orders.
234. HALE, REV. JOSEPH FRANCIS, M.A., S.T.L., J.C.L., The Pastor of Burial.
235. HENRY, REV. JOSEPH ARTHUR, A.B., J.C.L., The Mass and Holy Communion: Inter-Ritual Law, XII—138 pp., 1946.
236. LINENBERGER, REV. HERBERT, C.PP.S., J.C.L., The False Denunciation of an Innocent Confessor.
237. LOWRY, REV. JAMES MARTIN, A.B., J.C.L., Dispensation from Private Vows, XII—266 pp., 1946.
238. LYNCH, REV. GEORGE EDWARD, A.B., S.T.L., J.C.L., Coadjutors and Auxiliaries of Bishops, X—107 pp., 1947.
239. LYNCH, REV. TIMOTHY, M.S.SS.T., J.C.L., Contracts between Bishops and Religious Congregations, XIV—232 pp., 1946.
240. MCCLUNN, REV. JUSTIN DAVID, A.B., S.T.L., J.C.L., Administrative Recourse, VII—142 pp., 1946.
241. LOHMULLER, REV. MARTIN NICHOLAS, A.B., J.C.D., The Promulgation of Law, XII—140 pp., 1947.
242. MCGRATH, REV. JAMES, A.B., J.C.L., The Privilege of the Canon, XXII—156 pp., 1946.
243. MARBACH, REV. JOSEPH FRANCIS, A.B., J.C.D., Marriage Legislation for the Catholics of the Oriental Rites in the United States and Canada, XIV—314 pp., 1946.
244. SHIMKUS, REV. BERNARD ALOYSIUS, A.B., J.C.L., The Determination and Transfer of Rite.

245. SMITH, REV. VINCENT MICHAEL, A.B., S.T.L., J.C.L., Ignorance Affecting Matrimonial Consent.
246. WACHTRLE, REV. PAUL ANTHONY, A.B., J.C.L., The Baptism of the Children of Non-Catholics.
247. CROTTY, REV. MATTHEW M., J.C.D., The Recipient of First Holy Communion, X—142 pp., 1947.
248. EAGLETON, REV. GEORGE, J.C.L., The Quinquennial Faculties, Formula IV.
249. GIBBONS, REV. MARION L., C.M., LL.B., J.C.D., Domicile of The Wife Unlawfully Separated from Her Husband, XIV—171 pp., 1947.
250. KELLY, REV. BERNARD M., S.T.L., J.C.D., The Functions Reserved to Pastors, X—150 pp., 1947.
251. KILCULLEN, REV. THOMAS J., LL.M., J.C.D., The Collegiate Moral Person as Party Litigant, X—150 pp. 1947.
252. LAFONTAINE, REV. GERMAIN J., W.F., J.C.L., Relations Canoniques entre Le Missionnaire et Ses Superieurs.
253. LANE, REV. LORAS T., A.B., S.T.L., J.C.L., Matrimonial Procedure in the Ordinary Court of Second Instance.
254. LOVER, REV. JAMES F., C.SS.R., J.C.D., The Master of Novices, X—168 pp., 1947.
255. MCNICHOLAS, REV. TIMOTHY J., J.C.L., The *Septimae Manus* Witness.
256. MAROSITZ, REV. JOSEPH J., M.S.C., J.C.L., Obligations and Privileges of Religious Promoted to the Episcopal or Cardinalitial Dignities, XII—180 pp., 1947.
257. MURPHY, REV. FRANCIS J., A.B., J.C.L., Legislative Powers of the Provincial Council, XII—158 pp., 1947.
258. O'BRIEN, REV. ROMAEUS W., O.Carm., J.C.D., The Provincial Superior in Religious Orders of Men, X—294 pp., 1947.
259. PFALLER, REV. BENEDICT A., O.S.B., J.C.L., The *Ipso Facto* Effected Dismissal oi Religious.
260. POPEK, REV. ALPHONSE S., M.A., J.C.D., The Rights and Obligations of Metropolitans, XVIII—460 pp., 1947.
261. RISTUCCIA, REV. BERNARD JOSEPH, C.M., J.C.L., Quasi-Religious Societies, XVI—308 pp., 1949.
262. SONNTAG, REV. NATHANIEL LOUIS, O.F.M.Cap., J.C.D., Censorship of Special Classes of Books, XII—147 pp., 1947.
263. STADLER, REV. JOSEPH NICHOLAS, J.C.L., Frequent Holy Communion.
264. SZAL, REV. IGNATIUS JOSEPH, J.C.L., The Communication of Catholics with Schismatics.
265. WAGNER, REV. URBAN STANLEY, O.F.M.Conv., J.C.D., Parochial Substitute Vicars and Supplying Priests, IX—126 pp., 1947.

www.ingramcontent.com/pod-product-compliance
Lightning Source LLC
LaVergne TN
LVHW050257080826
844660LV00012B/653

* 9 7 8 0 8 1 3 2 2 4 3 9 8 *